RECKLESS HOMICIDE?
Ford's Pinto Trial

Lee Patrick Strobel

RECKLESS HOMICIDE?

Ford's Pinto Trial

South Bend, Indiana

RECKLESS HOMICIDE? Ford's Pinto Trial

and books
702 South Michigan, South Bend, Indiana 46618

Cover Photo: Taken by Neil B. Graves and admitted
into evidence as prosecution exhibit.

ISBN: 0-89708-022-X

First printing, March 1980.

Printed in the United States of America

Additional copies available:

the distributors
702 South Michigan
South Bend, IN 46618

To Leslie, Alison and Kyle

1

As a balmy August afternoon dissolved into evening, Lyn Ulrich scrambled into the cramped rear seat of her sister's subcompact car, anxious for a carefree drive through the Indiana countryside and a spirited volleyball game at a Baptist church about 20 miles away.

She pulled back the front seat to let her cousin, Donna Ulrich, slip inside next to the driver's seat. Donna pulled the door shut and rolled down her window to catch the soft, refreshing breeze. And then Lyn's sister, Judy, slid behind the steering wheel and started her yellow car.

There was no hint that they had just sealed themselves inside a death trap where they would be devoured by a raging inferno in only half an hour.

Judy was proud of her first set of wheels, even though her 1973 Pinto was five years old and had six other owners since rolling off the Ford Motor Company assembly line in Metuchen, New Jersey. Her father, Earl, who worked as a contractor, was helping her pay for it as a gift marking her graduation from Penn High School. Their decision to buy the Pinto, Ford's big-selling answer to popular small-car imports like the Volkswagen Beetle, was based on both practical and patriotic reasons – it was stingy with gasoline and it was made by Americans.

Judy, who was 18 years old and clad in pink shorts and a white short-sleeve blouse, glanced at the gas gauge and remembered she'd have to stop soon to fill up the tank. She recalled her mother's comment earlier that afternoon: "If you need gas, fill up at the Cheker Station; it's self-service and cheaper." Judy released the hand brake, put the car into gear, and eased away from her white, ranch-style home.

There was a lot for the girls to chatter about as they drove eastward along U.S. Highway 33, away from tiny Osceola and toward Elkhart, a city of 45,000 which dwarfs the small farming communities around it. Even if the three girls had not been related, they were so comfortable with each other and shared so many common interests that they surely would have been the best of friends anyway. Judy and Donna were especially close, having been born just one day apart in the same hospital in Peoria, Illinois. They were frequent playmates during their early childhood years when they lived near each other until Judy's family moved to Osceola when she was five.

Judy, who wore her shiny, dark-brown hair in waves stylishly swept back from her pretty face, was the quietest of the trio. She was a gentle-mannered girl who became popular in her circle of friends not because she pushed herself to the forefront, but because her easy-going friendliness and sincerity let everyone know she could be trusted with their confidences. Religion was at the core of her life, and she was active in the Missionary Youth Fellowship at her family's church. During the summer, she was earning money by working at a South Bend ice cream parlor and getting ready to enter a commercial college in September to pursue her long-held dream of becoming an interior designer.

Religion was equally important to Donna, a tall, athletic blonde who was visiting for a few days from her home in Roanoke, Illinois. Donna was just about to finish her year-long term as president of the Metamora Mennonite Church's youth group, which had flourished under her effervescent leadership. The other 22 young members marveled at her never-ending optimism and the way she talked so openly and enthusiastically about her deep commitment to Christianity. She was even thinking seriously of working full-time in the church's far-flung network of volunteer programs now that she had graduated from high school.

Lyn was 16 years old and excited about returning to Penn for her junior year. A well-liked, vivacious girl with shoulder-length chestnut hair and eyes as brown and inquisitive as a fawn's, Lynn already had compiled a perfect A average. She was more assertive than her older sister, and didn't hesitate to voice her opinions to anyone, including adults, although she was pleasant about it. Through her sister, she also had become involved in the church's youth group, and sometimes played hymns on the piano for evening services. During the summer, she was working as a cashier at the Park and Shop Supermarket in Osceola, hoping someday for a career in mathematics.

The girls' Pinto reached the edge of Elkhart, Indiana and a short distance later, the heavily traveled U.S. Highway 33 angled southeasterly toward Goshen, where the volleyball game was scheduled.

Judy and Lyn were probably talking excitedly about their upcoming trip to South Dakota with several churchmates for a week at an international youth retreat. Young people were coming from all over for the sports competition, talent shows, and worship sessions. In fact, that's why the Ulrich sisters were going to Goshen on that late August afternoon, so they could practice their volleyball in preparation for the retreat.

Donna undoubtedly told them all about the different kind of retreat from which she had just returned. Her church group traveled by bus to a poverty-stricken region of rural Kentucky where they volunteered their help in fixing up a mountain school. After working all day, they had spent their free time playing volleyball, visiting coal mines, having picnics on the bluffs, and singing hymns in a chapel. Donna loved the experience, especially the traveling and exposure to a different culture. But then, she always had an appetite for fresh places. In high school, she was involved in organizing the foreign exchange club and became best friends with a Rhodesian exchange student who captivated Donna with exotic stories of African life.

At a speck on the map called Dunlap, Judy pulled into the Cheker gas station. One of the girls jumped out to replenish the car's nearly dry tank, but she forgot to replace the gas cap on the Pinto, leaving it instead on the car's roof. A few minutes later, the three girls were back on the road, driving through the picturesque landscape of lush green cornfields. Bits of cloud flecked the azure sky. Visibility seemed unlimited. The temperature hovered around 83 degrees.

The time was getting close to 6:15, not quite half an hour since they left the Ulrich home. There was just enough time before the volleyball game to stop and visit their Aunt Esther in Goshen. Judy had called her after dinner and said they would try to stop by around 6:30 so Aunt Esther could see Donna during her visit.

What happened next with the gas cap became a mystery which would frustrate police for more than a year. According to the account which would finally emerge, the girls were about one-and-a-half miles away from the Cheker station when the chrome gas cap fell off the car and rolled across the five-lane highway, hitting the curb on the other side. The girls saw the cap as it meandered across the road and decided to retrieve it.

Judy drove until traffic was clear and then made a U-turn. She flipped on her four-way emergency flashers and was driving under the 55 mile-per-hour speed limit as she approached the area where the cap had come to rest. She probably wanted to pull off the road, but the eight-inch high cement curb blocked any exit.

Another high school girl was driving in the same direction after eating dinner at a McDonald's restaurant. She passed a fancy gold Chevrolet van with a mural of a train on its side and the words *Peace Train* emblazoned across its front. A little farther up the road, she passed the Ulrich Pinto, which was going down the right-hand lane.

Robert Duggar was driving the van. He had just come home from his job at a van conversion shop in Elkhart, ate a quick dinner with his roommate, and was on his way to a friend's house to tune up and clean out his van. He wanted it ready for a week-long vacation he was about to take.

There were two half-empty bottles of Budweiser beer on the console, a plastic "baggy" of legal caffein pills in the glove compartment (although Duggar thought they were amphetamines), and the remnants of a few marijuana cigarets with two packages of rolling paper under the passenger's seat.

The diminutive, shaggy-haired Duggar, who was 21 years old, was just getting used to the freedom of driving again. After convictions for running a stop sign, failing to yield, and twice for speeding, authorities had suspended his license. He just got it back a few weeks earlier.

Duggar glanced over into the opposite lanes of traffic and saw a police car coming toward him with a radar unit clinging to its side. Duggar checked his speed – 50 miles per hour. A short while later, Duggar decided he wanted a cigaret. The pack had fallen off the engine cover and onto the floor, so he took his eyes off the highway to search for them. When he looked back up, he was stunned to see his van was closing fast on the Ulrich Pinto, which was a scant 10 feet away.

At the same instant, Judy looked into her rearview mirror, feeling panic surge through her as her eyes met the image of the van's chrome grill looming behind. She knew she was helpless to avoid being hit.

There was no time for Duggar to brake or swerve. In less than half a second, the thick pine board used for the van's front bumper rammed the back of the Ulrich Pinto, forcing the car's rear down onto the highway where it left three long gouges. Duggar was jolted as his body was thrown into his custom steering wheel, although he didn't consider the crash very powerful. Almost instantaneously, he smelled the pungent odor of gasoline.

In a matter of milliseconds, the Pinto's soft rear end crushed up almost to the back axle. The 11-gallon gas tank, located between the flimsy bumper and the sturdy axle, was mangled and shoved into a sharp bolt which punched a small hole in it, letting gasoline trickle out.

The filler pipe, which is the tube that feeds gas into the tank, was yanked out, exposing a 2½-inch hole through which gasoline whooshed and spewed. Then the tank, squeezed smaller and smaller like someone stepping on a carton full of milk, burst open along a seam, and gasoline came gushing out.

A few inches away, the car's body welding pulled apart like a zipper, letting gasoline spill and spray into the passenger compartment, partially flooding it. And then, perhaps from the scraping of the car's body along the pavement, there was a spark.

A foot-long tongue of flame shot out from the left rear underside of Judy's Pinto, followed by the concussion of an explosion which one witness described as being like a large napalm bomb going off. A brilliant orange fireball engulfed the Pinto, sending fire and thick, black smoke curling 20 feet into the air, and then there was a second blast, shooting ragged shards of flame even higher. Cinder and bits of glass rained down across all five lanes of highway.

The van and Pinto were locked together, the blazing car scorching the asphalt as they careened in their embrace down the highway until the Pinto came loose, turning in a slow-motion clockwise rotation, finally coming to rest 154 feet away from the point of impact, facing backwards and straddling the eight-inch curb.

The car's interior was a roaring furnace, filled completely to the brim with luminous orange. Flames darted out the side windows, along the doors, and out the shattered rear glass, lapping five feet over the top of the car's bulging and blackened roof. The roadside grass was ablaze in a semicircle around the Pinto.

The piercing screams of Donna and Lyn lasted only a dozen seconds until both were seized by death, their mouths stretched open and locked in a contorted expression of horror. The frames of Lyn's sunglasses melted around her eyes. The inferno reached 1,292 degrees, melting the plastic dashboard and steering wheel and burning the vinyl seats down to the metal springs and backrest.

Judy, charred with third degree burns over 95 per cent of her body, was somehow flung from the car, ending up stretched out on the grass with her right ankle caught by the jammed door. The searing heat was melting her rubber tennis shoe onto her foot. With much of her ears burned away, her face disfigured, most of her hair and clothing gone, and her eyes rolled back so only white showed, she shouted over and over in a hoarse, husky voice: "Help me! Please help me!"

Albert J. Clark Jr., a retired carpenter, darted from his motorhome to help, and a farmer named Levi Hochstetler, who heard the crash while doing chores inside his barn near the highway, dashed toward the Pinto with a fire extinguisher. They were shocked to find that Judy, who was propping herself up on her elbows, could be so incredibly burned and still be alive.

Frantically, they tried opening the door to free her from the conflagration, but the deformed metal was stuck against her ankle and the intense heat kept pushing them back. Hochstetler scorched his hand while making a quick attempt to yank on the door. Finally, Clark found a board and was able to pry the door open, giving Hochstetler just enough time to grab Judy under her arms and pull her free.

"Thank you," she moaned. "Thank you, thank you."

Clark's wife, Pauline, ran over to Duggar, who had fallen to his knees near the fiery Pinto and was beating the earth with his fists. She grabbed him by his arm and pulled him away, then knelt beside him on the grass, put her arm around him and tried blocking his view of the holocaust.

"No, no, I'm all right," he sobbed, gesturing wildly toward the Pinto. "Just help them! Help them!"

Traffic in both directions halted, and several people ran to Judy, wanting to help but not knowing how. "Girls, the girls, are they okay?" she called out suddenly.

"Yes, they're okay," a tourist from New York assured her. "We got them out of the car." He turned around and gazed at the fire-packed Pinto, trying not to believe anyone else was actually inside.

The faint cry of sirens could be heard in the distance, and a few minutes later a pumper from the Concord Township Fire Department threaded its way through the backed-up traffic. Firemen tried to douse the Pinto while others sprayed water on Judy to cool her.

"I bet I'm ugly," she moaned. "I bet I smell."

Moments later, Bradley McLain, an emergency medical technician, pulled up in his car and ran to Judy. He hadn't seen such a severely burned patient since his days as a medic in Vietnam. Until he heard Judy talk, he thought she was dead.

"Help me," Judy pleaded to him. "I'm burning up." She asked him to take off her tennis shoe, but he said he couldn't do that yet. He began giving her oxygen.

When an ambulance arrived in a few minutes, firemen folded Judy's arms across her and lifted her onto a cot. "Thank you," she said. McLain climbed inside with her, and the ambulance sped toward Elkhart General Hospital.

"Will you be honest with me?" Judy, her throat burned from inhaling fire, asked McLain in a raspy, hesitant voice. He said he would.

"Do I still have ears?" she asked, and he said she did.

"Do I still have my nose?" she asked, and again he said yes.

"Be honest with me," she said. "Am I going to die?"

McLain knew she had no chance of survival. "No," he told her. "You're not."

Judy said she'd never been inside an ambulance before, and McLain told her she could come see it again when she got out of the hospital.

"You don't sound very hopeful," she said.

"Well," McLain replied, "you're going to be in the hospital for a while."

Another medic in the ambulance began touching her in different places to see if she could feel anything. Judy said she could, but she was unable to correctly say where she had been touched. Mercifully, the fire had destroyed the nerve endings over most of her body, sparing her excruciating pain, although her foot still tormented her.

At Judy's request, they prayed the rest of the way to the hospital.

As the ambulance arrived at the emergency room entrance, Terry Shewmaker, a young lawyer, watched from the window of an upper room where his daughter was recovering from minor surgery.

Shewmaker wondered what the commotion was about. At the time, he had no idea he was about to embark on an unprecedented, grueling 18-month legal battle seeking justice in the memory of three young girls he had never met – Judy, Lyn, and Donna.

The wide hospital doors flew open automatically as Judy was hurriedly wheeled inside. "Does anyone here know Jesus?" she called out. "Can anyone say any Bible verses?"

"Levi can," one of the nurses told her. "He'll talk to you."

Levi Woodard, a young orderly who had just finished preparing a sterile bed for Judy in Treatment Room 5, had seen many accident victims before. But he cringed at the sight of Judy.

A devout Seventh Day Adventist, Woodard waited until the doctors and nurses quit hovering over Judy for a moment to talk quietly to her about the Bible. Knowing she would die, he gently suggested she should ask forgiveness for any unconfessed sins, just in case she passed from this world.

Judy asked his name, "My name is Levi," he whispered. "Remember it when you're resurrected because I'll be there, too."

Judy was given an injection for pain, and about 90 minutes later she was wrapped in sterile sheets and put inside a medical van for a trip to a Fort Wayne burn center where she would be more comfortable.

During the 75-mile journey, Judy increasingly fretted about her sister and cousin. The two nurses told her the girls had been taken to the hospital and not to worry about them. Judy became more and more apprehensive, asking whether she would still be able to have children and if she was going to die. Finally, one of the nurses, with tears rolling down her face, recited from memory a Bible verse which proved the only medicine that could soothe and comfort Judy:

> *When thou passest through the waters,*
> *I will be with thee;*
> *And through the rivers, they shall not overflow thee.*
>
> *When thou walkest through the fire,*
> *Thou shalt not be burned;*
> *Neither shall the flame kindle upon thee.*
>
> *For I am the Lord, thy God, the Holy One of Israel,*
> *Thy Savior.*

Eight hours after her Ford Pinto exploded, Judy Ulrich died.

2

Indiana state trooper Neil B. Graves had just finished cleaning up the paperwork on a two-car, head-on crash in which four people were lucky to escape alive. Graves, an easy-going, boyishly handsome veteran of 6½ years on the force, was planning to pursue a few leads on a new child abuse investigation and then get off work on time for a change. His wife already had left for a garden party at a neighbor's house, and Graves was planning to show up right after his shift for a few beers and a steak.

But shortly before 6:30 p.m., Graves' radio crackled with an urgent call: "10-50 P.I. – bad," the dispatcher said, giving the location as 1½ miles north of Goshen on treacherous U.S. Highway 33. Graves flipped on his siren and flashing lights. The message meant a car accident with serious injuries, and Graves knew that instead of going to a party, he'd be spending his evening with his 987th traffic investigation.

Four minutes later, Graves maneuvered his squad car through the tangled traffic and pulled up to the scene just as firemen finally finished extinguishing the Pinto blaze. The dense, sooty smoke was beginning to clear from inside the car for the first time.

Graves walked over to the charred hulk and pulled the driver's door open wide. With the smoke dissipating, he was the first person to closely look inside the Pinto and confirm what firemen had hoped was not true – there were the remains of two bodies sprawled within, blackend and burned to the bone.

The heart-wrenching sight cut deep into the depths of Graves' brain, from which it would return for months to haunt him in persistent nightmares.

It took several minutes for Graves, the father of two young sons, to compose himself so he could begin his investigation. But as soon as he began examining the evidence, he found odd and troubling things.

Checking the interior of the car, which was virtually stripped to its metal shell, Graves found something unusual about the water which had accumulated on the front floorboard. Smelling it and rubbing it between his fingers, he concluded it was mixed with gasoline. "How the hell did that happen?" he asked aloud in his cowboy drawl.

Graves carefully took samples of the liquid, as well as bits of the ash-like seating from around the bodies, and put them in bottles for future scientific analysis. As it turned out Graves' suspicions would be proven – the Pinto's interior had been saturated with gasoline before the fire began.

After he checked the gear shift and found the transmission in second gear, Graves walked around the outside of the wreck and looked at its mashed-up and scorched rear-end. Then he examined the front of Duggar's van. Hardly any damage. That didn't make much sense either.

The descriptions of the crash by some eyewitnesses troubled Graves even more. They all seemed to agree the van and Pinto were both moving at the time of impact, and the van wasn't going much faster than the car. The words of Clark, who saw the entire accident from the opposite lanes of traffic before running to Judy's rescue, stuck in his mind: "If it was any kind of car, it should have been just a fender-bender."

And then Graves discovered something he had never seen before in an accident – the crash had ripped open the seam where the Pinto's body was attached to its floor, leaving gaping holes as large as six inches long and four inches wide. The holes were right next to where the gas tank ended up after being shoved forward by the van. Maybe that's how the gas got inside the car, he said to himself.

That wasn't all that was bothering Graves. As he stood on the blocked-off highway with his arms crossed, staring at the Pinto, he remembered seeing an article six months earlier in a magazine called *Mother Jones.* Graves, an insatiable reader, wasn't a subscriber to the California-based publication, but he recalled picking it up at a newsstand because the cover illustration had captured his curiosity.

The lead story was about the Ford Pinto, something about the car being susceptible to fire and explosion when hit from behind, Graves recalled. And didn't the article claim that Ford Motor Company knew about the hazard and put the car on the market anyway? Graves probed his memory, unable to recall many specifics. All he knew was that there was something odd about this crash. He decided to explore the *Mother Jones* angle further. The magnitude of the tragedy demanded it.

Indeed, Graves' memory had been accurate – *Mother Jones,* in its September-October issue of 1977, broke a major investigative story about the Ford Pinto. The article had followed numerous lawsuits filed by burn victims accusing Ford of defectively designing the Pinto's fuel system, and the unheeded warnings by a handful of safety experts of alleged hazards in the car.

Ironically, the Ulrich crash was on August 10, 1978 – exactly one year to the day after a press conference was held in Washington, D.C., to announce publication of the article, which was entitled, "Pinto Madness."

The 11-page story, which subsequently won several awards, contended that the gas tank placement on the Pinto, dating back to the original 1971 model year, made it unusually vulnerable to puncture and dangerous gas leakage when the car was hit from behind at low to moderate speeds. And based on "secret documents" obtained from Ford files, the article asserted that Ford management knew about the hazard when the subcompact was being developed, became aware of several possible ways to make the car safer, but retained the dangerous design because it was more cost-efficient than correcting the problem.

The cost of making the Pinto safer, the article concluded, could have been just a few dollars per car. Yet Ford's tremendous haste to enter the lucrative small-car market, and its self-imposed, rigidly-enforced goal of building the car to weigh under 2,000 pounds and cost under $2,000, meant that even minor changes were out of the question to Ford management.

Ford executives reacted angrily to the article, starting off by saying it contained "distortions and half-truths" and later issuing a press release assuring the public that "there is no 'serious fire hazard' in the fuel system of the Ford Pinto, nor are any Pinto models exceptionally vulnerable to rear-impact collision fires."

"The performance of the Pinto's fuel-tank system in actual accidents appears to be superior to that which might be expected of cars its size and weight," said the release issued by Herbert L. Misch, Ford's vice president of the environmental and safety engineering staff.

But on September 13, 1977 – 11 months before the Ulrich crash – the National Highway Traffic Safety Administration (NHTSA) launched a "formal defect investigation" of the Pinto, largely because of the magazine article. The inquiry uncovered 38 cases in which rear-end Pinto crashes resulted in fuel system damage, gasoline leakage, and fire. A total of 27 Pinto occupants died in those incidents (although one was reported to be from impact injuries) and another 24 suffered varying burn injuries. The numbers were considered minimums.

During the inquiry, Ford turned over to NHTSA summaries of 55 experimental crash tests conducted by the automaker on its Pinto and the car's virtually identical cousin, the Mercury Bobcat. These crash tests, dating back to a few weeks after the Pinto's introduction, consistently revealed that when the Pinto was crashed rearward into a wall at speeds as low as 21½ miles per hour, the fuel tank was punctured and the filler tube yanked out – causing gas to gush just as it did in the Ulrich crash – and the passenger doors jammed.

Aware of the problems years ago, Ford had studied several possible remedies, such as installing a plastic shield to protect the gas tank from puncture; using a "rubber bladder" inside the gas tank to retain gas even if the metal tank were punctured; using a tank made of molded polyethylene; reinforcing the car's rear end to make it stronger; and modifying the filler pipe to make it less likely to pull out in the event of a crash. None of the alternatives was adopted by Ford through the 1976 model, although some rear-end strength was added in increments starting in 1973.

Ford also was compelled to disclose that it already had been hit with 29 lawsuits stemming from Pinto burn injuries or alleging defective fuel system design in the car. By the time of the investigation, Ford had lost or settled eight of the cases, had won two, and the remaining 19 were still pending.

It was during the NHTSA investigation, in February, 1978, when the legal and automotive worlds were stunned by the milestone decision of a California jury in one of those lawsuits to award more than $128 million in damages in connection with a fatal fire in a 1972 Pinto.

The jury began by ruling that Ford must pay $600,000 to the survivors of Mrs. Lily Gray, who was burned to death when her Pinto stalled on the freeway, was rammed from behind by a car going 35 miles per hour, and exploded into a fireball.

Then the jury awarded another $2.8 million in damages to her passenger, Richard Grimshaw, who had been 13 years old at the time of the crash. Grimshaw, who was burned over 90 per cent of his body and lost four fingers, his nose and left ear, underwent 52 operations before the trial and faced dozens more to repair horrible scarring. In the jury's most controversial decision, Ford was ordered to pay $125 million to Grimshaw to punish the automaker because of evidence that Ford knew about the Pinto fire danger but failed to correct it. Grimshaw's lawyers had used Ford's own internal documents to show the jury that the company decided against spending $10 to $15 per car which could have made it safer in rear-end crashes.

Calling the Pinto "a lousy and unsafe product," the foreman of the jury was quoted as saying: "We came up with this high amount so that Ford wouldn't design cars this way again."

One of Grimshaw's lawyers, Mark P. Robinson, said the verdict was "probably the loudest noise that the jury has made in any civil suit in American jurisprudence."

The massive amount of money awarded by the jury, easily the highest for such a suit in American history, brought heightened media interest in the Pinto issue. Later, though, a judge reduced the $125 million in punitive damages to $3.5 million, and both sides appealed.

The same month as the Grimshaw verdict, still six months before the Ulrich crash, NHTSA arranged for Dynamic Science, Inc., of Phoenix, Arizona to conduct experimental crash testing of several Pintos as part of the ongoing NHTSA investigation. Dynamic Science used full-size Chevrolet Impalas to ram at various speeds into the rear-end of free-standing Pintos and then recorded the results with sophisticated photographic and scientific instruments.

In the first test, a 1971 Pinto was hit at 34.9 miles per hour. The result – A fireball exploded, consuming the car.

In the second test, a 1971 Pinto competitor, the Chevrolet Vega, was rear-ended at 35.3 miles per hour. The result – the Vega leaked a total of less than once ounce of fuel.

In the third test, a 1972 Pinto was hit from behind at the same speed as the Vega – again, fire erupted, engulfing the Pinto.

In all, Dynamic Science staged nine rear-end crashes of

1971-76 Pinto two-door sedans and three-door runabouts at speeds of about 30 to 35 miles per hour. Two blew up, and the other seven gushed gasoline ranging from 6 ounces to 5½ gallons per minute, with the average leakage at more than two gallons per minute.

As for the Vegas crashed at comparable speeds, two had virtually no leakage and two leaked fuel at 7 and 17 ounces per minute.

When a 1972 Pinto was backed into a cement wall at 21½ miles per hour, the gas tank was damaged and the filler pipe yanked out, letting fuel leak at more than 12 ounces per minute. In the same test, the Vega lost virtually no gas.

"Rear-end collision of Pinto vehicles," the agency's report concluded, "can result in puncture and other damage of the fuel tank and filler neck, creating substantial fuel leakage, and in the presence of external ignition sources fire can result."

The "fire threshold" of the 1971-76 Pintos was calculated to be at 30 to 35 miles per hour in rear-end crashes.

In May, 1978, three months before the Ulrich crash, NHTSA completed its initial investigation and sent a letter to Lee A. Iacocca, who was then president of Ford Motor Company and subsequently the head of rival Chrysler Corporation. Iacocca had bragged that the Pinto, developed under his reign, was "my car."

The letter notified Iacocca that, based on the NHTSA inquiry, there had been "an initial determination of the existence of a safety-related defect" in the 1971-76 Pintos and the 1975-76 Mercury Bobcats. The letter set June 14th for a public hearing at which Ford would be given an opportunity to present arguments against the finding.

But in what was widely seen as a successful move to head off that hearing, Ford on June 9th announced it was recalling the 1.5 million cars, even though Ford issued a statement disagreeing with NHTSA's determination that a safety defect existed.

Another press release was issued by Misch in which he insisted the Pinto's performance was comparable to other compact and subcompact cars. Yet he conceded that NHTSA "had identified areas in which the risk of fuel leakage could be reduced significantly on a practical basis. Accordingly, Ford decided to offer the modifications so as to end public concern that has resulted from criticism of the fuel systems in these vehicles."

The press release by Misch on the recall was two pages long, compared to the eight pages devoted a few months earlier to the release denouncing the *Mother Jones* accusations.

The recalled cars were to be modified by adding a polyethylene shield which would prevent the gas tank from being punctured by sharp bolts, and a longer and improved filler pipe and seal to lessen the chance of it being pulled out during a crash. Both species of safety improvements had been considered by Ford, and rejected, years earlier.

Ford's timetable called for tooling for the parts to begin promptly so that the modifications could be made for consumers in September, 1978 – which turned to be the month after Judy, Lyn, and Donna burned to death.

Mattie Ulrich, mother of Judy and Lyn, didn't hear about the recall. If she had, she said later, she would have gotten rid of the car well before that horrible August evening.

It wasn't until six months after they buried their daughters that Earl and Mattie Ulrich received their recall letter from Ford, notifying them of the government's conclusion that the Pinto posed an "unreasonable risk of substantial fuel leakage in low to moderate speed rear-end collisions."

"In the presence of an ignition source, fuel leakage can, of course, result in a fire that endangers persons in or near the vehicle," the form letter told the still-grieving parents.

"We urge that you have these important safety modifications made to your car."

3

When Terry Shewmaker returned home from visiting his daughter, Robin, in Elkhart General Hospital on the evening of August 10, 1978, he found a message to call the Elkhart County Sheriff's Department. For Shewmaker, a 30-year-old assistant prosecutor, this sort of call was routine. As the liaison between the prosecutor's office and the various police agencies, he constantly was getting calls about murders, assaults, robberies, car accidents, drug raids, and whatever else was happening in this Northern Indiana county of 126,500 that might involve criminal charges.

Shewmaker, a lanky native Hoosier with hair the color of straw, called the number and talked to a sheriff's deputy. The news was grim – fiery, two-vehicle accident; two girls dead; one girl dying; a man slightly injured with two cracked ribs. Shewmaker realized immediately that the ambulance he had seen speed up to the hospital during his visit had contained Judy Ulrich.

"Hey," the deputy mentioned casually. "Isn't there supposed to be something wrong with these Pintos?"

Shewmaker didn't take much note of the comment, although it did jog his memory. He recalled seeing a television show which contended the Pinto posed some sort of fire hazard.

The young prosecutor gave the deputy some instructions about impounding evidence. Realizing the gravity of the case, he also knew he had to call his boss, Michael A. Cosentino, at home immediately.

Cosentino, a 41-year-old conservative Republican, was Elkhart County's aggressive state's attorney, whose office was in charge of prosecuting everything from ax murders to speeding tickets to shoplifting charges. Although the $23,000 he earned each year as part-time prosecutor made up just part of his total income, most of which came from his successful private law practice catering to wealthy corporate clients, Cosentino was addicted to the challenge and excitement of criminal investigations and trials. His record of having personally tried 25 murder cases – and winning them all – had established his reputation as a tenacious, shrewd trial lawyer who was well-versed in the law and had a flair for courtroom theatrics.

A native of Aurora, Illinois, where he was raised by his divorced mother on her salary as a waitress, Cosentino was a high school football standout before going to study philosophy at Beloit College in Wisconsin. After graduation and two years in the Army, he worked his way through the University of Wisconsin College of Law by tending bar at night.

In 1967, he joined an Elkhart law firm headed by C. Whitney Slabaugh, who at the time was county prosecutor, and Cosentino began building experience by trying felony cases. Seven years later, when Slabaugh decided to retire from his prosecutor's post, Cosentino won the Republican nomination by 97 votes and clinched the job in the general election. With his first term coming to an end, Cosentino was unopposed in the November election.

Tall and solidly built, Cosentino had a prominent nose and slicked-down black hair which was streaked with gray. His intensely competitive nature bordered on the combative and seemed to be fueled as much by a strong fear of failure as by a desire to succeed. Two of his favorite sayings gave some insight into his personality: "No one likes a loser" and "Winning isn't everything; it's the only thing." Even playing cards for money with friends, he was merciless in plunging for the jugular. It appeared that one of the few times he relaxed his quest to be Number One was when he was bobbing on his boat on Lake Michigan during warm summer weekends, joking with friends and with a fishing line dipped into the water.

Cosentino received Shewmaker's call at 9 o'clock that night. Shewmaker briefed him on the accident and reported that a voluntary blood test showed that Duggar was being truthful when he said he had not been drinking. Shewmaker never mentioned anything special about the fact a Pinto was involved. Cosentino's own knowledge about the Pinto's problems was confined to having read a brief report about the recall a couple of months earlier.

Without even considering the Pinto controversy, Cosentino knew that three dead girls meant he had a serious case brewing. He ordered every angle thoroughly pursued as quickly as possible. "I want this handled as if it were a murder investigation," he said. "I want everything checked out."

Elkhart County, home of the recreational vehicle industry and generally populated by religious people with fundamental values, reacted with deep anguish over the tragic deaths. And the local news media was abuzz with reports that drugs had been found in Duggar's van. Shewmaker got a call the day after the accident from the sheriff's office saying a field test had preliminarily determined – although it was later found to be incorrect – that the pills found in Duggar's glove compartment were amphetamines. Shewmaker arranged for Duggar's arrest.

In the meantime, Graves was deluged with telephone calls from newspaper and television reporters from around the country wanting details about the Pinto angle to the crash, convincing him even more that this aspect of the case required a full investigation. Graves contacted Mark Dowie, author of the *Mother Jones* article, and obtained a reprint plus some help in getting in touch with three key figures in the Pinto controversy – auto safety consultant Byron Bloch; former Ford engineering executive Harley Copp; and Grimshaw case lawyer Mark Robinson.

Over the weekend, the police lab processed photographs of the accident scene, which were brought to a hastily called meeting in Cosentino's storefront office just off Main Street. Cosentino couldn't believe the difference between the devastated Pinto and the limited front-end damage to the van, which sustained a depressed grill and a slightly deformed hood.

"This doesn't make any sense," Cosentino muttered as he studied the color pictures taken from various angles. "Look at this – the left front headlight of the van isn't even broken, and the Pinto looks as if it was run over by a steamroller."

Like Graves, Cosentino also was troubled by comments from some eyewitnesses that the accident didn't look like it was going to be very serious until the fireball suddenly engulfed the car.

Cosentino and Shewmaker were repulsed by the grisly photos showing the incinerated bodies in their twisted positions inside the Pinto. Shewmaker shook his head. "No one ought to have to die like that," he said softly.

The next few days were packed with activity as the Pinto investigation was pursued at a hectic pace at the same time several other cases were coming into the office. Bits of evidence constantly were being funneled to Cosentino in a series of telephone calls, written reports, and informal meetings in his book-lined, dark-wood office.

Thanks to quick research, Cosentino was given the full background of the Pinto controversy, including accounts of the federal safety investigation, a synopsis of the evidence adduced in the Grimshaw trial, and circumstances surrounding the recall. A new light was being shed on the Ulrich accident.

Late one night not long after the crash, Cosentino was

sitting alone on the livingroom couch in his comfortable Elkhart home. His wife, Dianne, and their two sons were asleep, and he was taking advantage of the solitude to let his mind deftly sift through all of the evidence and data which had been gathered. Slowly, all the pieces began falling together into one picture.

Suddenly Cosentino snuffed out his ever-present cigaret, strode over to the telephone, and dialed Shewmaker's number. His top assistant and confidant came on the line.

"You know something," Cosentino said matter-of-factly, "I think Ford Motor Company ought to be held responsible for these deaths."

Stunned, Shewmaker nearly dropped the receiver. "Mike, are you crazy?" he exclaimed. "When we're finished with them, what are we going to do – take on the Soviet Union or Red China?"

"I don't know if I'm crazy or not," came the reply as Cosentino continued to mull over the disturbing evidence. "Things aren't adding up any other way."

Cosentino knew his suggestion was novel, but he did not consider it a radical departure from the basic rules of law. Based on the evidence he had seen so far, Cosentino was becoming convinced the three girls would have survived the impact of the crash without serious injuries, but that they burned to death because the Pinto's hazardous design caused the car to burst into flames. And that Ford knew about the car's fire-prone nature for years and decided not to spend the minimal amount of money needed to make the car safer.

If individuals are held responsible for their reckless actions which result in the death of someone, why shouldn't Ford be held responsible for its actions? To let the matter pass, Cosentino believed, would be giving the nation's second largest automaker immunity from the laws everyone else must follow.

And yet the idea was without precedent. No American manufacturer or individual executive had ever been criminally charged in connection with the marketing of an allegedly unsafe product.

Indeed, it wasn't too many years ago that corporations enjoyed immunity even from civil lawsuits by persons injured due to defective products. American courts had ruled that manufacturers could not be sued by persons injured by their products because no contract existed between them. This trend was reversed in a 1916 case from New York's highest court in which it was held that no such contract was required. That lawsuit, involving a defective wheel on a Buick, opened the door for injured persons and survivors of persons who were killed to recover money from manufacturers in instances in which the product was negligently made and caused the harm.

It was not until a 1960 landmark decision by the progressive California Supreme Court that modern product-liability law was born. This decision significantly expanded the earlier New York case by ruling that the injured person does not have to prove the manufacturer was negligent or at fault in order to be compensated. Instead, the injured person generally only has to prove the product was defective and "unreasonably dangerous;" that the defect existed when the product was sent out by the manufacturer; and that the defect caused the injuries.

No American prosecutor, though, had ever brought a similar criminal case, which would be considerably harder to prove than a routine civil lawsuit. For instance, in a case involving a death, the prosecutor would have to prove the manufacturer acted "recklessly" in designing or building the product or in failing to warn consumers of a dangerous defect, and that this was responsible for the death. This sort of evidence of willful misconduct is only needed in civil cases when extra, punitive damages are sought. In a criminal case, the evidence must be proven "beyond a reasonable doubt," which is a significantly higher degree of certainty than required in civil lawsuits.

And yet Cosentino was beginning to think this might be the next appropriate expansion of the law. He reasoned that small corporations can be seriously stung by multimillion dollar verdicts in the civil arena, and so they would be adequately deterred from designing or building their products in a defective manner.

But Cosentino believed that huge corporations, like the Ford Motor Company, are not affected by being ordered to pay a few million dollars in one civil case, a couple million in another, and a few hundred thousand in another. They take advantage of tax write-offs and return to business as usual despite injuries to consumers. The only way to make these corporations responsible for their actions, he concluded, was to resort to criminal law.

Was this unique kind of case even possisble to pursue under Indiana law? Cosentino wasn't sure. He assigned his assistants to research the issue, and then he called his friend, William Conour of the Indiana Prosecuting Attorney's office, and asked for an opinion. Conour helped draft the Indiana penal code and was very familiar with the intent of the legislature in passing the applicable laws.

A few days later, Conour called back with his conclusion – Ford could be prosecuted under Indiana's reckless homicide and reckless conduct statutes. Research by Cosentino's assistants yielded the same answer.

More evidence was flowing into Cosentino's office. Robinson sent one of the key investigators from the Grimshaw case to Elkhart to help. About that time, Cosentino obtained his first set of internal, once-confidential Ford crash tests and financial documents from lawyers who had been involved in civil lawsuits stemming from Pinto fires. The documents had been pried out of Ford during pretrial proceedings in civil cases or "leaked" by Ford employees. They provided a concrete, behind-the-scenes look at the steps taken by Ford in the development of the Pinto.

For Graves, the documents verified the essential allegations of the *Mother Jones* article and everything he had heard about the evidence in the Grimshaw case. He was now convinced that Ford should stand trial for the deaths of Judy, Lyn, and Donna.

Graves took some of the documents home to show his wife, Claudia, whose common-sense judgment he often sought in evaluating evidence. She read the documents and became just as adamant as her husband that Ford should be prosecuted.

"But what chance do you guys have playing Don Quixote?" she asked.

"That shouldn't matter," Graves replied. "What's right is right. We'll just have to wait and see what happens."

Graves continued to analyze the physical evidence from the accident and conduct in-depth interviews with witnesses who saw the vehicles collide. Billy Campbell, a former homicide investigator regularly assigned to Cosentino's office, interviewed others, including people at the hospitals where the girls had been taken.

But there was one puzzling element of the crash which bothered everyone connected with the case. If the girls were supposed to be headed south toward Goshen for a volleyball game, why did the accident occur as they were headed north? And why were they going so slow on a five-lane highway?

Their only clue was a brief conversation between Judy and Dean Neterer, a sheriff's deputy, shortly before Judy was moved out of Elkhart General Hospital.

"Judy, you had your flashers on, did you have car trouble?" Neterer asked through a gauze face mask as he leaned close to hear her answer.

"No," Judy said.

"Did you run out of gas?" he asked, and she told him, "No." When he asked what happened, Judy replied only, "Gas ca- -," which she repeated two more times. Then, apparently because she was succumbing to the effects of a potent pain-killer a nurse had injected moments earlier, Judy stopped talking. Neteter was asked by the hospital staff to leave the room because nurses were getting Judy ready for her trip to the burn center.

What was Judy trying to tell him about the gas cap? All sorts of theories were advanced. One explanation was that the girls thought they left the cap at the Cheker station, had turned around, and were stopping to make sure the cap was missing before proceeding any farther. Maybe the cap was left on top of the car. The cap itself was not recovered during the initial investigation but was brought in by someone who found it later. When investigators checked photographs of the accident scene, they could see the cap sitting on the highway next to the curb. How did it all fit together? All the investigators had was speculation. As far as they knew, the truth had been buried with Judy.

Cosentino decided to have a grand jury start hearing some of the evidence being developed in the case. Under Indiana law, Cosentino had the power to file criminal charges against Ford on his own if he wished, but he figured that the reaction of the six grand jurors would help him predict how jurors would respond to evidence in an actual trial. If the panel decided Ford should be indicted and forced to stand trial, Cosentino would plunge ahead. If the reaction was negative, Cosentino figured he would be wasting his time with a trial. Like any prosecutor, he knew he could influence the grand jurors to do just about whatever he wanted. He vowed, though, that he would not push them one way or the other during the secret proceedings.

The astonishing news that a grand jury would even be asked to consider criminal charges in a Pinto crash sent two questions ricocheting through Ford's corporate headquarters in Dearborn, Michigan – "Who in the hell is this guy Cosentino and what is he trying to pull?" Ford management was especially concerned because of the possibility that Cosentino would seek criminal charges against individual corporate officers, even though Cosentino made up his mind at the outset that taking on the corporation itself would be enough for him to handle.

Ford assigned teams of lawyers to research the law and find support for the conclusion that any reckless homicide charge would be impermissible under the Indiana and United States constitutions. In an attempt to head off the case before it got started, Ford sent several lawyers, headed by Roger W. Barrett of Chicago's prestigous law firm of Mayer, Brown & Platt, and Richard Malloy, Ford's internal Pinto litigation expert, to visit Cosentino. The tactic backfired.

Cosentino considered the Ford lawyers condescending in their implication that he was just a small-town prosecutor who didn't quite know what he was doing. With his competitive nature aroused, each argument by Ford lawyers against the case merely strengthened Cosentino's resolve to press forward. And Cosentino completely rejected their contentions that the Ulrich crash involved such high speeds that no car could have been expected to withstand it without gas leakage. The evidence, Cosentino was convinced, disproved that notion.

When it became apparent their visit failed, Ford lawyers considered seeking a federal court injunction barring the prosecution, which would have been a legal maneuver nearly as radical as the charges the grand jury was to consider. That plan, however, was later abandoned.

Providing key testimony before the grand jury was Harley Copp, 57 years old, who started out during the summer of 1938 as a laborer on an experimental Ford farm and worked his way to the upper levels of Ford's corporate hierarchy until he was forced to retire in 1976. During his career, Copp was in charge of designing the original Ford Falcon, was involved with producing the popular compact Capri, served as director of engineering at Ford of Europe, and became director of Ford's engineering and technical services office. He reportedly earned $250,000 a year at his peak.

At one point in his career, Copp helped blow the whistle on the hazardous tendency of the General Motors Corvair to roll over, prompting consumer advocate Ralph Nader to comment approvingly that this marked "the first time an engineering expert of one company has so decisively repudiated the safety of another company's vehicle." In self-defense, carmakers have traditionally refrained from directly attacking the safety of another's cars.

Copp was forced to retire at age 55 on December 23, 1976, on grounds that his "extended and unauthorized absenses" prevented him from carrying out his responsibilities "in a satisfactory manner." But many people, including Cosentino, were convinced that Copp was forced out because he was too concerned and too vocal about auto safety.

After leaving Ford, and while still getting his hefty Ford pension, Copp became an engineering consultant to lawyers who were suing automakers in product-liability cases. His two weeks of testimony played a crucial role in winning the historic verdict in the Grimshaw case.

The gray-haired, grandfatherly Copp brought with him some internal Ford documents to add to Cosentino's growing collection. Some more were contributed by Byron Bloch, a colorful auto safety consultant who worked behind-the-scenes in the Grimshaw case and who also testified before Cosentino's grand jury. Both men closely examined the Ulrich Pinto, taking extensive notes, measurements, and photographs. Thinking that a faulty carburetor might have been responsible for the car slowing down on the highway, just as one had caused the Grimshaw Pinto to stall, Copp removed it for study. He concluded it was functioning normally.

On September 6, 1978, the grand jury issued summonses for corporate chairman Henry Ford II and former Ford President Lee A. Iacocca to testify about the design of the Pinto fuel system. "We would hope they will attend and give us Ford's side of the case," Cosentino told reporters at a press conference. "I would hope to have some information as to why the Pinto was constructed as it was."

Cosentino, indicating he didn't want to delay the grand jury's considerations, said he would be willing to receive testimony from anyone else designated by the automaker. In the end, two Ford executives were dispatched to Elkhart and spent hours telling Ford's story to the grand jurors.

After examining the physical evidence in the case, hearing evaluations of the Ulrich car by Copp and Bloch, seeing the internal Ford documents, and listening to Copp's fascinating inside account of Ford's decision-making, Cosentino came away personally convinced that Ford had sacrificed human life for corporate profit in selling its subcompact Pinto.

When a vote was taken, the grand jury's decision was unanimous – Ford Motor Company, just 34 days after the fatal crash, was indicted on three charges of reckless homicide and one misdemeanor charge of reckless conduct.

The three felony charges accused Ford of recklessly designing and building the 1973 Ulrich Pinto "in such a manner as would likely cause said automobile to flame and burn upon rear-end impact." Also, Ford was charged with failing to repair and modify the defective car. As a result, the indictment contended, the three Ulrich girls "did languish and die by incineration."

The misdemeanor charge was later dropped by Cosentino before trial because of fears that if Ford pleaded guilty to it, this would preclude prosecution of the more serious felony charges.

As for Duggar, the grand jury issued a one-page statement saying: "Although he may have been negligent in his conduct at or prior to the time of the collision, we do not believe that his conduct constituted a criminal act."

The grand jurors added that they "sincerely believe" that the curbs on Highway 33 "*must* be removed and provisions made by the appropriate officials to permit a motor vehicle to leave the roadway when necessary." Ten months later, construction crews began tearing away some of the curbing on the highway between Elkhart and Goshen and adding bays for disabled vehicles.

The indictment caused a nationwide sensation. Newspapers across the country gave the story front-page treatment and it got major play on the network news shows. Joseph Tybor of the *National Law Journal* put a large picture of Cosentino on the front page and profiled him in a lengthy article. Cosentino's telephone wouldn't stop ringing as he was beseiged by other interview requests.

Nader called the indictment "marvelous," saying it was "a lack of moral courage that put 1.5 million Pintos on the road with that atrocious gas tank." Using his forefinger as if to beckon Ford forward, he commented: "It's the only time a prosecutor has said to a company like Ford, 'c'mere.' "

Some of Cosentino's conservative friends reacted with skepticism, wondering what he was trying to do and speculating that he was attempting to make a name for himself so he could run for governor or Indiana attorney general. As he would end up doing repeatedly for the next 18 months, Cosentino disavowed any political aspirations beyond his job as part-time prosecutor.

Cosentino would admit later that he was naive when he obtained the indictment and had no idea of the scope of his undertaking. He had committed himself to trying to prove unprecedented criminal accusations against the nation's third largest industrial corporation, a mammoth, international business with $42 billion in annual sales, a net income of $1.6 billion a year, more than half a million employes, a giant and impressive legal staff and access to law firms employing some of the brightest minds in the country.

As for Cosentino, he had one full-time investigator, a handful of part-time assistants to handle the county's entire criminal caseload, and a total budget of $200,000 which was already committed. His only background in products liability was negotiating small settlements in three cases involving a spoiled sandwich, a can of food, and a bottle of soda.

"Terry," he said as he slapped Shewmaker on the back the day after they made legal history. "I think we've bitten off quite a bit here."

4

As news of the indictment reverberated through America, the initial reaction at Ford headquarters outside Detroit was a mixture of mild releif overshadowed by indignant anger.

The relief came because Cosentino had not obtained any criminal charges against individual corporate executives, and so no one person would be pushed into the humiliating position of having to defend himself under a threat of prison. And the intense anger stemmed from the deep-seated belief among Ford's highest echelon that the company's prized Pinto was once again being unfairly maligned.

The fact that conviction on the three felony charges would bring only a maximum fine of $30,000 was of little comfort. Everyone at Ford, and indeed throughout the automotive industry, knew there was much more at stake than that.

The recall itself had sent Ford's Pinto sales plunging 40 per cent for several weeks, and the car had only partially rebounded. Ford was in the midst of mounting a concentrated sales effort to try to cut into the resultant massive inventories by offering dealers an incentive of $325 for each

Pinto they sold. However, there was widespread skepticism among dealers as to whether this would be sufficient to overcome increasing public doubts about the car.

Just two days before the grand jury indictment, Andy Pasztor, who monitored the auto industry for the *Wall Street Journal,* described Ford's planned sales blitz and added that the Pinto "still threatens to become the company's biggest albatross since the ill-fated Edsel of two decades ago." He also quoted Henry Ford II as saying that the Pinto was "the biggest problem we've got."

One crucial aspect of the problem was that, under government regulations, the sales of gas-efficient cars like the Pinto helped determine the number of highly profitable, gas-guzzling big cars automakers could sell. A plummet in Pinto sales could cause a damaging ripple effect through much of the rest of the corporation's car line. And as one Wall Street analyst was quoted as saying: "There's no way Ford can sell its quota of 1979 Pintos unless it starts giving them away – and there aren't enough quiz shows for that."

Dealers were faced with the painful possibility of having to slash Pinto prices below wholesale cost in order to clear them from their crowded lots, even though the Pintos they were trying to sell had never been implicated in the controversy over the 1971-76 models.

Ford management knew that the additional bad publicity over the criminal charges could further aggravate the Pinto's sales downslide and compound the company's financial problems. More than that, though, they feared long-term damage to the corporate image, which already had been dragged through the mud as the Pinto controversy escalated to its climax at the time of the recall.

When a New York research firm completed a wide-ranging study of consumer opinions a few months after the indictment, it found that 38 per cent of those polled had heard that Ford cars were somehow unsafe. This was dramatically more than the rate for General Motors (six per cent); Chrysler and various imports (four per cent); and American Motors (one per cent).

Worse yet, in the critical under-35 age category, the level of persons saying they had heard or read negative things about the safety of Ford cars reached 47 per cent.

Although such statistics tend to fluctuate, Ford management was deeply concerned that the intense media reporting of a protracted trial, and the repeated image of burning Pintos seen on the evening news as part of the coverage, could translate into long-range financial woes for the company's already sagging domestic auto operation.

And there were other nagging concerns. With the number of Pinto and Bobcat lawsuits continuing to rise toward 50, and total damages of more than one billion dollars being sought, Ford lawyers feared a conviction could cause plaintiffs' lawyers to hold out for higher civil court settlements and even encourage new lawsuits. The evidence disclosed during a criminal trial also might be used by lawyers in civil lawsuits to strengthen their cases if they wound up in front of a jury.

In addition, there was the ominous possibility that a success by Cosentino could set a precedent encouraging prosecutors elsewhere to pursue similar criminal cases in the future – and the next time, perhaps individual executives would not be spared.

More subtle problems also troubled Ford management. Even though no executives were formally charged, prosecutors had to present evidence that the car had been defectively designed and that the corporation had been reckless in failing to warn consumers. A corporation acts through its executives, and so the prosecutors, in effect, would be trying individual members of Ford management for their decisions regarding the Pinto. Ford executives, accustomed to receiving community respect commensurate with their high social status and lucrative salaries, cringed at such a degrading possibility. Even if they felt they had done nothing wrong, the idea of undergoing public interrogation and being the target of a prosecutor's allegations and insinuations was a humiliating thought.

Ford lawyers knew, of course, that there was a way

to avoid most of these problems. If they were able to get the indictment declared unconstitutional as soon as possible, it would pull the plug on Cosentino's planned trial and all the publicity that would accompany it. The decision was made to spare no expense in launching a massive attack on the legality of the charges.

A team of about 10 lawyers, headed by Roger Barrett of the 185-member Mayer, Brown & Platt law firm, was given responsibility for drafting a broad-based motion to dismiss the indictment. According to James Warren and Brian Kelly, two reporters who looked into this phase of the case, Ford also assigned the respected New York firm of Hughes, Hubbard & Reed to work on the issues involved. Among those analyzing the indictment for that firm was Philip Lacovara, a former Watergate prosecutor described as a "young hotshot" in the firm's Washington office. Henry Ford II, who supposedly scrutinized the legal papers, preferred the constitutional rhetoric employed by Lacovara and his firm, and in the end part of the Hughes, Hubbard approach was worked into the legal document submitted by Barrett to Judge Donald W. Jones of Elkhart County Superior Court.

The 55-page motion to dismiss the indictment, containing more than 15 different arguments and citing cases dating back to the dawn of American jurisprudence, became Ford's first comprehensive attack on Cosentino's untried legal theory. Ford lawyers were confident of success to the point of being cocky.

"The state," began the document, "seeks to transform an incident that traditionally is judged under the civil law into a basis for criminal prosecution. A decision to apply the criminal process to manufacturers whose products may be involved in an accident. . .presents so major a policy question that it must, in the first instance, be addressed by the legislature.

"Such an application of the criminal law would drastically expand common conceptions of criminal responsibility and would wipe out the basic distinction between civil wrongs and criminal offenses."

Civil lawsuits, Ford lawyers asserted, would be "more than adequate" to deal with any allegedly improper Ford actions which might have contributed to injuries. "There is neither a need nor a proper basis for this court to strain to entertain these criminal charges which, as the prosecuting attorney has acknowledged, are a novel and unprecedented effort to stretch the criminal process to fit the allegations of a product liability case," the motion said.

The constitutional arguments centered on the fear of what would happen if criminal juries in various states were allowed to judge whether automakers had recklessly strayed from standards of conduct which the jurors determined where appropriate for them to follow.

Ford lawyers asserted that when Congress passed the National Traffic and Motor Vehicle Safety Act of 1966, setting up auto safety standards and a mechanism for investigating alleged safety defects in cars, it preempted the states from using their own criminal laws to regulate the design and manufacture of cars.

"An automobile manufacturer cannot, as a practical matter, produce an automobile according to two sets of standards, one established by a federal agency and the other constructed by a state criminal jury," the motion said.

In a related argument, Ford lawyers contended that letting Indiana impose criminal sanctions would "unreasonably burden the free flow of commerce" between the states.

"The automobile industry is essentially a national industry, and basic matters of safety in design cannot be fragmented on a state-by-state basis. If each of the 50 states were permitted to base drastic criminal sanctions on its individualized notions of how an automobile 'should' have been designed, manufactured, or modified, the entire industry would be tied in regulatory knots."

Also, Ford lawyers claimed the indictment violated the *ex post facto* provisions of the state and United States constitutions because the alleged reckless design and manufacture of the Ulrich car occurred before the 1977 enactment of the Indiana reckless homicide statute. The *ex post facto* clauses prohibit retroactive application of criminal laws. Because of a new provision of the Indiana law which went into effect later, the most Ford could be charged with would be acting recklessly by failing to warn about the allegedly dangerous Pinto during a 41-day time period prior to the Ulrich crash, Ford lawyers said.

And there were other arguments. Ford lawyers contended that 'there are clearly crimes – essentially crimes of violence against other human beings – where it is irrational to read the statutes as applying to corporations." They also said the allegation that Ford failed to "repair and modify" the Ulrich car made no sense because "research has not uncovered a single case that holds a manufacturer is legally required to go out and physically retrieve a product from its owner and then repair and modify it."

They added that the indictment was vague, providing "not the slightest clue as to how the design and manufacture (of the 1973 Pinto) were reckless."

"It is regrettable but true, of course, that even an automobile built like a tank cannot assure the absolute safety of the occupants when an automobile is involved in a rear-end collision," the lawyers asserted.

At times using sarcasm and poking fun at Cosentino's effort ("the indictment makes no sense at all"), the motion went on to explore numerous other legal theories before concluding with the self-assured statement that "the entire indictment must be dismissed."

With a resounding swat, Ford had returned Cosentino's opening serve. And the small-town, part-time prosecutor was going to need some help in keeping the volley going.

5

Mike Cosentino and Terry Shewmaker realized right away that they desperately needed two things to plunge ahead with their historic case – Money and manpower.

"The way I figure it," Shewmaker said in his flat Indiana drawl, "somehow we've got to find a way to imitate a 100-man law firm. Otherwise, we won't stand a chance."

Cosentino knew where they could at least get some extra money for the case. "I'll ask the County Council for $20,000," he said. "That's all. I've got to promise them up-front that I won't come back in six months begging for more."

In a tax-strapped county whose primary industry was suffering a nose-dive because of the soaring price of gasoline, Cosentino knew he couldn't dare ask for more than $20,000. That meant they would have to be frugal, but he figured they could make it without much problem unless Ford decided to drag out the case for years or was able to get the trial transferred to a far-away county. If that happened, he knew the money squeeze would become acute.

In addition to the cash, Cosentino knew he could draw

on some of the resources of the state and federal governments to help him. The state police already agreed to cooperate by assigning Graves to the case on a full-time basis, and they offered to make their planes and helicopters available if they were needed. The crime lab would analyze evidence without charge. Some evidence, such as internal Ford documents as well as movies and reports on the Pinto crash tests run by NHTSA during its investigation, could be obtained free from the federal government. And Conour promised back-up help in researching the many novel legal questions raised by the case.

But there was no question the $20,000 would be a handicap in the face of what Cosentino expected to be an all-out, open-checkbook defense by Ford. Cosentino knew he could forget about retaining some expert technical witnesses he wanted to use to bolster his case – they wanted their standard rate of up to $750 a day. And he had to abandon his idea of running an experimental crash test of his own on a 1973 Pinto as part of the investigation. The bill on just one independent test would eat up half his entire budget.

Because of their keen interest in the Pinto controversy, Bloch and Copp agreed to work on the case for free, even paying their own air fare to Indiana. In a way, their volunteer help also was an investment for them. Their participation in such a landmark trial could pay them benefits later by enhancing their reputations and giving them national publicity which might bring them more profitable consulting work in civil lawsuits.

But if Bloch and Copp were interested enough in the case to donate their time, wouldn't some lawyers be intrigued enough by the novelty and significance of the indictment to provide some free help? Cosentino and Shewmaker already had received some tentative inquiries from law professors who said they might want to assist, although they were at schools located too far away to be of much help.

They decided to make a few telephone calls and find out if anyone closer to Elkhart County would offer their legal services in return for working on a case which was destined to be part of tomorrow's law books. An intern from Valparaiso University's law school who was working in Cosentino's office suggested they try Bruce Berner, a professor at nearby Valparaiso. Berner, who looked like comedian Woody Allen and could rattle off puns and jokes in the machinegun style of Henny Youngman, had a reputation for having a quick, well-trained legal mind and a photographic memory. One of the first bits of advice law students would get through the grapevine when they started at Valparaiso was always: "You've *got* to take a course from Professor Berner."

Late on a Friday afternoon, Shewmaker called Berner at his house, finding the professor hard at work improving his golf game by hitting plastic balls around his back yard.

"Have you been following the newspaper accounts of the Ford Pinto prosecution?" Shewmaker asked after identifying himself.

"Sure," Berner replied.

"Do you think we're all crazy?"

"Absolutely not," Berner said immediately. "It sounds theoretically sound to me."

Shewmaker asked if he would like to get involved, and Berner agreed to attend a meeting in Elkhart that weekend to discuss the possibility. At the time, he didn't know if getting involved with the case would mean receiving an occasional telephone call about a legal point or, as it turned out to be, a virtual full-time commitment.

A 34-year-old professor of criminal law, Berner was intrigued with the issues raised by the unprecedented indictment. Although he was a liberal Democrat who had worked on Eugene McCarthy's ill-fated presidential bid, Berner didn't consider himself a "Ralph Nader-type" consumed with trying to reform corporations. He was more interested in the case from an intellectual standpoint because it posed stimulating and challenging legal problems in his area of academic expertise.

Except for a burning childhood ambition to become a short-stop for the New York Giants, Berner always wanted to be a lawyer. He attended Valparaiso University and then its law school, graduating in 1967 and returning to his native New Jersey where he was a prosecutor of traffic and misdemeanor cases. He joined a four-man litigation firm and got extensively involved with civil cases before returning to teach law at Valparaiso in 1971. His wife, Linda, and their three children had just returned a few months earlier from a leave of absence during which Berner earned an advanced law degree from Yale Law School.

He was slightly built, with brown hair cropped short and glasses with thick lenses that magnified his eyes. Despite his book-worm appearance, he was considered a sociable, easy-going and conscientious teacher whose off-beat brand of humor provided a much-needed change of pace from the grind of law school.

Shewmaker had another possibility in mind. He remembered that when he briefly attended law school at DePaul University in Chicago a few years earlier, he took a course in torts and products liability from Terrence Kiely, a burly, bearded professor who had strong opinions about corporations. Shewmaker called him at his office, described the project, and asked if he would be willing to help.

Kiely, whose bulldog appearance made him look more like a nightclub bouncer than a professor, had only a vague acquaintance with the criminal case but was quite familiar with the Grimshaw trial because he talked about it during his classes. He told Shewmaker he might be interested in helping and would be willing to attend the meeting in Elkhart.

Kiely strongly believed that corporations were unaccountable to the American public – he called them "out of control" – and that this was doing profound damage to the American economic system. A 36-year-old Chicago native with law degrees from DePaul and New York University, Kiely believed that civil lawsuits had failed to deter big corporations from producing dangerous products and that the time was ripe for the step to be taken into the arena of criminal law. That was the only way, he felt, that a message could be sent to corporate executives that they are personally responsible to the public for the decisions they make.

Ironically, Kiely once received funding from the Ford Foundation for a prison legal clinic program he conducted while teaching law in Columbus, Ohio. His trial experience, which did not include any product-liability cases, involved primarily contract and accident litigation while he worked for an insurance defense firm. A popular professor, he had a low-key personality and a wry, sometimes biting sense of humor, and was often kidded about his constant snacking on almonds and grapefruit juice.

At the Elkhart meeting, Cosentino went over the legal theory behind the indictment and showed the professors some of the evidence and internal Ford documents. Their initial interest intensified when they saw the inside of the case, and when Cosentino asked them for a commitment, there was no hesitation, although neither professor understood they would end up sacrificing all their free time for months to the pressing demands of the complex case.

Two other important decisions were made at that meeting. The first was that the workload would be divided between the professors, with Berner handling the legal theories and Kiely working on the evidence, including the Ford documents. Later, a Goshen lawyer named John Ulmer would donate his time in helping Cosentino with trial preparation. The other decision was that the professors would each choose a select cadre of second and third-year law students to provide the manpower needed to research legal questions, help draft motions, and compile and catalog the evidence.

Cosentino, who was successful in getting his special $20,000 allocation for the case from the county, would say later that bringing in Kiely, Berner, and the students was the smartest move he ever made. Without them, the case would have overwhelmed his office and the prosecution effort would have capsized.

The case, with its first-ever legal issues and its intricate, often-technical evidence, was a natural work-study project for the students, giving them a chance to escape from the stale cases in lawbooks and work instead on real-life issues with national ramifications. Kiely and Berner chose their teams carefully from among their brightest students. They generally skipped the younger students in favor of those with more maturity and backgrounds which included military, business, or some other experience that required the efficient fulfillment of responsibilities. From each one, they elicited a pledge of total commitment to the project. "One hundred percent is a minimum," Kiely warned each one before they signed up.

Before it was over, about 15 students would be involved with the project. As a few would graduate, others would be selected to replace them, although a few that went on to law firms continued to contribute some time. Often working in teams, they camped out in the law library late into the night and on weekends, sandwiching in some research time during their lunch hours and between classes. Kiely's cramped, drafty office seven stories above downtown Chicago was the scene of constant informal meetings as students flowed in and out according to their various schedules. As Kiely would say later, "They all gave a lot more than 100 per cent."

One of the students was Don Seberger, the 26-year-old editor of the Valparaiso Law Review who was raised by his widowed mother in Schererville, Indiana, just down the highway from the law school. Seberger studied for the priesthood as a student before quitting for a stint as a $3.51-an-hour steelworker, throwing scrap iron into a 3,200-degree furnace. After finishing college with a degree in history and political science, getting married to a nurse, and working as an insurance claims adjuster, he decided to become a lawyer.

Known as the law school's "resident Tory" because of his adamant conservative views and pro-business attitude, Seberger's motive for getting involved was to learn about the practical aspects of law by working closely with Berner, a professor he respected. He also saw it as a rare opportunity to play a role in a case with the potential of becoming as reknowned as the Scopes Monkey Trial.

His big-business sympathies initially kept him form endorsing much of the corporate-reform rhetoric associated with the case. But when he read the accounts of eyewitnesses to the accident and what happened to Judy and the girls, Seberger's eyes filled with tears and he became outraged, wanting retribution for the deaths Later he realized there was more to the case than that, and became convinced that the case had an important mission – to send a message to American industry that they must stop producing dangerous products. Seberger strongly believed American manufacturers were capable of making healthy profits and at the same time protecting consumers. From a pure business standpoint, he concluded, Ford's action in producing the Pinto was plain stupid.

Seberger, whose choir-boy complexion and black-rimmed glasses gave him a studious look, intended at the outset to pursue the case only on an intellectual level as a learning experience. That fell apart as he got deeper and deeper into the case and the objective, analytical approach of a student gave way to the passionate zeal of an advocate. He felt each setback as a personal blow and celebrated each victory, however minor, with elation. Seberger devoted as much as 30 to 35 hours a week to the case at the peak of his activity, letting much of his other schoolwork slide but getting an education few students ever receive.

The first assignment given the students was to plunge into the lawbooks and come up with solid legal reasoning to answer the voluminous motion to dismiss the indictment which had been filed by Ford's lawyers. Four of Berner's students worked hundreds of hours in the library to provide him with the ammunition to write the 73-page response.

"This case is not about big business. It is about homicide," the prosecution brief said in its introduction. "Although Ford Motor Company wishes to paint the State of Indiana as ad-hoc regulators of industry, the fact remains that the state has simply responded in its traditional manner to three local deaths which it claims resulted from criminal misconduct.

"Ford cries surprise. Yet, where is the surprise? Three homicides have occurred and the state has responded with indictment and prosecution as it has always responded when crimes are committed. Surely Ford's surprise, like that of all persons accused of crime, lies in the fact that it's crime has been discovered and that the state has the temerity to bring Ford to account for its conduct."

Prosecutors said that there was no basis for Ford's fear that this case would "open the floodgates" to similar prosecutions across the country. The brief pointed out that to prosecute under the reckless homicide statute, the state must prove the defendant acted in "plain, conscious, and unjustifiable disregard of the harm that might result" and the disregard "involved a substantial deviation from acceptable standards of conduct."

"This statute cannot be violated by inadvertence or mistake. It requires proof that a manufacturer was aware of an intolerable risk to the consumer of its products and *consciously* chose to visit risk on them in service of its own interest.

"The state alleges that Ford did just that when it marketed the Pinto. Although the state does not desire to 'chill' manufacturers generally, it does desire to *deter* outrageous decisions to sacrifice human life for private profit."

In response to statements by Ford lawyers that the indictment was "novel" and "bizarre," the brief said: "it is not the prosecutor's legal theory which is 'novel' or 'bizarre.' The novel element, instead, is Ford's alleged conduct of deliberately placing on the nation's highways over one million vehicles, known by it to possess an intolerably unsafe design which would predictably and unnecessarily take human life."

Saying Ford "is not being asked to observe any higher standard of care than any other member of society," the brief added:

"Reckless Homicide is an offense against the peace and dignity of this sovereign, which is endowed with the right, the power, and the duty to prosecute the offender to the fullest extent of the law. The state has no desire to regulate the auto industry; yet, Ford's position as a member of that industry does not grant it exemption from those laws which every member of society is expected to observe."

The brief then painstakingly went through each of what prosecutors called the "spurious, albeit ingenious, arguments" made by Ford lawyers and attempted to rebut each one.

Cosentino's filing of the document two days before Christmas, 1978, marked the end of the first round of combat involving his ragtag band of volunteers and students against Ford's polished legion of corporate attorneys. The task of deciding the winner fell to Donald W. Jones, a judge who had just been elected to the bench and suddenly found himself in the national spotlight.

6

Donald W. Jones assumed the bench promptly at 1 p.m. on Friday, February 2, 1979, and looked out at a courtroom crowded with lawyers, news reporters, and spectators. Jones, a youthful former public defender still getting acclimated to his new position as judge, wasted little time in issuing what he knew they were all waiting for – his decision on whether to dismiss Ford's indictment.

The courtroom fell silent. "There are substantial factors in this case for which there are no precedents in law," he said from atop his marble-adorned bench. Tension built as lawyers on each side weighed every word for clues as to which way he would rule.

Then Jones, known for his straight-forward style, added simply: "The indictment is sufficient. I therefore deny the motion to dismiss."

An audible sigh of relief swept through the courtroom; Cosentino broke into a broad smile as he shook hands with his assistants and patted them on the back. Ford lawyers, including Roger Barrett of Chicago, stared down at their tables and gathered up their papers.

Jones set February 15 for the automaker's arraignment.

Reporters and television cameramen surged around Cosentino as the courtroom doors swung open onto the second floor corridor. "The court has justified our position," Cosentino said, obviously savoring the moment. "As far as the law is concerned, a corporation can be indicted for homicide. This was the main motion. We're over our major hurdle."

Earl and Mattie Ulrich, who sat motionless during the brief proceeding, found themselves surrounded by newsmen as they walked arm-in-arm down the hallway. "There comes a day of reckoning," the slender, graying father of Judy and Lyn said quietly into the microphones. "And I think that day of reckoning is here."

For Ford lawyers, it was a day of few public words. "I'm disappointed, naturally," was all Barrett would say.

Jones accompanied his verbal ruling with a 20-page decision in which he rejected Ford's constitutional arguments as well as its attack on the sufficiency of the indictment itself.

As for Ford's argument that the federal regulatory system for auto safety preempted states from using criminal laws in connection with auto design, Jones said that "this action is a criminal prosecution and is not being brought for a violation of any federal standard, nor for the violation of any regulatory scheme adopted by the State of Indiana. . .

"Inasmuch as there appears to be an absense of any clear, manifest purpose of Congress to supersede the general criminal laws of the state, the allegations in the defendant's motion to dismiss on the theory that the federal legislation has preempted the state are not well taken and must fail."

In rejecting the argument by Ford lawyers that the case would impermissibly disrupt interstate commerce, Jones said that "states have paramount jurisdiction in matters of intrastate commerce and where protection of public health and safety is necessary. . . .Even if the statute does affect interstate commerce, it is not necessarily unconstitutional. If the statute is a reasonable and legitimate exercise of the police power and does not discriminate against interstate commerce or disrupt the area where uniformity is required, it will be upheld unless the burden imposed on commerce is clearly excessive in relation to the local benefits."

Jones pointed out that Ford lawyers failed to submit any sworn allegations supporting "all of the essential facts necessary for the court's determination" of the interstate commerce issue.

The judge also rejected assertions by Ford lawyers that the automaker had no duty to remove the car from the road or modify it before the accident. "Further," he wrote, "the enactment of the reckless homicide statute did not create this long-standing duty, but only applied criminal sanctions where reckless breach of that duty caused the death of a human being."

In addition, Jones had little difficulty in disposing of Ford's contention that a corporation cannot be accused of violating the reckless homicide law. "The rule of no corporate criminal liability has been somewhat eroded and it now appears to be an accepted view that a corporation can have imputed to it the guilty mind of its agents," he wrote. "A common sense reading (of Indiana law) discloses that a corporation can be prosecuted for any offense and can be convicted of that offense when the offense was committed by (a corporate) agent acting within the scope of his authority."

Jones, however, had some problems with the wording of the indictment. "The indictment in this case does not appear to allege the fact of recklessness causing the death, but rather seems to allege that the impact caused the defendant's recklessness," he wrote. He resolved the problem by calling it a grammatical error and saying, "This language is clearly not intended to mean what is stated."

Yet was this instance of sloppy draftsmanship on such an important indictment more than that – perhaps a hint of haste and lack of thoroughness which might have crept into part of the criminal investigation itself? This troubling question would not even begin to be answered for more than a year.

The most important part of Jones' ruling dealt with the

assertion by Ford that the indictment violated the *ex post facto* provisions of the state and federal constitutions. Ford lawyers had charged that the automaker's allegedly reckless design of the 1973 Pinto occurred more than four years before the October 1, 1977 enactment of the Indiana reckless homicide statute, and therefore that statute could not be retroactively imposed against Ford.

However, a new provision of the reckless homicide law went into effect 41 days before the Ulrich accident and permitted criminal charges against anyone who *failed* to perform a required act and thus caused the death of someone. Ford's indictment accused the company not only of recklessly designing and building the car, but also *failing* to repair and modify the allegedly dangerous vehicle.

Jones ruled that the indictment was constitutional only when read to charge that Ford acted recklessly by failing to repair or warn about the Pinto during that 41-day time period before the Ulrich crash. The elements of the indictment concerning the car's defective and dangerous design were relevant only to establish the reason why Ford should have warned the public or fixed the car during that 41-day period.

Now that Ford's attempt to head off a trial had failed, management of the corporation decided to attack the situation on two fronts. First, a major effort would be mounted to get the trial moved out of Elkhart County, where publicity about the case was so intense that Ford lawyers believed an impartial jury would be impossible. They knew that they would have a better chance of winning the trial if they could get it transferred to a rural Indiana community populated by conservative, pro-business townspeople who might not accept Cosentino's legal theories. And this would have the advantage of getting out of Cosentino's backyard where he was well-known and respected, and into another county where Cosentino was unknown and would have to spend much of his paltry budget for travel, living expenses and office space.

The second objective was to find a top-notch criminal

defense lawyer to head the case. Barrett had told Ford all along that his expertise was civil law, not criminal, and that Ford would have to find itself an outstanding criminal defense specialist if it appeared the case would end up in front of a jury.

Ford officials had definite ideas about the kind of lawyer they wanted. He would have to be superb in the field of criminal defense work, with a track record of being able to win extremely complicated and protracted trials. He would have to have leadership qualities in order to supervise and coordinate a multi-faceted defense effort involving dozens of people. He should have at least some experience with product-liability cases because this prosecution borrowed much of its theories from that area of the law. Preferably, he would be able to communicate well with a small-town jury in case Ford was successful in getting the trial moved to a rural county. And it was crucial to have someone who was comfortable and effective in dealing with the news media. Ford officials knew, although they didn't like it that the case would attract heavy national coverage and that there would be two trials – one in court and one in the media. It would be possible to win the jury's verdict but lose the public relations war if consumers were left with a strong impression that Ford was an evil corporation that produced dangerous products.

Members of Ford's law department began calling their friends in the legal community and discretely fishing for the names of possible candidates. One of those called was Philip Lacovara, the Hughes, Hubbard & Reed lawyer who impressed Ford officials during the early stages of the case. Lacovara didn't have to think long before coming up with the name of a Nashville, Tennessee, lawyer he had worked with on part of the Watergate case. The attorney, James Foster Neal, fit Ford's criteria as if he had been grooming himself for the job for years.

Neal, a short, sturdy, broad-shouldered man with piercing blue eyes who smoked cigars that were so big they looked like inflated toys, served as a special assistant to U.S. Attorney

General Robert F. Kennedy and gained national attention as the first prosecutor to win a conviction against Jimmy Hoffa, who at the time headed the International Brotherhood of Teamsters. After that, Neal served a term as a federal prosecutor in Tennessee before opening a private law practice with a newspaperman-turned-lawyer named Aubrey Harwell.

In 1973, Neal again stepped into the national spotlight as a special Watergate prosecutor who handled the politically explosive trials stemming from that scandal. Despite his success in Washington, he chose to go back to Nashville afterward to rejoin his burgeoning law practice, which handled primarily white-collar criminal cases and also performed legal work for such country-western stars as Johnny Cash and Dolly Parton. At one point he was a top candidate to become director of the Federal Bureau of Investigation until he withdrew his name from consideration.

Neal grew up on a tobacco farm near tiny Oak Grove, Tennessee, learning early in life to appreciate education because he found that the more hours he spent in school, the less time he had to spend toiling in the tobacco fields. For entertainment, he sometimes walked over to the local courthouse to watch the proceedings.

A star fullback, Neal went through the University of Wyoming on a sports scholarship and later served as a Marine captain in the Korean War. At Vanderbilt University Law School, he graduated first in his class and went on to earn an advanced law degree from Georgetown University.

Neal and Harwell, also a Vanderbilt law graduate, built their private practice into an eight-man firm which often roamed the country trying criminal cases having regional notoriety. When Nashville millionaire-socialite Bronson Ingram, head of the Ingram Corporation, was indicted in Chicago in an intricate bribery case, Neal was paid a reputed $800,000 to win his acquittal. A Texas oilman, in trouble with federal sleuths, once offered to send Neal a $100,000 check just to get Neal's attention so he would listen to his story. At the same time, Neal's firm was expanding into the defense of product-liability lawsuits, representing such automotive clients as General Motors, Volkswagen, and Suburu.

Through it all, Neal, whose nickname was "Flash" (although it was once embarrassingly misspelled as "Flush" in the *New York Times*), tried to maintain his down-home, country image. He sprinkled his conversation with words like "doggone it" and "ah reckon," pronounced words like automobile as "autoMObile," and vehicle as "veHICLE," and made a flourish of being chivalrous and polite in court. Instead of simply telling a judge that it would be unrealistic to expect a jury to disregard something, Neal would say: "If it please the court, you can't throw a polecat into a jury box and expect the jury not to smell it."

Among the news media, he was considered popular, accessible and quoteable, seldom refusing to answer a question with "no comment" but being careful to reveal only what he wanted. His relaxed style of lighting up a fat cigar, sipping on a scotch-and-water, and spinning colorful tales of his legal conquests gave reporters the false feeling of being in his confidence. And he would often bolster the egos of reporters and give them an inflated feeling of self-importance by pulling them aside and, in a concerned and serious tone, asking them their opinion about a legal issue or tactic.

A fierce competitor, the 49-year-old Neal hated to lose any contest, including tennis matches. "Flip him to see who buys lunch and he loses – the day's a disaster," Harwell told the *New York Times* in one of several articles in which Neal was profiled. He also had a tendency to become hyperdefensive whenever he felt someone had even subtly questioned his Southern honor.

Neal's first contact about the case came from Lacovara, who asked him whether he would be interested in talking to Ford about the job. Neal's reaction was mixed at first. He realized the case would require him to become knowledgeable about complex engineering and automotive concepts and terminology, which was something he wouldn't enjoy. And he knew the case would require an extended absense from his office.

But Neal also was flattered by being approached, and he knew Ford was a client fully capable of paying his hefty fee. In addition, he was intrigued by the broad and significant legal questions and the potential impact of the case on American industry. Neal had strongly held opinions that American corporations were becoming underdogs in society, entities with few friends among the public, even though the success of American industry had given the United States the highest standard of living in the world. He was gravely concerned about what he considered serious problems facing corporations – deteriorating plant equipment, declining productivity, dependence on foreign oil, lack of capital, massive government controls, foreign competition – and was convinced that Cosentino's attempt to add another burden would lead to further disruption of the economic system.

Neal believed that not only Cosentino's hybrid criminal case, but also civil product-liability cases should be outlawed when Congress has undertaken to intimately regulate a particular industry, such as the auto industry. When federal government standards for safety are set and a manufacturer meets those minimum standards, he believed no civil or criminal jury should have the power to hold the manufacturer accountable for failing to meet a higher standard. Only when a corporation failed to meet the requirements of a minimum federal standard should it ever face liability in a civil or criminal case, in Neal's view.

Neal said he would be interested in talking about the case, and flew to Dearborn a few days later for a meeting with Ford's chief corporate counsel, Henry Nolte. After several follow-up conversations, and getting permission from his client General Motors, Neal accepted the case. As it turned out, General Motors was so interested in the ramifications of the case that it sent its own lawyers to attend the trial and report back on the proceedings.

Part of Neal's deal with Ford was that Harwell would be his partner on the case. Although they hadn't worked together on a trial for more than seven years, Neal knew the complexity of the case would require someone with Harwell's extensive product-liability background as well as his considerable talents as an investigator.

And there was one more lawyer who would make up the core of Ford's defense effort – Malcolm Wheeler, a 34-year-old anti-trust expert in the Los Angeles office of Hughes, Hubbard & Reed. After the massive jury verdict against Ford in the Grimshaw case, Wheeler was sent to the automaker with the assignment of trying to devise an entirely new legal strategy to cope with future Pinto litigation. Even before the Ulrich tragedy occurred, Wheeler was working closely with Ford lawyers and engineers to become completely familiar with the technical and legal ends of the Pinto controversy. Unlike most attorneys, he felt at ease with the technical aspects because of his extensive background in physics, which included a degree from the Massachusetts Institute of Technology. Wheeler's fortuitous head-start in digging into the Pinto controversy would prove invaluable to the defense team in the criminal case.

Wheeler, who once represented billionaire Howard Hughes in a libel case, was in the process of abandoning his successful career as a legal practitioner to become a professor of law at the University of Iowa in Iowa City. His long black hair, which hung over his collar, made him look like he would be more comfortable handling the prisoner and Indian rights cases he once championed than representing a straight-laced corporate giant like Ford. But Wheeler, like Neal, believed there was a danger in the growing tendency of the American public to automatically consider corporations as enemies of society. American industry, he believed, needed someone to stand up for it and tell its side of the story. He was anxious to do it.

7

It took only one afternoon to conduct the entire formal court hearing into the question of whether Ford's trial should be moved out of Elkhart County, but the short duration belied the amount of time and money Ford invested in this crucial issue.

"Since the time of the accident underlying this case, the people of Elkhart County and the surrounding counties have been subjected to a massive amount of publicity which must have irrevocably convinced a great many of them that Ford is guilty of the offenses charged in the indictment," Ford lawyers told Judge Jones in a thick written request for a change of venue.

To back up their assertions, Ford attorneys compiled voluminous records of newspaper articles and television tapes. They also arranged for a sophisticated telephone survey to be conducted in which more than 600 residents of Elkhart and adjacent counties were contacted and interviewed about their views of the case. The cost of the survey, conducted by an Iowa firm, was just about equal to Cosentino's budget for the entire prosecution.

Then Ford hired the well-respected Hans Zeisel, a 72-year-old professor emeritus of law and sociology at the University of Chicago Law School, to provide testimony about the effects of the publicity. Zeisel was an expert on juries, having written the highly regarded text *The American Jury* with the late Harry Kalven in 1966. His fee was $1,000 a day.

Ford had attorneys from two firms working on the motion – Barrett's giant firm and the Elkhart firm of Thornburg, McGill, Deahl, Harmon, Carey & Murray. Neal, who was just beginning his involvement in the case, attended the proceedings in an advisory capacity.

The telephone survey, analyzed by a nationally known consultant, disclosed that 56 per cent of the people quetioned in Elkhart County believed Ford was either guilty or probably guilty of the reckless homicide charge. The poll also showed that about 69 per cent believed that neither side could get a fair hearing in Elkhart County.

Barrett bolstered the survey results with testimony by Zeisel, who said he found 86 news reports he considered extremely prejudicial to Ford. He said that in his opinion, it was "highly unlikely" that Ford could get a fair trial in Elkhart or any adjacent county.

Cosentino knew that a change of venue to a far-away county would be a severe blow to his team's morale and budget. He subpenaed Ford television commercials from three local stations, arguing that "Ford's advertisements for the Pinto are plainly calculated, among other things, to offset any negative opinion flowing from this prosecution. . . Ford's prominence has permitted it to make its position on the case clear."

He pointed out that changes of venue were denied in such celebrated cases as the Patty Hearst, Charles Manson, and Watergate trials. And he used the results of Ford's own survey to point out that about 66 per cent of the persons interviewed declined to say that Ford was "probably guilty."

Berner and Cosentino also tried to call into question the validity of the survey by introducing into evidence a letter from a communications specialist who had been asked by

Ford to help with conducting part of the survey. "I must honestly tell you that I do not believe a case can be made from it (the publicity) to the effect that the company you represent has been prejudiced in the news media," Joseph M. Webb, head of the communications department at the University of Evansville, wrote in the letter to Ford.

When Jones' three-page ruling came on April 10, 1979, Cosentino was disappointed but not surprised. "Based on all the evidence of pretrial publicity," Jones wrote, "the court finds it highly probable that Ford would be prevented from obtaining a fair and impartial trial in this county and in the five surrounding counties and that in the interest of justice the defendant should be entitled to a change of venue."

The decision was Ford's first clear-cut victory in the case. As for Cosentino, he already had promised not to seek any more money from the county and now he would be faced with paying travel and living expenses for himself, his assistants, the volunteers, and some witnesses during a trial which could last two or three months. And his home-court advantage was gone.

Jones said Ford lawyers and Cosentino could have three days to decide on a new site for the trial – something everyone knew was impossible given the animosity between the opposing sides – or he would submit a list of five counties for them to choose from. When no agreement was reached, each side was allowed to alternately strike a name from the list until just one remained – Pulaski County.

Down in Pulaski (pronounced locally as "Pulask-eye") County, situated about 55 miles southwest of Elkhart, the change of venue was the biggest news since someone shot the sheriff back in 1967. News reporters and television crews flocked to Winamac (population 2,450), the county seat where the 84-year-old limestone-and-slate courthouse was located, to interview local residents about their reaction. What they found was a slice of rural Americana and a very hospitable atmosphere for Ford Motor Company.

One guitar-strumming Winamac cafe owner who drove a Ford truck was so swept away by the righteousness of

Ford's defense that he wrote a song commemorating the change of venue:

Ford Motor Company has turned down
Every courtroom around,
Now they've found them a good little town,
They've come here to fight
And we're gonna treat them right
'Cause a good old company is all they'll ever be!
Refrain: *They're not gonna take the blame*
For something they didn't do.

Named after Revolutionary War hero Casimir Pulaski, the county was the home of 12,500 people, 650 soybean and corn farms, and some notorious wild patches of marijuana which often attracted quite a few cars with out-of-state license plates. The Pulaski County Historical Society's history of the area was summarized on only one side of a piece of paper, concluding with the concession: "Nothing of general historical significance has transpired within the bounds of Pulaski County."

Winamac, a quiet, homey community which borrowed its name from an Indian chief, had eight churches, 10 lawyers, three taverns, and a quaint swinging bridge over the Tippecanoe River. The parking meters in the four-block downtown area, on streets with names like "Main" and "Market," demanded only a penny. If a visitor forgot to pay, a parking ticket was $1. And if they forgot to pay that, no problem. The city had no local court to prosecute anyway.

The gray courthouse, squatting in the middle of town, was a hulking, fortress-like three-story building with a lighted clock in its tower and a lobby decorated with rows upon rows of pictures showing proud-looking local boys in their World War I uniforms. Downtown merchants could spot strangers right away; they're the ones who locked their car doors. And strangers were treated just like everyone else — with a cheery "hello" when passed on the sidewalk.

Reaction to the news of the coming trial was varied. Rick Sutton, editor of a weekly advertising circular and tabloid, said he was insulted by the implication that Winamac was a backward community that was uninformed about the Pinto case and other affairs. "You have to wonder what was going through the minds of the lawyers when they chose Winamac," he told the *South Bend Tribune.* "I think they'll find that we're not a bunch of country bumpkins and are well-informed."

A lot of other people, including Mike Garrigan, the kindly bailiff at the courthouse, were excited. "I'm on cloud nine," he said. "This will put Winamac on the map."

Transferring the case to Pulaski County meant that the presiding judge would be Harold R. Staffeldt, a 60-year-old lifelong resident of the area whose self-confessed lack of math skills kept him from his dream of becoming an engineer. Staffeldt followed the advice of his father, a farmer who emigrated from Germany, and became a lawyer instead, getting a degree in 1947 from Tulane Law School in New Orleans.

He returned to Winamac to begin his private practice and shared office space for two decades with another lawyer, Lester Wilson, who became one of his closest friends. Wilson, who still maintained a thriving practice on Pearl Street, continued to be a frequent luncheon partner with the judge at Miller's Restaurant (which, incidently, had the tastiest homemade fruit pies in the county).

In 1969, the newly elected governor called Staffeldt, who was an acquaintance, and offered to appoint him to fill a judicial vacancy. Staffeldt politely declined, saying he would like to assume the bench someday but he still needed his higher salary as a private lawyer to help put his two sons through school. "Too late," the governor replied. "Your commission's in the mail." Staffeldt became a judge.

A slender, balding man with wispy gray hair, silver-rimmed bifocals and a hesitant manner of speech, Staffeldt was fond of wearing colossal, polka-dot bow ties and brown boots. One reporter observed that he looked like a Dr. Seuss character. Staffeldt and his wife of 21 years, Helen, were music buffs who often travelled to symphonies in Indianapolis, She was the organist at St. Luke's Lutheran

Church in Winamac.

Staffeldt was informal and disarmingly friendly as a judge and enjoyed chatting with visitors in his office just off the second-floor courtroom. Sometimes he would conduct hearings in court, sitting in front of a picture of George Washington and next to an American flag, wearing a sports-coat instead of the traditional black robes. When Alan Lenhoff, automotive specialist for the *Detroit Free Press,* came to interview him for a profile before the trial, Staffeldt responded by taking him to his nearby colonial-style house for a lunch of bologna sandwiches, homemade apple sauce, and fruitcake served by his white-haired wife.

In a quote later regarded as a joke when reporters discovered his timidity and indecisiveness, Staffeldt told Lenhoff at the time: "I think most people see me as being a little brash."

Staffeldt's judicial experience with product-liability cases was generally limited to lawsuits in which farmers sought damages from feed companies because their cattle failed to fatten. But when the word came that he would be presiding over a new criminal-law concoction with strong product-liability flavoring, Staffeldt told reporters he wasn't at all intimidated.

"It's just part of the daily work," he told them. "It's a job to be done. We'll take it as it comes."

Ford officials wasted little time in getting to Winamac and paying an attractive salary to hire the judge's close friend, Lester Wilson, as their local counsel. "At least we know these Ford people are smart," one local merchant commented when word swept through town about Wilson's job.

Ford's move raised quite a few eyebrows, although Staffeldt said he was unconcerned. He told Lenhoff that he and Wilson "just shared a secretary" for about "five or six years," while Wilson disclosed to other reporters that they practiced together for more like 22 years. They never entered into a formal partnership agreement.

Ford lawyers considered Wilson's office too small for their headquarters, so they took over the barbershop next door, had a contractor knock out the wall between them, and divided the new space into tasteful offices. "We'll put the wall back when we leave," one Ford lawyer said.

Then they rented a spacious former restaurant on Market Street, filling it with sophisticated word-processing and copying equipment and making room for a flock of legal researchers and secretaries. Partitions were erected to keep curious townspeople from peering inside. For housing, they leased nine apartments for a reported $27,000 a month as well as four rooms at an inflated rate at Winamac's only motel, the Indian Head. Other living quarters would be added later as they were needed. Winamac residents got their first indication of the size of the coming Ford contingent when a Ford advance team asked a church group whether it would be able to cater three meals a day for 45 to 50 people.

"Ford must be planning on just pouring all kinds of money in here to win," mused John Stombaugh, owner of a downtown corner drug store.

Realizing he would need a local lawyer, Cosentino used part of his budget to hire, at a reduced rate, a youthful Winamac attorney named Daniel Tankersley, whose office was located down the block from the courthouse. One of Tankersley's first roles was to brief Cosentino on everything he knew about Staffeldt so Cosentino could decide whether to seek a new judge within the specified time period allowed by the law. Cosentino decided to gamble on Staffeldt.

When Cosentino asked the judge whether his team could get some room in the courthouse for temporary office space, Staffeldt said the antiquated building was already too crowded. Instead, Cosentino set up his headquarters in Tankersley's already-cramped offices. As for living accommodations, Cosentino turned down the offer of one profit-minded local entrepreneur who wanted $7,800 a month for a few apartments. He ended up renting two drafty cottages located next to Bass Lake about ten miles north of Winamac. Lawyers and students would have to sleep two to a room, with some on cots in the livingroom, and cook their own meals. Rent was a total of $800 a month and Cosentino knew his budget couldn't handle it, so he decided to pay the rent, telephone, and utilities out of his own pocket. Everyone would chip in to buy groceries.

The closer the time got to the trial, the more Winamac's usual sleepy tranquility became disrupted. Print and broadcast reporters from places like New York, Washington, D.C., Georgia, Florida, Illinois, California, Ohio, Michigan, Tennessee and Pennsylvania trooped into town to write the obligatory "color" story about how the once-ignored small community was coping with the impending major trial.

"There's been so many color stories written that Winamac's been bled to black and white," Nick Miller, the young editor of the weekly ***Pulaski County Journal,*** lamented after a while. Miller quickly lost track of how many reporters stopped by his office to pump him for background about the area.

The out-spoken Stombaugh was interviewed half a dozen times by reporters. At Matilda's Cafe, located in the shadow of the courthouse, gregarious waitress Karen Hopkins became something of a celebrity before it was over, having been interviewed 14 times by reporters from ABC-TV, *Newsweek, The Detroit News,* and other papers. "Some of the other waitresses are getting a little tired of all the questions," she said in the midst of all the hoopla. "But I think being interviewed is fun."

Over at the local Oldsmobile-Pontiac dealership, owner Bill Goble was interviewed three times in one day alone. At one point, a network camera crew, complete with a soundman scurrying around with an elongated microphone, barged into his showroom and chased away a customer.

At the Schultz Brothers Dime Store, tee-shirts with "Where In the Hell is Winamac?" written across the front were being snapped up at a record clip for $3.99 each. Another store featured a special on plastic models of the Pinto. To raise money, a local mental-health organization started selling $1 bags of Pinto beans with a label commemorating the case. One restaurant was rebuffed in its attempt to place a newspaper ad promoting its "Red-Hot Pinto Bean Chili."

It didn't take long for the townspeople to get perturbed at the hillbilly image of Winamac being flashed across television screens and portrayed in articles. "We don't like the media coming in here and painting us as hicks or yokels or rednecks or know-nothings," Stombaugh fumed at the height of the publicity.

"I don't mind people laughing with us," Nick Shank, a 36-year-old clothing store owner added over a drink at Rudy's Roost tavern. "I just don't like them laughing at us. We don't deserve that. Sure, Winamac doesn't have the night-life of a bigger city. But our wives can walk down the street at night and not be afraid, we know everybody walking down the sidewalk, and this is a nice place to raise a family and not have to worry about something bad happening."

But what stung the pride of the community the most were news reports accusing some businesses of price-gouging by taking advantage of the expected influx of visitors and the town's limited facilities. At the Indian Head Motel, prices were raised for the trial from the usual $22 per night to $40, although the owner denied she was profiteering. "If I wanted to gouge, I could get $100 a night," she said indignantly. One magazine writer, angered over the rate hike, filed a complaint about the motel with the Federal Council on Wage and Price Stability.

A network camera crew was charged $975 a month for a furnished apartment. Other newsmen escaped the high prices by arranging to stay in motels as far as 25 miles away or by sleeping in the home of a local resident (Rate: $25 a night, including a free dinner party on Mondays). *Newsweek* caused a stir by sniping at the Indian Head's rates and saying that Goble asked for $100 a day to rent a reporter a furnished apartment with maid and linen service, although the usual price was $265 a month unfurnished. Goble thought he was being unfairly criticized but said he understood why some rates were going up around town. "Look, this is the Indianapolis 500 for Winamac. They raise rates for everything there. I can see where some people would do that here. I can't blame them."

However, most merchants maintained their regular prices, many of which the visiting newsmen found astondingly low. "Down at Matilda's Cafe on Main Street, where they have the friendliest waitresses and the sweetest butterscotch pie in town, a belt-busting breakfast is still less than $2," Lenhoff marveled in one of his color stories.

At Rich's Cafe, its jukebox crammed with records by singers like Tom T. Hall and Loretta Lynn, its wall decorated by a collection of farm hats, and a shotgun dangling from the ceiling, the generous luncheon special stayed at $2.50. Across town, one delicatessen charged so little for its enormous sandwiches that visiting reporters felt guilty and kept urging the owner to raise her prices. She finally did, but just by pennies. On the outskirts of Winamac, the Colonial Inn held the line on its price for a roast beef dinner – $2.65.

As the trial got closer, one of the fastest growing local pasttimes became thinking of ways to avoid jury duty. The trial was expected to take between six weeks and three months and few people wanted to disrupt their daily lives to sit inside a stuffy courtroom that long. At a party, one local man asked a lawyer for some advice on what to say if he was questioned as a potential juror: "How about if I say I used to drive a Ford and it was so bad I'd like to see the whole outfit behind bars? Think that'd work?"

Jury selection was scheduled to begin in November, 1979, but Staffeldt granted a delay. His final ruling was that selection of the jury would commence at 9:30 a.m. on January 7, 1980, with opening statements starting as soon as 12 jurors and three alternates were chosen.

In an editorial, Sutton urged patience to Winamac residents during the trial. "There will be times," he wrote, "when you will wish they'd never heard of Winamac."

8

They were called simply, "The Pinto Papers."

Terry Kiely kept them locked in four black filing cabinets in his seventh-floor office at DePaul Law School in downtown Chicago. They were internal engineering studies, crash test reports, cost analyses, recommendations, and corporate orders from Ford Motor Company. Many of them had the word "confidential" stamped across the top. A large number had the names of key corporate executives on them.

Kiely was in charge of collecting, analyzing, and cataloguing the hundreds of papers. He knew they were the key to the Pinto prosecution. They detailed, in black and white, what Ford officials knew, when they knew it, and what steps they took during the development of the Pinto and shortly after the car went on sale. Kiely was convinced that unless the jury was allowed to see a substantial amount of this concrete, hard-to-refute evidence, proving the reckless homicide charges would be extremely difficult, if not impossible.

The documents came to Kiely from several sources – some from Harley Copp and Byron Bloch; some from the federal government's own files; and many from civil lawyers involved in private lawsuits against Ford in connection with people killed or disfigured in Pinto fires. The documents originally reached the outside world through "leaks" by Ford employes, through Ford executives who took their papers with them when they left the company, or through pretrial proceedings in civil cases during which lawyers can demand that certain documents be disclosed.

During the investigation, Kiely, Cosentino, and sometimes Berner met with numerous civil lawyers to obtain documents or get background information explaining the significance of documents they had already received from other sources. Several lawyers with civil Pinto cases refused to cooperate because they felt Cosentino's criminal case was intruding on their turf. Others, though, were generous with their assistance. As one said: "I was at D-Day, and I know that when you hit the beach and someone is running in the same direction, he's on your side."

When the scathing *Mother Jones* article was published in 1977, it largely based its conclusions on a core of significant internal Ford documents which the magazine had obtained. Those documents provided a revealing, shocking glimpse inside Ford Motor Company. But since then, a flurry of civil litigation had pried loose new documents which put the Pinto controversy into sharper focus and provided important additional evidence concerning Ford's conduct.

Most of these recent documents had never been made public. One reason was that when Ford was sued in a civil case involving a fire in a Pinto or some other Ford model, it sought and usually obtained a court order sealing the case file from public view. These "protective orders" meant that if Ford was forced into disclosing some of its internal documents during that case, the lawyer for the plaintiff could see them but they would be kept secret from everyone else unless they were ever successfully introduced into evidence at a trial.

Ford often obtained these protective orders by claiming the documents contained "trade secrets" which must be kept away from other automakers for competitive reasons. Lawyers fighting Ford, though, contended that Ford's true motive was "to prevent highly incriminating documents from becoming generally known." Ford's record of disclosure of documents during civil cases has been stained with dishonesty. Courts have censured Ford for deliberately withholding and secreting documents, providing false answers under oath about documents, and other misconduct.

Kiely and Cosentino were able to piece together their unusually comprehensive file of Pinto documents by meticulously tracking down lawyers in the lawsuits where protective orders had been denied, collecting a few documents at a time as if building a giant ball out of bits of string.

What did the documents say? What was contained in those hundreds of pages of papers, photographs, and charts that so thoroughly convinced Cosentino and his assistants that Ford had purposely sacrificed human lives for private profit in the development of the Pinto?

Ford lawyers tried hard to prevent those questions from being answered. In the fall of 1979, copies of many of the Ford documents were inserted by Cosentino into the case's public file as part of a motion. Neal promptly asked Judge Staffeldt for a protective order sealing the file from public scrutiny on grounds that disclosure of its contents in the news media might prove prejudicial to the automaker. Neal hoped he would later be able to block the documents from being made public or seen by the jury during the trial itself.

Cosentino vigorously objected to Neal's request, saying public court files should be kept public. But Staffeldt, who admitted later he had no idea of the contents of the documents because he hadn't read them, granted Neal's request by issuing a broad verbal order blocking the public from seeing any part of the file which even discussed potential evidence. Later, when a reporter asked for clarification as to how broad the order was, Staffeldt appeared puzzled and said the reporter should go ask Neal.

When it came to signing a written order to seal the file, Staffeldt adopted the exact contents of an order proposed by Neal, even though the judge hadn't read Cosentino's lengthy written objections. The judge told journalist Joseph Tybor later that he didn't read Cosentino's submission before signing because he was about to leave on a fishing trip and didn't have time.

Neal's success in cutting off public access to the sensitive papers, though, came a little too late. The day before Staffeldt issued his verbal order, this author spent an entire day combing the public file and photocopying many of the internal Ford documents. By adding other material available from public sources, such as the U.S. Patent Office, and documents from some civil Pinto cases, it was possible to compile an accurate set of Ford documents similar to the one in Kiely's possession.

The documents, some of which were veterans of the *Mother Jones* article but more than a dozen of which contained important new material never before published, formed the basis of a series of widely reprinted articles in *The Chicago Tribune* in October, 1979. The documents proved to be so much in demand that one private attorney unsuccessfully offered $5,000 in cash for just one of them he wanted to use against Ford in a civil trial.

Since publication of *The Tribune* series, a few more internal Ford documents have been obtained which disclose even more evidence concerning the Pinto controversy. The details of these documents, such as the so-called "Pricor Report," have never been published before this book, although statements made in court indicate Kiely had the documents and intended to use them as part of the criminal case against Ford.

Kiely, who had little technical background, had to meet with several engineers so he could understand the significance of the technical jargon in the Pinto Papers.

For instance, there were three different kinds of crash tests involving Pintos. One was a car-to-car test in which a free-standing Pinto would be smashed from behind by another car to determine the amount of damage sustained by the Pinto at a certain speed. This sort of crash gave an accurate idea of what would happen in an actual highway collision.

The second was a moving-barrier test in which a 4,000 pound wall was moved into the back of a free-standing Pinto. Because the wall was flat, it could not duplicate an actual highway crash involving another vehicle. However, this kind of test resulted in damage which was close to what a car would suffer in a car-to-car collision at the same speed.

The third was a fixed-barrier test in which a Pinto would be towed rearward into a stationary cement wall. A fixed-barrier test caused much more damage to a car than a moving-barrier test at the same speed. For instance, the amount of damage sustained by a car in a 20 mile-per-hour fixed-barrier crash would be the same as a car in a moving-barrier crash at 28 miles per hour.

To Cosentino and Kiely, the Ford documents they obtained told a story which went back to June, 1967, when Ford, using the code-name "G-Car," began working on plans to build an American-made subcompact to compete against the popular imports which dominated the small-car market. According to Cosentino's information, this was a rushed project in which corporate executives rigidly enforced an edict that the car must weigh under 2,000 pounds and cost under $2,000 when it was introduced.

An early question in the car's design stage, of course, was where to safely put the gas tank, which had the explosive power of dozens of sticks of dynamite when it was full. To see how other small cars handled the problem, Ford in 1967 bought a Rover, an English-built subcompact which featured its gas tank in a location above the car's rear axle. Ford engineers smashed the Rover from behind with a moving-barrier at 30 miles per hour and, according to the test report, "there was no deformation, puncture, or leakage of the fuel tank." A rousing success for the over-the-axle design.

Ford engineers at that time were already familiar with how to move the gas tank away from the rear of the car. According to records from the U.S. Patent Office, Ford was granted a patent in 1961 for a "saddle-type" tank which could fit above and mostly forward of the car's rear axle. The patent pointed out that this design would remove the tank "from possible puncture or damage as a result of the vehicle dropping into holes or hitting obstructions."

Not long after Ford's successful Rover test, researchers at the University of California at Los Angeles announced the results of a detailed engineering study on how cars should be designed to protect passengers from fire in high-speed, rear-end crashes. Ford helped finance the study with a research grant and donated some of the cars that were crash-tested.

The study concluded that "much progress can be made" in cutting down the risk of gas spillage and subsequent fire in rear-end crashes by using "relatively inexpensive design considerations relating to fuel tanks and related fuel system."

The study also concluded that "fuel tanks should *not* be located directly adjacent to the rear bumper or behind the rear wheels adjacent to the fender sheet-metal as this location exposes them to rupture at very low speeds of impact."

Instead of putting the tank at the car's rear, the study said that "an improved location" appeared to be *above the rear axle,* as in the Rover tested by Ford. "This location is least often compromised in collision of all types," the researchers said. The reason was that this would put the tank away from the back of the vehicle where crushing occurs in rear-end crashes.

The study warned that care must be taken in designing the filler pipe so that it would not be yanked out of the tank during a crash, exposing a hole through which gasoline could gush. In a summary of the UCLA study published in a journal for automotive engineers, the researchers said that a design in which the filler pipe was rigidly attached to the car's body at the gas-cap end, and then merely inserted into the gas tank, could cause the pipe to pull out during rear-end crashes as low as 20 miles per hour because the tank would be shoved forward.

After the study was released, Ford engineers tried designing the future Pinto – now code-named the "Phoenix" – with its gas tank located over the axle as in the Rover. In a report dated January 21,1969, Ford engineers in the "product development group" evaluated this design.

The conclusion: "Due to the undesirable luggage space attained... it was decided to continue with the strap-on tank arrangement." This meant abandoning the over-the-axle location in favor of putting the tank at the car's rear. Apparently, the over-the-axle design resulted in a luggage compartment which would be limited in its ability to carry long objects, such as golf clubs.

The same memo also illustrated how concerned the engineers were to slice off pennies from the car's cost to stay as far below the $2,000 price limit as possible. They proudly reported under "significant accomplishments" that the use of a certain type of control lever would shave 18 cents off the cost of an alternative lever. They reported that another 50 cents per car could be shaved by redesigning the car's floor, and another $1.84 per car could be eliminated by relocating the headlight dimmer switch.

Six months later, Ford engineers took a Japanese Toyota and modified its rear-end so it would be similar to the proposed Pinto. This involved not only putting the gas tank at the rear of the car, but also eliminating any rear frame which would strengthen the car against excessive crushing. The car was rammed from behind by a moving barrier at 21 miles per hour. The results: The tank was severely deformed and ruptured, resulting in gas spilling out.

It was about this time that Ford, after several years of planning, introduced in Europe its Capri model, a compact car similar in shape to the Pinto but with its gas tank located over the axle. The Capri, largely the creation of Harley Copp, was launched with a major advertising blitz which bragged that its gas tank was "safely cradled between the rear wheels and protected on all sides."

In mid-1969 – more than a year before the Pinto was introduced – Ford engineers took three Capris and modified their rear-ends to be similar to the proposed Pinto. This meant moving the gas tank from the over-the-axle position and placing it at the car's rear.

When one of them was backed into a wall at 17.8 miles-per-hour, the welds on the gas tank split open, the tank was damaged when it hit the axle, the filler pipe pulled out, and the tank fell out of the car, resulting in massive gas spillage. The welds on the car's floor also pulled apart, which could let gasoline spill inside the car.

In two other tests in which the car was rear-ended by moving barriers at 21 miles per hour, gas leaked either from the filler pipe pulling out or because sharp objects punctured the fuel tank.

Nevertheless, the Pinto was put on sale on September 11,1970, with its gas tank located at the car's rear just six inches away from the largely ornamental bumper. Sharp bolts on the differential housing were situated three inches from the front of the tank in the exact path the tank would be pushed in a rear-end crash. Other sharp metal edges also were dangerously located just inches away from the tank.

In addition, the filler pipe was rigidly attached to the car's body at the gas cap end and then only loosely inserted into the gas tank to a depth of 2.6 inches, the sort of design which UCLA researchers warned earlier would cause the pipe to pull out in low-speed crashes. Unlike Ford's own Capri, the Pinto had no added rear frame to strengthen against excessive crushing when the car was hit from behind.

The Pinto was billed as "the carefree little American car" and boasted a pricetag of $1,919 – about $170 less than the price announced for its soon-to-be-released competitor, the Chevrolet Vega, and within $80 of the big-selling Volkswagen Beetle.

Embarrassingly, within six months there would be two recalls of the Pinto – one because of a tendancy of the engine compartment to burst into flames when the car was started, and the other because the accelerator pedal sometimes got stuck.

One of the most significant experimental crash tests occurred less than a month after the Pinto appeared in showrooms. On October 9,1970, Ford engineers took a Capri – with its over-the-axle gas tank design – and subjected it to a 31 mile-per-hour rear crash into a cement wall. This test, which was the equivalent of about a 45 mile-per-hour car-to-car crash, was a tremendous success – "No leakage was observed from the fuel tank or lines."

There was a dramatic contrast between this impressive result and the next one conducted at Ford's Dearborn testing facility. This time engineers took a standard Pinto and crashed it backwards into a concrete was at 21 miles per hour, which would be equal to a car-to-car crash of about 31 miles per hour.

In a report marked "confidential," engineer H. P. Snider said that the Pinto's soft rear-end crushed up 18 inches in 91 milliseconds. He said: "The filler pipe was pulled out of the fuel tank and fluid discharged through the outlet. Additional leakage occurred through a puncture in the upper right front surface of the fuel tank which was caused by contact between the fuel tank and a bolt on the differential housing."

In addition, there were two more punctures of the tank from nearby sharp metal objects and both passenger doors jammed shut, which would have prevented any quick escape or rescue in an actual crash.

This pattern of devastation and hazardous gasoline spillage was repeated in other Pinto tests conducted in the following months, at even lower speeds. When a Pinto was rear-ended by a moving barrier at 19.5 miles per hour on December 15,1970, the filler pipe pulled out, causing gas to escape, and the left door jammed shut.

When the Pinto went on sale, the federal government had no standards concerning how safe a car must be from gas leakage in rear-end crashes. However, within days of the Pinto's introduction, the government announced strict proposals that cars must be able to withstand a 20 mile-per-hour fixed-barrier crash without gasoline leakage as of 1972. This would be equal to about a 30 mile-per-hour car-to-car crash. And by 1973, cars would have to be able to survive a 30 mile-per hour fixed-barrier rear-crash, which would be equal to about a 44 mile-per-hour car-to-car collision.

Automakers panicked because they knew that cars like the Pinto would fall far short of meeting those requirements. Ford's response was to join other automakers in an aggressive lobbying campaign in an attempt to block the proposals from ever becoming law. In an internal Ford memo dated November 10,1970, Ford officials developed some lesser safety standards which they believed "the Department of Transportation can be expected to buy."

This opposition by Ford came even though its own crash test of the Capri demonstrated it knew how to build cars safe enough to pass even the government's most stringent proposed standard.

Apparently believing its lobbying would be successful in eliminating the government proposals, Ford then adopted its own internal standard for rear-end crashes. In a policy-setting memo from key corporate executives dated November 20, 1970, Ford adopted a requirement that its cars must pass a 20 mile-per-hour moving-barrier rear-end crash without gasoline leakage starting with the 1973 models. This was less than half as stringent as the government's proposal for that year.

The same memo added that for the Pinto even to meet this lesser requirement by 1973, its filler pipe would have to be fixed so that it wouldn't pull out as easily and the car's structure would have to be beefed up.

At the same time, Ford assigned engineers to develop ways of making the Pinto substantially safer from the risk of fire in rear-end crashes, just in case the strict government proposals or similar standards did become law.

It was only 12 days after the Pinto's introduction when Ford engineers spelled out in an internal memo what would be necessary to greatly improve the Pinto's ability to withstand rear-end collisions without gas leakage and to comply with even the government's strictest proposals:

"This will probably require repackaging of the fuel tanks in a *protected area* such as above the rear axle." The memo added: "Currently there are no plans for (future) models to repackage the fuel tanks."

In an internal memo two months later, Ford engineers reiterated that an over-the-axle gas tank designed would be among the necessary changes to significantly improve the

Pinto's safety from fire in rear-end crashes. "Fuel tanks must be repackaged to afford maximum protection from impact at any angle," the memo said. Engineers even submitted a diagram showing precisely how the tank could be placed over the axle in the Pinto and listed some pros and cons of the change.

On February 9,1971, in a study titled, "Confidential Cost Engineering Report," Ford engineers concluded that the cost of an over-the-axle tank design, including a protective sheet metal barrier, would be $9.95 for the average car. This figure was not broken down according to different models.

In another approach to making the Pinto safer, engineers tried installing a heavy rubber bladder, reinforced with nylon, inside the metal gas tank. In a 20 mile-per-hour rear crash into a cement wall – equal to a 30 mile-per-hour car-to-car collision – the gas tank ruptured as it had in all Pinto tests at that speed. But the inner bladder kept any gasoline from spilling out. The engineers tried the bladder again in a 26 miles-per-hour crash into a cement wall, and again the bladder successfully retained the gas even though the metal tank was punctured in several places.

"The bladder tank provides a substantial improvement in crashworthiness when compared against a conventional steel tank in which any rupture leads to fuel spillage," said a memo dated January, 1971.

The memo said that the Goodyear Tire & Rubber Co. gave a preliminary price estimate of $6 per bladder, although engineers were skeptical of this figure and said that developmental problems would have to be ironed out.

The following month, the Advanced Chassis Engineering Department reported that the bladder would greatly improve the Pinto's safety in rear-end crashes, but recommended further testing only "in the event that future legislation should require the . . . liner."

Another alternative was a "tank-in-tank" system in which polyurethane foam was added between an inner and outer metal fuel tank shell. According to a confidential cost study in February, 1971, this design would help to significantly boost rear-end safety from fire at a cost of $5.08 per car. Figures were not given for individual Ford models.

It was only two months after the Pinto went on sale when engineers first raised the idea of adding a shield to the car to protect the gas tank from being punctured by sharp bolts on the differential housing. The idea was repeated in another internal memo three months later.

When engineers obtained price estimates, they found the "material cost" for a rugged nylon shield would be 44 cents apiece, or 22 cents each for an ultra-high molecular polyethylene shield. "Both materials appear to have the potential of stopping fuel tank penetration by the differential housing at a reasonable cost," said a memo dated March 20,1974.

The memo added that a shield made of polyethylene "is likely to offer better fuel tank protection for a lower cost than any other plastic material and . . . will simplify vehicle installation."

In the Grimshaw trial, Copp testified the design cost of a shield for the Pinto would have been $2.35 per car or the axle could have been made smooth for a design cost of $2.10 per car. A design cost is the price of direct material and labor.

A 30-page study of gas tank safety for Ford's "light cars" was issued just five months after the Pinto's introduction. Called the "Pricor Report" after its author, Ford engineer A. J. Pricor, the analysis involved nine experimental crash tests of several light-car models, including the Pinto. Its conclusion listed several concrete recommendations for how to make the car substantially safer from fuel leakage and fire in rear-end crashes.

Among its conclusions was that by positioning the spare tire properly, it would absorb up to 10 per cent of the energy in a rear-end crash and cushion the gas tank from deformation.

The Capri was an example of how Ford designers had used this system successfully. In a memo dated October 27, 1970, Ford engineers concluded Capri's ability to withstand the equivalent of a 45 mile-per-hour car-to-car crash was based not only on its over-the-axle tank design, but also on the "favorable location of the spare tire which carried the impact force directly into the rear axle."

However, engineers did not position the Pinto's spare tire in a manner which would protect the gas tank when the car was hit from behind.

Also, the Pricor study concluded that the "desirable fuel tank location" appeared to be 13 to 17 inches away from the rear bumper – not six inches as in the Pinto.

In addition, the report stated that small cars should have "body rails" installed on both sides. These are steel rails which run lengthwise in the car and attach to the rear to absorb some of the impact during a rear-end crash. Pricor said these were "necessary to absorb and control vehicle collapse on a predictable basis" and were effective in "preventing surrounding sheet metal from total collapse."

Early in 1971, Ford engineers installed two side rails on a Pinto to see what would happen when it was crashed backward into a cement wall at 21 miles per hour. This was the same speed – equal to about a 31 mile-per-hour car-to-car crash – at which Pintos without rails demonstrated a history of massive damage and extensive spilling of gas.

The result was that the Pinto with the side rails crushed considerably less than the standard Pinto and there was no leakage from the tank or filler pipe.

The Pricor analysis did not provide any cost estimate for side rails. However, during his Grimshaw testimony, Copp said the design cost of adding rails to both sides of the Pinto would have been $2.40 per car.

Ford management, though, decided against putting any side rails on the Pinto until the 1973 model, at which time only one rail was added instead of two, providing much less protection than Pricor recommended. A second rail was added starting in the 1974 Pinto, but an internal memo dated April 26,1972, described those rails of being of a type "which is poor, undesirable for energy absorption."

Pricor also warned that the type of filler pipe used in the Pinto "invites fuel leakage" and that an alternate design like that used in the Capri would be the "most desirable" system. Other memos written during this time period also cited the necessity of improving the filler pipe to make the Pinto safer. And a memo dated October, 1970, from Ford's "product development group" included a diagram of a design "which would eliminate filler neck leakage."

Still other memos reported during the autumn of 1970 that "heavier gauge tank metal" could contribute to improving the Pinto's ability to withstand gas spillage in rear-end crashes.

In the spring of 1971, Ford engineers were coming to believe that a "flak suit" would be the answer to making the Pinto significantly safer from gas leakage in rear-end crashes if some structural improvements were also made. A flak suit was like a rubber tire that fit around the tank to cushion it from impact and prevent puncture. Another 1971 memo said the flak suit design "has merit in high-energy situations and should be considered as an alternative."

A "confidential" memo dated April 22,1971, said that the design cost of the flak suit or the bladder would be $8 per car. But the same memo said that based on this amount, executives recommended that the company "defer adoption of the flak suit or bladder on all affected cars until 1976 to realize a design cost savings of $20.9 million compared to incorporation in 1974."

They said they hoped that in the meantime "cost reductions can be achieved or the need for the flak suit or bladder eliminated after further engineering development."

During this time, Ford and other automakers continued to lobby vigorously against the stringent government safety proposals. In the end, they were successful. The strict fixed-barrier proposals were abandoned.

It was at a meeting in the fall of 1971 – a year after the Pinto appeared in showrooms – that a committee of high-ranking Ford executives got together to decide whether any of the various improvements would be adopted to make the Pinto safer from gas spillage and the risk of fire in rear-end crashes.

In an October 26,1971 memo labeled "confidential," the decision was disclosed: There would be no additional

improvements for the 1973 and later models of the Pinto until "required by law."

It wasn't until six years later – after 1,513,339 Pinto sedans were built and sold – when the government finally imposed its first safety requirement designed to protect against gas leakage and fire risk in rear-end crashes. The standard was that all 1977 cars must be able to withstand a 30 mile-per-hour moving-barrier crash in the rear without gas leakage, a regulation which was considerably weaker than the earlier proposal which had aroused the ire of the auto industry.

To make the 1977 Pinto capable of passing the test, Ford dusted off some of its old ideas and added a polyethylene shield to prevent puncturing of the gas tank; improved the filler pipe so it wouldn't pull out so easily; and added some rear-ended strength by making the bumper stronger.

The shield and improved filler pipe were, of course, the same changes made to improve the 1971-76 Pintos and 1975-76 Mercury Bobcats in the recall which was announced in 1978 after the government determined that those cars were prone to spill gas when hit from behind.

Among the most controversial documents obtained by Kiely and Cosentino was a "cost-benefit" study which Ford developed as part of its campaign against plans by the government to adopt regulations concerning auto safety.

A cost-benefit analysis is a business tool used to determine whether the cost of a project would justify the dollar value of the benefits which would be derived. If the price of achieving the benefit is greater than the value of the benefit itself, the project is viewed as not being financially worthwhile.

According to the *Mother Jones* article, the auto industry pressured NHTSA into setting a price tag on human lives and suffering, and then the automakers plugged those figures into cost-benefit equations in order to argue why safety improvements were too expensive to be worthwhile.

One of these Ford cost-benefit studies, originally excerpted in the *Mother Jones* article, concluded that it would not be worth the cost of making an $11 improvement per car in order to save 180 people from burning to death and another 180 from suffering serious burn injuries each year.

On the "benefit" side of the equation, Ford calculated that making the improvement would result in the saving of those 180 lives and 180 serious injuries. Ford then translated this human suffering into dollars according to NHTSA's figures – $200,000 for the life of a burn victim; $67,000 for each serious burn injury; and $700 for each fire-ravaged vehicle. Ford referred to dead and injured persons as "units."

When all of this was added up, the "total benefit" of making the safety improvement and eliminating the death and pain was calculated to be $49.5 million.

This was balanced against the cost of making the $11 improvement to 1.5 million light trucks and 11 million cars throughout the auto industry, for a "total cost" of $137 million.

"Thus," the report concluded, "the cost is almost three times the benefits, even using a number of highly favorable benefit assumptions."

The study added that NHTSA's dollar figures for lives and injuries (Ford called it a "casualty-to-dollars conversion") were higher than some other sources "and their use does not signify that Ford accepts or concurs in the values."

Ford officials submitted this analysis to NHTSA in 1973 as part of its campaign against the government's plans to adopt a regulation concerning how safe cars must be from fire risk in crashes in which the vehicle rolls over.

Ford executives indignantly responded to disclosure of this study by saying they only used NHTSA's own figures and had been asked by the government to perform the study. They contended the analysis was never intended for the purpose of making engineering decisions and never affected the design of the Pinto or any other car.

However, an associate administrator of NHTSA insisted that the dollar figures were developed for other purposes and "were never intended to be used in such a cost-benefit analysis." He said the figures were created to estimate the loss to society when a person dies, based largely on lost productivity, so the agency could study what traffic fatalities cost the nation.

When Ford submitted this study to the government, it said the analysis concerned the proposed rollover safety requirement but added that "analyses of other portions of the proposed regulation would also be expected to yield poor benefit-to-cost ratios."

Yet shortly after this was submitted, a Ford executive completed another cost-benefit study concerning another portion of the proposed law that dealt with limiting fuel leakage in side and rear crashes. And, as it turned out, the results were quite different from the rollover proposal.

In this instance, the study concluded there was some financial sense in spending $8 per car throughout the industry for safety improvements which would save 370 lives and 370 serious injuries a year from fiery side and rear crashes.

The "benefit" of saving those lives and injuries was calculated at $102 million, based on the same formula of each life being worth $200,000 and each serious burn injury being valued at $67,000. On the other side of the equation, the "cost" of making the $8 improvement was estimated to total $100 million.

"Thus, the costs are comparable to the most generously estimated benefits, indicating marginal cost-effectiveness," the study concluded.

This analysis, then, tended to justify in dollar terms the side and rear impact portions of the government's proposed safety regulations. However, Ford never submitted this study to the government.

At that time, Ford was not opposing the proposed side and rear impact requirements, which included the later-adopted standard that cars must be able to withstand a 30 mile-per-hour moving-barrier rear-end crash as of the 1977 model year. Yet this study confirmed that at least as far back as 1973, Ford management was aware that it would be relatively inexpensive per vehicle to achieve this degree of added safety.

All of these documents – plus dozens of other internal Ford papers which added more insight into the automaker's conduct – were contained within Kiely's four bulging filing cabinets.

Did they tell an accurate story? Kiely was convinced that they did. But he also knew there were going to be a lot of difficult legal obstacles in his way before the prosecution could ever hope to let the documents tell their story to a jury.

9

Cosentino and his corps of volunteers expected that the battle over the Pinto Papers would begin early and be waged throughout the trial because the documents were so important to the case. But what they did not expect was to suffer so many demoralizing defeats even before the first juror was seated in the historic trial. And, as it turned out, those losses were just the beginning.

Cosentino's main problem was how to authenticate the Pinto Papers as being actual Ford documents. Even though most of them had "Ford Motor Co." and the corporate logo across the top and what appeared to be the signatures of Ford executives at the bottom, the court had to be satisfied that they were what they purported to be. Otherwise, the jurors would never get to see them.

At a meeting held in June, 1979, the prosecutors worked out what they thought was a solution. They decided to ask Judge Staffeldt to require Ford to participate in the kind of wide-ranging pretrial "discovery" proceedings typical in civil lawsuits. Under these procedures, Ford could be forced to admit the documents were authentic and even be compelled to turn over more documents for Cosentino to use against the automaker at the trial.

In civil cases, discovery is the legal process in which each side is required to disclose to the other side any relevant evidence which is specifically requested. The rules are much stricter in criminal cases because the defendant, under the Fifth Amendment to the U.S. Constitution, cannot be compelled to incriminate himself.

But in this case, the defendant was a corporation and corporate entities do not enjoy Fifth Amendment privileges against self-incrimination. Cosentino thought that this fact, coupled with Indiana's increasingly liberal discovery rules in criminal cases, would be enough to allow broad discovery in this trial.

Not so, Neal protested. He contended that no Indiana Supreme Court decision "holds that the state can force a defendant to assist in preparing the prosecution's case."

Staffeldt agreed with Neal and ruled that he would only require Ford to submit to discovery if Ford first initiated the process by seeking evidence from Cosentino under the discovery rules. Anxious not to open up Ford's files to Cosentino, Neal opted to ask for no information from the prosecution.

Cosentino tried again. He filed a slightly different motion seeking to force Ford to authenticate the documents Cosentino already had in his possession. But Neal called this "nothing but a transparent attempt to obtain discovery." Staffeldt agreed. Strike two for Cosentino.

At this point, Cosentino had a choice. He could try to find another way to authenticate the documents, which might require a lot of time and money. Or, he could try to get a higher court to reverse Staffeldt's rulings and risk alienating the judge who would try the case. Not being one to back down from a fight, Cosentino filed an appeal with the Indiana Supreme Court.

"We don't think a corporation has any right to withhold evidence of its own guilt," Conour told justices during arguments for the prosecution. "Ford thinks that if it denies what exists long enough, it will convince others that it does not exist."

"They want us to convict ourselves," Neal contended. "We have the right not to take the time to adjust the hood on our head while it's on the block."

The decision was 4 to 1 to uphold Staffeldt's rulings. That may have been strike three for Cosentino, but he continued to swing away. A short time later, he and his partners thought of another legal maneuver which might work to the prosecution's advantage. They would issue a subpena demanding that Ford turn over copies of the same documents which Cosentino already had in his possession, plus some new ones. In complying with the subpena by removing the original copies from their own files and turning them over, Ford would, in effect, be admitting the documents were authentic, Cosentino figured.

The subpena went out for Henry Ford II and 29 other Ford executives, demanding that they appear in court and bring the documents with them. Some of the prosecution team members conceded privately that going after Ford himself was something of a grandstand play. "The reporters loved it," one commented later.

To serve the subpena in another state, Cosentino had to go through a Detroit judge and convince him to issue it. Sorry, a judge in Wayne County, Michigan, told him. He killed the subpena on the grounds that there was a lack of proof these executives were material witnesses in the case.

That only made Cosentino more determined. This time he served another subpena on Neal during a pretrial court hearing. Staffeldt dismissed that subpena on grounds that it was improperly served. Cosentino tried once more, this time serving another subpena on the CT Corporation, an Indiana entity which represented Ford in the state.

Cosentino's tenacity proven, Neal agreed to enter into a compromise. Neal said he would give Cosentino the original copies of individual documents he was seeking, but if the judge refused to let any of them into evidence, Cosentino would have to return those documents to Neal without making any photocopies.

The reason for this procedure was because Neal wanted to make sure none of the documents which would be new to Cosentino would find their way into the hands of any civil lawyers who could use them against Ford in lawsuits. Ford attorneys were very careful about keeping the Pinto Papers as private as possible, even to the extent of using a computer to keep track of who had them and where.

Neal added another proviso to his deal with Cosentino. He refused to concede that just because the documents were produced from Ford files and had "Property of Ford Motor Co." stamped across them, that they were necessarily authentic Ford documents. Staffeldt would have to resolve that issue later.

This pre-trial wrangling over the Pinto Papers merely foreshadowed the increasingly bitter fight which would permeate the entire marathon trial. And it gave Cosentino just a taste of the frustration he would have to endure in trying to get as many of the documents as he could into the jury's hands.

As the trial date neared, both sides continued pursuing full investigations into all of the circumstances that surrounded the case. Cosentino was somewhat hampered by a lack of money, but Ford lawyers had difficulties, too.

In a typical criminal case, lawyers for the defendant would be entitled under the discovery rules to obtain a lot of information – such as police and autopsy reports – from the prosecutor. In this case, though, Ford didn't dare ask for any information because of fears that, under Judge Staffeldt's ruling, they could trigger Cosentino's right to demand information from Ford.

When Aubrey Harwell, Neal's partner and head of the accident investigation, tried as an alternative to go directly to the state police office to obtain the crucial accident reports, he was told they had all been turned over to Cosentino.

So Harwell, a tall, smooth-talking one-time Washington reporter for a Memphis newspaper, began his investigation where he was most comfortable – sitting among a heaping pile of newspaper clippings.

Harwell, whose receding hairline made him look older than his 37 years, obtained the extensive number of clips about the accident and grand jury investigation from Ford's public relations office and Ford-associated law firms in Chicago and Indiana. Then he went to the "morgue" or clippings library of two Indiana newspapers to search for more background.

Every time a name was mentioned in an article, it was added to a list with a brief description of how the person fit into the case. More than 100 names eventually were compiled and then cross-indexed in a master file. Harwell was determined to try to interview every one of them – policemen, firemen, eyewitnesses, and technical experts.

With the help of three lawyers from his firm, Harwell traveled thousands of miles tracking down each person, sometimes talking to as many as 10 people just to find out where he could find the individual he was looking for. One former nurse was finally located in California, another in Costa Rica. Harwell made as many as 30 trips to Elkhart and South Bend during the investigation. In an area still angered over the deaths of the Ulrich girls, he found that just mentioning that he was representing Ford resulted in hostility and doors being slammed in his face, literally and figuratively.

He discovered that some people wouldn't talk to him because Cosentino happened to be their personal attorney. Others, such as some firemen and law enforcement officers, indicated there was pressure from their superiors not to talk to Ford representatives. But many others did cooperate, even to the extent of giving more names of potential witnesses.

The second phase of the defense investigation was to find out everything possible about Robert Duggar and try to reconstruct his life starting with the day of the accident and extending two days later. Harwell and his assistants, working simultaneously in contacting various people to preserve the element of surprise, tracked down Duggar's friends, former roommates, and people who had worked with him. Every detail was recorded, down to what he ate for lunch the day of the crash.

Then each former owner of the Ulrich Pinto was interviewed to see whether they had modified or damaged the car. Even Esther Ulrich, the aunt of the dead girls, agreed to be questioned.

At the same time, Neal moved his operations from Nashville to Ford headquarters outside Detroit, occupying a makeshift office just beyond a sign reading, "Office of the General Counsel." Neal was given top priority in talking to anyone at Ford in connection with the defense.

Cosentino's headaches centered on cash problems. Not knowing how much he could expect in expenses in Winamac and having decided to hire at least two technical experts as potential witnesses, Cosentino was being extremely frugal with his $20,000.

Even photocopying costs became a problem because several copies of hundreds of pages of internal Ford documents and legal briefs had to be reproduced. Sometimes the law professors would send their students scurrying around town in an effort to hunt down discount copying centers to save a penny or two per page in expenses.

When it became necessary to go out of town to interview potential witnesses, Cosentino tried to avoid buying airline tickets. Once one of his assistants had to drive 14 hours in his car to meet with a witness for a discussion. At another time, several members of the team had to travel to California for meetings with technical experts. Trooper Graves arranged for an antiquated twin-prop police plane to transport them on a bumpy, frustratingly slow 200 mile-per-hour flight.

And there were always manpower problems, with his assistants repeatedly getting tied up with other pressing cases and trials. More and more, Cosentino had to rely on his volunteer help, and his volunteers were constantly reshuffling their schedules to fit the Pinto case into pockets of free time.

Cosentino had his advantages, too. He generally had community support on his side, and his investigators carried official badges which were very effective in convincing people to answer questions instead of slamming the door.

Just before the trial, though, Cosentino discovered one of the more aggravating repercussions of his limited funds. At Ford's request, a team of court stenographers was brought to Winamac to prepare the trial's official transcript on an hourly basis because the court's usual court reporter couldn't handle the load. Included were two court reporters, a team of typists, and a professional jogger whose job was to run the raw notes from the courtroom to the typing pool across town where the transcript was hurriedly put together.

Ford lawyers agreed to pay $9 per page for the transcript – in the end they would pay more than $50,000 – and Cosentino knew he couldn't afford to buy a copy. As Neal would demonstrate several times during the trial, having a transcript to work with was a valuable tool in cross-examining witnesses and building a precise catalogue of previous testimony. Being without one, Cosentino found out, was a considerable handicap.

As the first day of Jury selection approached, new figures were disclosed concerning the Pinto – more than 60 Pinto occupants had died in fire-accompanied crashes since 1975 alone, including at least 23 in fiery rear-end collisions.

"I know this sounds corny," Shewmaker told a friend in explaining why he was packing his weekends and evenings with work on the case. "But if we can prevent someone else from having to die like those girls did, then this is worth it."

10

Fifteen seconds after the rap of Judge Harold Staffeldt's gavel signalled the opening of the long-awaited Ford Pinto trial, Mike Cosentino and Jim Neal got into the first of what would become a long string of heated, and often petty, verbal brawls.

With the first group of potential jurors getting ready to file into the courtroom, Cosentino pulled the lecturn close to the jury box so he could question them.

"I don't see why Mr. Cosentino has to sit in their laps," Neal griped. "I can't see their reactions when he's standing in front of them."

Cosentino spun around and pointed at his adversary. "This is merely a sham by Ford to upset the state from properly selecting a jury!" he blared.

The two opponents argued back and forth about where to put the podium until finally the quiet-mannered Staffeldt hesitantly stepped between them. "I don't want to say where we'll put the furniture, or I'll take it all out and you'll stand," he gently admonished the pair.

Neal emerged the victor in this trivial altercation when Staffeldt suggested Cosentino move the lecturn back and closer to the bench.

Neal commented that when it was his turn to question the potential jurors, "I will do my doggondest to stay behind the podium."

"Well, Mr. Neal, I'll do my *DOGGONDEST*, too," Cosentino retorted with a sour look on his face as he mocked the Tennessee lawyer's down-home, folksy speech.

It may not have been the smoothest way to start a major trial that was being conducted in the national limelight, but the opening few minutes did set the tone for much of what was to follow during the next ten weeks. Almost daily, Cosentino's scrappy pugnacity and hair-trigger temper clashed with Neal's shrewed but reserved aggressiveness and often-biting humor.

This pattern began to emerge even before the trial began when the two competitors bickered during pretrial court hearings. Neal, who learned early how to light Cosentino's fuse, told the judge at one point, "Mr. Cosentino seems to have a statute of limitations on pleasantness – it sort of runs out after an hour or so."

And Cosentino demonstrated during one pretrial session that his style was about as subtle – and explosive – as a hand grenade. When Neal suggested he might file a lawsuit to obtain some documents, Cosentino thundered: "That's just a threat! I've been threatened before! File any number of actions, Mr. Neal. File this afternoon!"

At another pretrial proceeding, Neal taunted his rival by starting a sentence with the sarcastic comment, "If Mr. Cosentino gets lucky and wins this case – "

"It won't be luck!" Cosentino snapped back.

"Well, then," Neal replied smugly, "It will be a miracle."

Staffeldt was generally reluctant to interject himself when the lawyers got into a fray, preferring to let them burn themselves out. As he told one reporter, "I kind of get a kick out of all the legal antics in court."

The audience on the opening day of the much-anticipated trial also seemed to get a kick out of the early fireworks. Some of the local townspeople hoped the trial would provide enough rousing entertainment to keep them amused during what were usually the sleepy months of the year. As it turned out, the squabbling lawyers were so much fun to watch that some regular spectators stopped calling it the Pinto trial and referred to the case as "The Mike & Jim Show."

Staffeldt's courtroom was packed on the morning of January 7,1980, when jury selection was to begin. Eager spectators claimed each of the regular seats and the extra folding chairs in the aisles, others stood in the rear and along the sides of the court, and a crowd of others was turned away downstairs because there was no more room. The news media, numbering more than two dozen, were herded into a roped-off section at the far side of the courtroom after a bailiff checked to make certain each reporter had a special press pass issued by Staffeldt. Others, such as cameramen and sound technicians, waited in the lobby. Represented were many of the country's most prestigious newspapers, the wire services, all three television networks, and newspapers from throughout Indiana.

Sketchers wearing blue smocks wandered freely around the courtroom, using colored chalk or watercolors to portray the likeness of the participants for the evening network news shows.

Staffeldt's courtoom was a curious mixture of turn-of-the-century flavoring and odd modern touches. The walls were green-and-gold patterned wallpaper, the wooden trim was a light shade, and the high white ceiling was arched. An old-fashioned clock with a swinging pendulum hung near the jury box. Hissing radiators were situated beneath the large, bullet-shaped windows which were decorated with yellow curtains. The carpet was green and both wooden doors had a large pane of frosted glass, one stenciled in black with *COURT* and the other with *ROOM.*

But contrasting with the room's antique atmosphere were the unusual light fixtures, which were nothing more than long fluorescent tubes clustered together and dangling vertically, and the modern-looking theater-type seats which, the reporters came to appreciate, were amply padded.

Cosentino's counsel table, located near the jury box, was fully occupied, with the chief prosecutor at one end, Trooper Graves sitting in full uniform at the other end, and Berner, Kiely, Shewmaker, local counsel Dan Tankersley, and volunteer attorney John Ulmer in the middle. When a few law students could get away from their classes, they sat in the first row of audience seats directly behind the prosecution table.

Ford preferred to have only Neal, Wheeler, Harwell, and Winamac lawyer Lester Wilson sitting at the counsel table, perhaps to counteract the generally held impression that they were overwhelming the prosecution with their resources. Other Ford attorneys and paralegals sat scattered among the spectators, ready at a moment's notice to rush out to a nearby law library to dig up precedents for Neal if he got engaged in an unexpected legal debate with Cosentino.

The total number of Ford-employed lawyers in Winamac varied during the trial, but sometimes there were more than fifteen, plus a support staff of typists, secretaries, and college students who kept coffee cups filled and carted around boxes containing documents and transcripts. Wilson's office became virtually a 24-hour-a-day headquarters were the attorneys and staff would churn out voluminous legal briefs on the many unusual points of law which were raised during the trial.

Ford's Pinto litigation specialist, Richard Malloy, always sat in the courtroom's second row next to Jerry Sloan, an assistant director of Ford's public relations staff whose job was to keep the reporters advised of Ford's position on the case.

Through an electronic receiver he kept in Wilson's office, Sloan received daily copies of articles published about the trial in newspapers around the country. He would sometimes corner a reporter the following day to chide him about the way he wrote his story or complain, "We don't think your paper's giving us a fair break."

The first set of 12 potential jurors, looking apprehensive and a little embarrassed at all the attention, was led into the courtroom by Mike Garrigan, the bailiff, and Cosentino began the tedious process of questioning them. Each lawyer was given ten free opportunities to eliminate anyone from the panel, and the judge could be asked at any time to remove a potential juror for a specific reason.

Staffeldt demonstrated from the outset, though, that he was going to be very strict about letting anyone escape jury duty. Even when a woman said she had watched television accounts of the case and had concluded that "Ford knew something was wrong with the car," Staffeldt refused to let her go. Neal had to use one of his precious 10 challenges to bump her from the panel. Staffeldt also balked at removing a farmer who had hearing problems and said his mind would sometimes wander because he would be thinking about his livestock.

In a typical criminal case, Cosentino would be looking for conservative, blue-collar jurors with strict law-and-order views, but here he was searching for liberal, free-thinking individuals who might be more comfortable with his theory of the case.

He asked the members of the panel what kinds of magazines they read, seeking well-informed jurors who liked news and commentary publications instead of farm journals. He asked if they were joggers or hikers, looking for people who enjoy the outdoors and might have a little hostility toward big corporations because they foul the environment. He inquired if they smoked cigarets, cigars, or pipes, believing perhaps pipe-puffers would be more thoughtful and independent.

When one husky steel-worker said he owned a 1976 Pinto, Cosentino asked him whether that would influence his outlook on the case. "I don't think so," came the reply. "I once drove a Corvair."

His answer brought howls from the audience because of the Corvair's bad safety reputation, and won a place for the Pinto-owner, Raymond Schramm, on the jury.

Neal used his questions to probe for jurors he thought would be conservative and sympathetic to big business. "Would you say a person who works for a large corporation is less concerned than other people?" he inquired.

He wanted to know their attitudes toward Ralph Nader

and liberal groups such as Common Cause, whether they thought the government should require the installation of air bags in cars, and if they thought that small cars should be expected to be as safe as big ones.

"Do you think big corporations can be trusted?" he asked one former Navy mechanic.

"No, especially if you're a little peon out there," he responded. "They don't care if you live or die."

That ended his chances for jury duty.

Sitting inconspicuously toward the back of the courtroom was Hans Zeisel, the $1,000-a-day jury expert from the University of Chicago Law School, who scribbled notes at a furious pace and then huddled with Neal during breaks.

Neal was hardly shy about using his country-flavored twang and homespun comments to try to ingratiate himself with the small-town jurors. Alan Lenhoff of the *Detroit Free Press,* noting how Neal "smiled warmly and chattered away excitedly whenever the talk turned toward farmin', fishin', or berry pickin'," wondered if this would endear him to the jurors or make him appear patronizing.

In a humorous story about what he called "the good ol' boys at the defense table," Lenhoff poked fun at Neal for the backwoods philosophy he spouted to the potential jurors ("Here's a li'l story mah minister frien' tole me. . . .") and observed that "from Ford's side of the courtroom, the accepted way of addressing the jury seems to be "you-all.'

"Thanks to Neal's folksy Southern charm and self-effacing humor," Lenhoff added, "Ford is managing to out-country the real country boys here."

The consensus among the press corps was that Neal was successful in scoring quite a few points during this important get-acquainted session, especially compared to the dour and down-to-business Cosentino, who eschewed levity because he felt it was inappropriate at a homicide trial.

It took four days of repetitous and mind-numbing questioning to choose the 12 jurors and three alternates. Among the seven men, five women, and three male alternates were two farmers, a mobile-home salesman, a woman truck driver, a woman coal-shoveler, a retired grocer, an x-ray technician, and a junk-hauler. Their average age was 41 and half of them owned Ford cars or trucks.

Both sides expressed satisfaction with the final panel. But Neal added with a smile, "If the verdict is right, it's a good jury. If it ain't, it's a bad one."

Once the jury was chosen, there would be another crucial legal step before opening statements could start. Neal knew the outcome of these arguments could well determine the final result of the case even before the jury heard what it was all about.

The arguments could concern almost 20 legal motions filed by Ford and asking the judge to severely limit the sort of evidence Cosentino would be allowed to talk about in front of the jurors. For instance, Neal wanted the prosecution blocked from discussing any internal Ford documents or crash tests which did not specifically relate to the 1973 model of the Pinto, which was the one involved in the Ulrich crash.

Cosentino had only a handful of crash tests of the 1973 Pinto and they would not be of much help. They were run at speeds below the car's breaking point, so they failed to demonstrate the widespread damage sustained by the car when it was hit at slightly higher speeds.

Cosentino wanted to show the jurors the sequence of crash tests starting with the 1967 Rover, through the Capri models which were modified like the Pinto, and including the tests run shortly after the Pinto's introduction which showed dramatic and devastating damage to the car. He believed that those tests, plus the other Ford documents about alternative gas tank and decisions made by Ford management, designs told the entire Pinto story which led up to the building of the fatal 1973 model.

The legal arguments, which took place without the jury present on Monday, January 14, were heated and tumultuous at times. Wheeler accused Cosentino of making "absolutely false" statements and playing to the press. Cosentino charged that the entire defense team did not know what the case was all about. Wheeler said that the prosecution just wants to "confuse the jury" by showing it internal Ford documents. Kiely accused Ford of having "lied to the government again and again" and trying to "frustrate, delay, and stop" the NHTSA investigation which led to the Pinto's recall.

The scope of some of Staffeldt's rulings were so ambiguous that lawyers would cluster in the hallways during the recesses to try to come to a consensus as to what he was trying to say. Compounding the confusion was the judge's seeming uncertainty about some of his decisions. "I don't believe that's wrong, but it might be," he commented about one of his rulings.

In short, though, Staffeldt granted Ford's request to limit the evidence, but he said he would allow Cosentino to introduce the documents during the trial if he could "lay the proper foundation" first. This meant, in addition to proving the authenticity of the documents, Cosentino must first elicit expert testimony outside the jury's presence to establish enough preliminary facts to prove that the documents were relevant to the case. Until he did that, he could not specifically discuss them in front of the jury.

This would have a serious impact on Cosentino's opening statements, which were scheduled to be held the following day. Opening statements provide a forum for lawyers to give the jurors an overview of the evidence they intend to produce and an explanation of what it means and how it all fits together.

Cosentino, though, would be precluded from mentioning details of many of the documents he considered crucial to his case. Even if he were successful later in laying a foundation and getting the documents into evidence, the damage may already have been done. The jurors might not understand how the documents fit into the prosecution's case, or they might conclude the documents must be not very important since the prosecutor did not bother to discuss them at length during his opening remarks.

By deleting the references to the excluded documents, the length of Cosentino's planned opening remarks was cut from 2½ hours to about an hour.

Even more seriously, the prosecution team saw this as

at least an initial indication that Staffeldt felt the documents should be barred altogether from the trial. They wondered whether they would be able to convince him later that they were an integral part of the prosecution's case.

Staffeldt also ruled that two of Cosentino's documents– the controversial cost-benefit analyses – were inadmissible and would be excluded from evidence. "I think they're pretty far removed from the issue of any defects in the '73 Pinto," he said. Unlike his other rulings, he did not qualify his statement by saying that the documents could be admitted later if a foundation were laid.

Although the cost-benefit studies were dramatic, their loss was not considered a setback for the prosecution.

Ford was victorious in most of its motions to temporarily limit the evidence, but it was denied its most important request which, had it been granted, would have forced the prosecutors to pack up their briefcases and go home. The issues raised by this motion went to the heart of the case and had broad ramifications stretching far beyond the country courthouse in Winamac.

The issue concerned standards. Under the reckless homicide law, prosecutors had to prove Ford acted in a "plain, conscious, and unjustifiable disregard of harm that might result, and the disregard involved a ***substantial deviation*** from ***acceptable standards of conduct.***"

What constituted "acceptable standards of conduct?" Neal contended there could be only one standard that the jury should be allowed to impose and that was the 30 mile-per-hour moving-barrier, rear-end standard which NHSTA finally adopted for the 1977 model year cars.

If the judge agreed, the prosecution's case would be virtually destroyed. Cosentino expected much of the credible evidence to establish that the Ulrich impact occurred at a speed between 30 and 35 miles per hour. How could Ford be found guilty if the crash occurred at a speed greater than the only standard the automaker was supposed to comply with?

Neal was forceful and adamant in his arguments. "NHTSA has said a 30 mile-per-hour moving-barrier test is a reasonable standard that meets the needs of auto safety," he said. "The state should be precluded from saying that some higher standard than 30 miles-per-hour is reasonable."

Neal conceded there were no federal rear-end safety standards in effect when the 1973 Pinto model was built, but added "it would be the height of foolishness to say that if the standard was 30 miles-per-hour in 1977, that it should have been something higher in 1973."

"I see disaster, absoulute disaster if the prosecutor in this case can offer evidence of an acceptable standard of conduct which is higher than 30 miles per hour. If they're successful, that means you can prosecute (an automaker) for a car manufactured today even though it meets the federal standard. The prosecutor is saying, 'I don't care if the manufacturer made the car to meet a 30 mile per hour impact standard – I'm entitled to indict because I have the right to have a jury determine a higher standard."

Neal acknowledged that in civil lawsuits, juries can conclude the federal standard was not high enough and award damages to the plaintiff even if the automaker complied with the federal requirements. "But there's a difference between money claims and prison," he said. "The state is saying you can meet federal standards and still go to prison."

"That is a horrendous, horrendous proposition. Alabama and Alaska can say some different standard is appropriate. What you'd have is the total destruction of the auto industry."

Neal said that the auto industry "needs uniform standards and if the State of Indiana thinks there should be a higher standard, it can go to NHTSA and say it wants a 50 mile per hour standard."

Rising to rebut Neal in a low-key but assertive manner, Berner replied that "federal standards may be *some evidence* of what is an acceptable standard, but they are minimum standards and minimum means minimum."

He said that prosecutors intended to offer evidence of another standard – the "state of the art" – which is what automakers knew was technically possible and economically feasible to achieve when the car was built. "Ford Motor Co. knew at the time it could build a car much more safely than it did. It had already produced the Capri, with a safe, over-the-axle design," he said.

Berner emphasized that there were no federal standards for rear-end crashes in 1973. "NHTSA would have let the gas tank be strapped to the rear bumper. A jury could surely say it was reckless to be put there," he said.

"Everyone else, whatever they do, they do knowing that a jury may find what they did was negligent or reckless or criminal. By what right does Ford claim immunity? By Ford's logic, if one gains profits in 50 states, one can ignore the rules in those places that everyone else has to live by."

Berner's argument came down to a core question of the trial: "Who sets the standard in this case – Washington or this jury? In Indiana, the constitution says in criminal cases, the jury has the right to determine the law and the facts. Yet Ford wants to tell the jury it can find the law is no more than a 30 mile per hour standard. To limit this jury now would be to invade its province and block it from its constitutional duty to weigh all of the evidence and determine the facts and the law."

Neal appeared frustrated in his final comments. "Ford once built a safety vehicle for $50,000 – it weighed several tons," he said. "Detroit can build a car that looks and drives like a tank, that floats on the water, if safety at any cost is the requirement, without regard to durability, fuel economy, and comfort. Apparently that's what Mr. Berner is saying – you build a car as safe as possible or you subject yourself to criminal prosecution."

There was a tremendous amount of tension in the courtroom as Staffeldt pondered his decision. "The question is an awesome one," he began. But then he ruled against Ford and said that prosecutors could present evidence going beyond the NHTSA standard.

"That's not to say the court will not, when the trial is going on, reverse its ruling depending on the facts, circumstances, and evidence presented to the jury," he cautioned.

At the end of the day, the lawyers seemed to agree the rulings had been a draw. The state was limited, at least for a while, in the evidence it could present. But prosecutors did win the one motion which, by itself, might have scuttled the entire case.

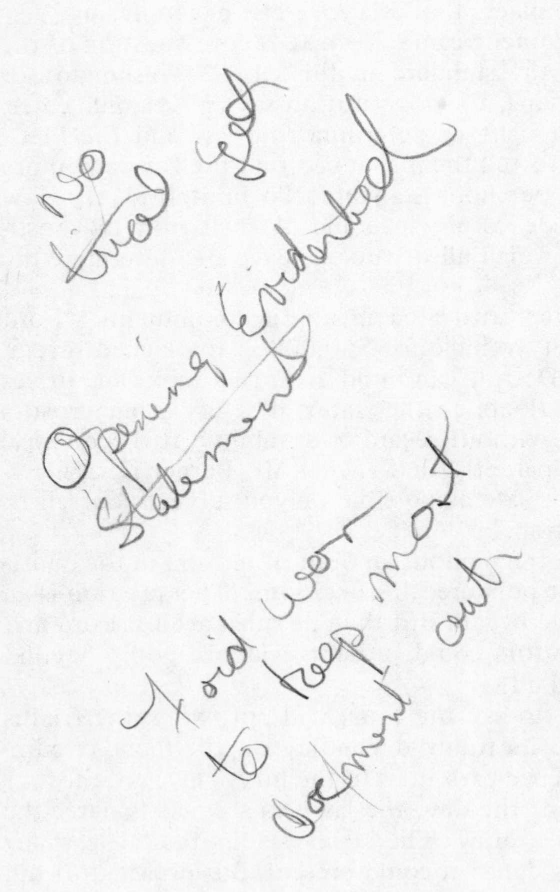

11

Five hundred and twenty-two days after Robert Duggar's van sparked the inferno which killed three young girls, the opening statements were set to begin in Ford's reckless homicide trial.

The weather in Winamac was frigid that Tuesday morning, but the community had been spared the mountains of snow that kept it buried for much of the previous winter. Inside Staffeldt's courtroom, it was warm and stuffy. Some of the windows were fogged and the two state troopers who watched over the proceedings would periodically open the doors to let some cool air flow in. The spectators settled into their seats and whispered among themselves as if waiting for the curtain to go up on opening night of a new play.

Before the case could begin, though, James Neal had one more crucial legal maneuver to accomplish.

Neal wanted Cosentino to be blocked from showing the jurors the grotesque photographs of the victims taken after the accident and from eliciting gruesome testimony from eyewitnesses about the accident scene. He knew that such evidence would be dramatic and powerful, and if the jurors were to become enraged by it there was only one thing they could lash out against – Ford Motor Company.

So Neal told the judge that Ford was filing a document in which it admitted the identities of the girls and that each one of them died from burns. This resolved the issue of whether the force of the impact itself or the ensuing fire claimed the three lives.

Because Ford admitted the manner in which the girls died, Neal said to Staffeldt, there would be no need for Cosentino to present photographs or testimony in an attempt to prove they were killed by fire. He also said that any evidence about the girls' lives or religious practices would be irrelevent to the issues in the case. "They were nice girls, we don't have any doubt about that," he said.

"Ford cannot plead partly guilty," Berner protested. "This is a sanitized admission to keep the uncomfortable realities of homicide from the jury. . . . This is an attempt to render these victims to the jury as less than real people."

Berner argued that the state has an obligation to prove every element of the crime, even in face of an admission by the defendant. "Just because there may be a full confession in a case doesn't mean the prosecution can't present other evidence of guilt," he said.

Neal countered that he wanted to prevent the case from turning into "a melodramatic spectacle" or "a soap opera."

Staffeldt ruled in favor of Ford, barring any pictures of the girls taken after the accident, any "gruesome testimony" or any statements made by Judy Ulrich unless they dealt with the crash itself.

Cosentino asked whether he could show to the jury some pictures of the girls taken before the accident. "Really," Neal said in disgust. "I thought this prosecution was going to get to the question of whether we were reckless or not."

"What you want to do is sanitize the state's case," Cosentino charged. "These girls are not statistics. Someday at NHTSA, maybe they'll be statistics, but I'm entitled to show these were living, breathing people."

Staffeldt ruled, though, that he did not see "any particular reason" to let the jurors see high school pictures of the victims.

Cosentino was angry. "I guess we can't prove anything about the victims – whether they lived or died or anything else – even though the victims are what this case is all about," he told the television cameras in the courtroom lobby as he left for lunch.

"All we want to do is preclude proof that's unnecessary," Neal told the press corps. "We've got plenty of issues to try. This isn't a matter to be tried on emotion; it deserves to be tried on the issues."

The prosecution team was convinced that Staffeldt's ruling was wrong. But Cosentino commented later that Neal's maneuver was "a very good strategic move for Ford." Cosentino had wanted the jurors to know something about the girls so they would see the case as being more than just an antiseptic bundle of issues. And he had hoped to give them a vivid idea of the accident scene and injuries to the girls because "if you can see what fire can do to somebody in this kind of collision, maybe you'd want to save somebody else's life out there."

When it came time for opening statements, Cosentino used a straight-forward approach in a firm voice tinged with a hint of controlled outrage. Standing erect behind the lecturn, he spent 58 minutes on his presentation, much of which he read from 20 typewritten, legal-sized pages of notes.

He charged that a rushed schedule and the strictly enforced limitations that the car weigh under 2,000 pounds and cost under $2,000 resulted in the Pinto being built "with utter disregard for fuel system safety."

"The Ulrich car," he said, "had a fuel system design that invited fire in the event of normal highway collisions. . . . The state will prove to you that Ford management was aware of the fire risk to its Pinto customers and totally disregarded it."

Cosentino went through a litany of safety problems with the car, including what he called "inadequate crush space." He said that most American cars provide 26 inches of crush space between the bumper and the gas tank, compared to the Pinto's six inches, and that the Pinto lacked the rear structure present in previous Ford compacts.

"Although the Pinto was the first subcompact Ford had built in this country," he said, "the great majority of the foreign-designed subcompacts locate the gas tank above the rear axle or in front of the rear axle, which provides much more crush space and structural protection."

Cosentino conceded that "standing alone, there is nothing wrong with making an automobile soft" in its rear because it can help cushion the passengers from the force of impact. "However," he added, "you do not put a gasoline tank in this crush zone."

"Ford engineers repeatedly revealed to management the danger of the Pinto fuel system design as well as alternative safe designs which eliminate the fire danger to Pinto customers," Cosentino charged. "The state will prove to you that Ford management decided to totally ignore 1973 Pinto fuel system safety, and that these decisions were made in the face of overwhelming knowledge of the great potential for the Pinto to burst into fire at clearly foreseeable highway collision speeds."

In addition, he said, "documents will prove to you that the defendant engaged in an intentional effort to hide their knowledge of the Pinto fire hazard."

Ford, he said, "had ample time to alter the fuel system design of the 1973 Pinto. The state will prove that Ford Motor Company management refused to do so for the sole reason that they would save money by not doing it. . . . The state will prove to you that the Pinto was designed for profit, not safety."

In light of Staffeldt's rulings limiting the evidence he could discuss, Cosentino talked only in rather sketchy terms of how Ford rejected the over-the-axle Pinto design because of luggage space, how the "prototype" tests demonstrated the Pinto's design was prone to fuel leakage, and how engineers came up with alternative designs such as the bladder and flak suits.

"Even with direct evidence of Pinto fire hazards and

additional direct evidence of feasible ways to eliminate Pinto fire deaths, Ford management deliberately chose profit over human life," he said.

Cosentino said that Ford management "did not give the public one hint" of the car's danger, and that when the Pinto controversy erupted a year before the Ulrich crash, Ford officials issued a statement saying that "Ford wishes to reassure Pinto owners and the public that the Pinto does not pose any undue hazard to its occupants."

He concluded by asserting that Judy, Lyn, and Donna Ulrich "needlessly died as a result of the callous, indifferent, and reckless acts and omissions of the defendant, Ford Motor Company."

Later, Neal would accuse Cosentino of violating Staffeldt's orders at least three times by discussing material which had been prohibited by the judge. Cosentino replied by accusing Neal of doing the same thing.

Neal began his opening remarks in a somewhat confused and harried manner by attempting to specifically rebut a few points Cosentino had made. His presentation, though, became smoother when he began referring to the stack of index cards he brought with him to the lecturn. His aw-shucks country-boy demeanor was shelved for a stern, serious approach as he spent 75 minutes unveiling Ford's million-dollar defense.

"We won't deny we could make mistakes," he told the jurors. "We don't even deny that we could be wrong. But we do deny that we are reckless killers."

Then Neal began listing nine points which formed the core of Ford's case. The first was that Highway 33 was a poorly designed road with curbs so high that the girls could not get their car off. "No one is called to answer for that," he said.

His second point was that Duggar rammed the Ulrich car "at 50 miles-per-hour even though the Pinto had its emergency lights on. . . but Mr. Duggar is not called to answer."

Third, he said, was that the 1973 Pinto "met every fuel system safety standard required by any government." And the fourth was that the 1973 model met Ford's own internal standard that the car be able to withstand a 20 mile-per-hour moving-barrier test, even though "no other manufacturer had any standard."

"Mr. Cosentino said to you that Ford stopped with a 20 mile-per-hour standard for the 1973 model, as if that is some sort of castigation of Ford," he said.

Neal said, though, that "practically every organization up to" the time of the Pinto's introduction had suggested a 20 mile-per-hour moving-barrier rear-end standard for fuel system safety.

In what would become a major cornerstone of the Ford defense, Neal's fifth point was that "the Pinto was comparable in design and manufacture to other 1973 subcompacts."

His sixth assertion, and what he termed "the best evidence that we are not reckless killers," was that the same engineers who designed the Pinto also drove them and bought them for their families. "We will bring these people in," he said. "We will have them take the stand."

His next point was that information collected by the federal government and the State of Washington and given to Ford in 1977 and 1978 "showed that the Pinto performed as well or better with respect to fires and collisions than most other subcompacts."

Neal then emphasized that when Ford in June, 1978 – two months before the Ulrich crash – decided to recall the Pintos "in an effort to even improve their fuel systems," Ford acted as quickly as possible.

This was important because Cosentino had to prove that Ford acted recklessly by failing to warn of a dangerous defect in the Pinto during the 41-day period just before the Ulrich crash. This time frame was after a public announcement of the recall and during the time the recall process was at full steam, Neal contended.

This narrow band on time was established by Staffeldt as the essential element in the case because of Judge Jone's earlier opinion which upheld the indictment. This meant it would not be enough for the prosecution to prove the car had been recklessly designed and built. Ford's alleged reckless failure to warn consumers was the key to the case.

Neal's final point was that with the speeds involved in the Ulrich collision, and the fact the van weighed almost twice as much as the Pinto, "other subcompacts, and even larger cars, would have suffered the same consequences."

Neal maintained that the Pinto had been stopped when it was rammed from behind – not moving as Cosentino had claimed – and that the van smashed into it at 50 miles-per-hour. "No subcompact could have withstood the assault of the van in this case," he said.

In addition, Neal pointed out that Cosentino never explained why the three girls had turned their car around and were headed back toward Elkhart when the crash occurred. The reason Cosentino omitted this, of course, was that all he had was speculation. But Neal surprised the prosecution team by saying confidently, "We will establish why they turned around."

Even before the jurors heard testimony from them, Neal attacked the credibility of Harley Copp and Byron Bloch, the government's two top technical witnesses, and labeled them "Howard Cosells."

"I've never known of Howard Cosell to miscall a play," Neal said, "because he always waits until the play is over and sometimes waits for the instant replay and then he says, 'Oh, they did this, but they should have done that.'"

Pinto engineers, on the other hand, were "the quarterbacks on the spot who must make on-the-spot decisions."

Neal also contended that "when the Pinto came off the line, no one thought that fire on rear-impact and deaths and serious injuries from fire on rear-impact were a high risk problem."

He said there were 50,000 traffic fatalities a year, but only about 100 people died annually from fire in rear-end crashes. "That's not to belittle lives. It's simply to say that when you are dealing with a problem, you address. . . the serious, high-risk (areas) first," he said.

As he neared the conclusion of his remarks, Neal told the jurors that reckless homicide "is a nice term for reckless killing." Then he repeated slowly, stressing each word: "*We are not reckless killers.*"

It was 4:30 in the afternoon by the time Neal sat down, and Staffeldt decided to dismiss the jury until the following day when testimony would begin.

Jerry Sloan's work, though, was just beginning. His public relations staff took the official transcript of Neal's opening statements, made dozens of copies, and shipped them out to editorial writers at newspapers across the country – just in case they needed some material.

12

Cosentino and Neal exchanged vehement charges accusing each other of having violated the judge's orders during opening statements. Neal vowed not to be "Mr. Nice Guy" anymore. Cosentino accused the defense team of harassing a prosecution witness with a late-night telephone call, leaving the witness "upset and shaken." Ford lawyers claimed they had been "very polite" in asking the witness for an interview. Cosentino warned that *he* would start making late-night calls to Ford's witnesses if Staffeldt refused to order a stop to the defense team's calls.

It was, in sum, another typical morning of bickering at the Ford Pinto trial.

When all of that was finally cleared out of the way, the jury was brought in and Cosentino stood to announce: "The State of Indiana calls its first witness, Trooper Neil B. Graves." It seemed appropriate that the first investigator to notice oddities about the Ulrich crash should lead off the prosecution's case.

After being sworn in by the judge, Graves sat down on the witness stand adjacent to the jury box and began recounting the sequence of events beginning with his arrival at the scene of the Ulrich collision 17 months earlier.

He recalled how he was puzzled when he found "a mixture of gas and water" on the right floor of the Pinto. He said he found "a large gaping hole on the left side of the fuel tank where it had split" and then found splits in the seam between the car's body and the floor where the gas had apparently entered the passenger compartment.

Cosentino interrupted his questioning to reach inside a large paper bag next to the counsel table and pull out the severely mangled and twisted gas tank from the Ulrich Pinto. After marking the scorched, rusty tank with a sticker designating it "State's Exhibit No. 1," he strode over to Graves and handed it to him. In a dramatic demonstration, the trooper then illustrated the size of the hole in the tank by sticking his entire hand and forearm inside. The sketch artists frantically tried to capture the moment on paper. Graves spent quite a while attempting to wipe stubborn black soot off his hands with a handkerchief.

In further testimony, Graves described the position of the vehicles at the scene and the various measurements of the gouges and scorch marks left on the asphalt by the Pinto. He added that the Pinto had been in second gear. Under Staffeldt's previous order, he could not describe the bodies he found inside the car except to say they were "incinerated." He also testified that the curb along the highway was eight inches high, but then added, "The curbs didn't cause the fire in the Pinto." Neal objected to the remark.

Graves told of finding the beer bottles and five grams of marijuana inside the van and said that a blood test showed Duggar had not been drinking or taking drugs. He conceded, though, that the test was not designed to detect marijuana use.

Under cross-examination, Neal asked if Graves had seen the gas cap when he investigated the crash. "No, I did not," the trooper replied. Based on photographs showing the gas cap at the scene, Neal then elicited testimony that if the Pinto were to be placed on the highway at the point of impact, the gas cap would have been found just to the right of the car's front fender. The importance of that fact would only become clear several weeks later.

With the jury dismissed, Neal and Cosentino got into another argument, this time because Neal wanted to ask the trooper whether Duggar had been charged with possession of the marijuana.

"This has absolutely nothing to do with this case," Cosentino exclaimed angrily. "You're the most highly overpaid counsel I've ever seen in my life!" He loudly accused Neal of perpetrating "a hoax and a fraud" by trying to ask the question.

"Are you talking so the jurors can hear you?" Neal demanded, pointing to the small room at the rear of the courtroom where the jury was taken during its absenses.

Staffeldt ruled it would be improper to ask Graves whether Duggar had been charged with a crime. "If (Duggar) has been convicted, that may be proper," he said.

With the jurors still out of the courtroom, Cosentino asked the trooper his opinion about whether the Pinto had been stopped or moving at the time of the crash. "I concluded it was not stopped; the Pinto was moving," he replied. But because Graves was not qualified as an expert in this area, Staffeldt ruled the testimony could not be repeated in front of the jury.

The next battle between the lawyers broke out a few minutes later when Cosentino said he wanted to show the jury a 40-second television news clip of the accident scene. The film showed the Pinto, the van, firemen trying to pry the door off the car, and the victims being removed, although they were not visible.

"How this has anything to do with the issues before this court is beyond me," Neal argued. Cosentino contended the movie was "not grotesque or horrible" and that it demonstrated the damage to the vehicles and how the Pinto's door had jammed. "You just can't sanitize the state's evidence," he said.

Staffeldt sided with the prosecution and said the jurors could view the movie. "Is there sound?" Neal asked. "You wouldn't like the audio," Cosentino replied.

After the film was shown, the sudden appearance of the next witness in the doorway quickly silenced the whispering among the audience. Mrs. Mattie Ulrich, mother of Judy and Lyn, walked into the courtroom accompanied by investigator Billy Campbell.

A petite woman with curly brown hair and wearing a black pants suit and a rust-colored blouse, she looked solemn and composed as she sat on the witness stand and was asked to remember the day her daughters died.

She described how Judy and Lyn were taking their house guest, Donna, over to Goshen for a church volleyball game driving in Judy's yellow Ford Pinto.

"Why did you buy the Pinto?" Cosentino asked gently.

"We bought it because it was gas-saving and it was an American-made car," she replied in a clear, unwavering voice.

"Did you ever get a warning from Ford relative to the Ford Pinto?"

"Yes, sir."

"When did you receive it?"

"February of 1979."

"That was several months after the girls had been killed?"

"Yes, sir."

Cosentino handed her the recall notice she had received from Ford, but Neal objected to her describing it. Instead, the two-page letter was passed among the jurors so they could read it for themselves.

"Did you receive any warning at all before August 10, 1978?" Cosentino inquired.

"No, sir."

"What would you have done if you had received a warning about the Pinto on or before August 10,1978?"

"I would have gotten rid of it."

"Would you have let the girls drive the car that evening?"

"No, sir."

Neal blocked Cosentino from asking whether she would receive any money from Ford if the automaker were convicted in this trial. Cosentino had wanted to emphasize to the jurors that this was a criminal, not a civil, case and that the Ulrich family did not stand to gain anything financially from it. Under Indiana law, there would only be a limited amount of damages the family could expect to receive under a civil case. At the time, no case had been filed but the family lawyer was negotiating with Ford about a possible settlement.

With the jury absent, Cosentino tried to convince the judge to let her identify for the jurors some high school photographs of the three girls. Staffeldt refused. So that the official record of the case would be complete, Cosentino then had her identify the pictures of all three girls without the jurors present.

She gazed several moments at each photograph as it was handed to her by Cosentino and before she said the name of the girl who was shown. The only emotion her face betrayed was a slight, forlorn smile as she examined the picture of her daughter Lyn.

Neal had tried earlier to prevent Mrs. Ulrich from testifying at all, and during her short time on the witness stand he was pushed into objecting five times to questions by Cosentino or her answers. Like any defense attorney, Neal knew it can leave a bad impression with jurors when a lawyer makes repeated objections because it tends to make the attorney look like he has something to hide. Part of Cosentino's strategy, it seemed, was to force Neal as much as possible into a position where he would be forced to object in front of the jury.

At the end of the day, the lawyers were confronted in the courthouse lobby with a crescent-shaped crowd of reporters and television cameras. What started as impromptu press conferences at the foot of the courthouse stairs had evolved into a twice-a-day ritual in which Cosentino and Neal, one at a time, would step in front of a cluster of microphones to answer reporters' questions before lunch and at the conclusion of the day's proceedings.

Cosentino was asked about his frequent courtroom skirmishes with Neal and his characterization of his adversary as being overpaid. "Well," he said, "I guess it's going to be a harsh trial."

Neal, who was generally much more reticent in front of the cameras than his rival, said only, "No trial is any picnic."

Cosentino's next group of witnesses was among his most crucial because their testimony would deal with the vital question of how fast the Pinto and van were moving at the time of the crash.

A central part of Cosentino's case was that the force of the impact itself was not very powerful and that the girls would have survived it with few, if any, injuries. But he contended that the defective fuel system design of the Pinto was responsible for causing the fireball that burned them to death instead.

He believed that the "closing speed" in the accident was between 30 and 35 miles per hour. The closing speed represented how much faster the van was going than the Pinto at the time of the crash. Cosentino contended that much of the evidence would prove the van was going 50 miles per hour and the Pinto was moving at 15 to 20 miles per hour at the time, thus giving the 30-to-35 mile-per-hour closing speed.

Neal's assertion, though, was that the Pinto was stopped on the highway at the time and that the van was going 50 miles per hour or faster when it plowed into the car. As Neal said in his opening remarks, Ford believed that *any* subcompact, or even a standard-sized car, would have leaked gas and possibly burned in such a tremendous impact and that the cause of the fire was not any defect in the Pinto.

The prosecution's first eyewitness to testify was Albert J. Clark Jr., the retired carpenter who was driving in his motorhome down the opposite lane of traffic when the crash occurred and who had pried open the Pinto's door to free Judy from the inferno.

Clark was a wiry, nervous man with a heart condition who was so overcome with the emotion of having to relive the tragedy that he had to halt his testimony several times to put nitroglycerine pills under his tongue. He said he believed the Pinto was traveling 30 to 35 miles per hour and the van was moving 40 to 45 miles per hour when the crash took place, which would yield a closing speed of between 5 and 15 miles per hour.

"The force (of the impact) was not that terrific, as far as I can tell," Clark recalled. "I thought at the time it would be a fender-bender."

Under questioning by John Ulmer, the volunteer prosecutor from Goshen, Clark described how a "puff of flame" shot out from the rear underside of the Pinto after the impact.

"A second later, the whole thing was engulfed in flames. I'm an old G.I., and it was like a large napalm bomb going off; it just blew up." He snapped his fingers. "The car just went."

He said the car was "nothing but flame, just like a ball of flame" as it careened down the highway and that fire was shooting out the windows and lapping over the car's top when he ran up to try to help.

Although Clark was allowed to say that he saw "a body" in the grass with its foot caught in the door of the fiery Pinto, he was precluded under Staffeldt's previous ruling from going into details. Ulmer asked for the jury to be excused and then asked the judge if Clark could at least testify that Judy was conscious, moving, and talking. This, he said, would help prove that the force of the crash was not tremendous because she would have been knocked unconscious or suffered severe impact-related injuries.

"Neal said he would prove there was a 50 mile per hour closing speed," said Ulmer, a short, balding lawyer with a penchant for pointed cowboy boots. "Traumatic injuries go with a crash of that speed."

At that point, Staffeldt issued a ruling which had the prosecutors shaking their heads. "The issue is the recklessness on the part of Ford and the cause of the accident; the fact of traumatic injury doesn't go to that issue."

But the issue in the case was not the cause of the *accident,* which already had been established as being the van ramming the car due to Duggar's driving and the fact the Pinto was slowing or stopping on the road. The issue was what caused the *fire* which killed the girls – was it the defective design of the Pinto which Ford had recklessly failed to warn about, or was it the force of the tremendous impact itself which would have caused virtually any car to explode.

Some of the prosecutors began wondering whether Staffeldt understood what the case was all about. When Cosentino raised this point with the judge a few days later, Staffeldt replied, "Maybe my language didn't convey what I thought. . . . My semantics were bad; that's a common fault of mine."

And yet, several weeks later, Staffeldt again said from the bench, when talking about a defect in the Pinto, that "it's a matter of proving what was wrong (with the car) was the cause of the accident." When two prosecutors immediately said that was not right, Staffeldt replied, "It has to be."

Staffeldt did let Clark testify about the jammed door on the Ulrich Pinto because of evidence this was a typical problem when Pintos were hit from behind in Ford tests years earlier.

"There was an awful lot of flame," Clark said. " I pulled on the door, I couldn't get it open. I tried opening the door again; the heat and flame coming out of the car were so intense I couldn't get it open. It was caught. Finally I got a board and pried the door open."

Clark was becoming visibly shaken and wiped his eyes with a handkerchief. "Will you ever forget that day?" Ulmer asked.

"No," Clark said, shaking his head and becoming choked up. "No."

During cross-examination, Neal tried to cast doubt on Clark's estimate of the speed of the vehicles by questioning the angle from which he saw the crash. Then he showed Clark a photograph which Neal only identified as "Defendant's Exhibit H" and which looked like a Pinto with a smashed rear-end. He asked Clark to compare this damage with a picture of the Ulrich Pinto which he handed him.

"They're pretty close," Clark responded, adding, "Well there's a heck of a lot more damage" to the Ulrich car.

Neal gathered up the pictures and began walking back to

his table. As he went, he commented loud enough for everyone to hear that Exhibit H showed a Pinto that had been hit from behind "with a closing speed of 50 miles per hour."

"That's a cheap shot and you know it," Ulmer charged. But even though Staffeldt ordered Neal's comment stricken from the record, Neal's point had been made.

The next witness was Clark's wife, Pauline, who, ironically, used to work for Ford as a keypunch operator. She testified both the van and the Pinto had been moving, but did not know how fast.

"The van hit the Pinto," she recalled. "There was a small flame like 12 or 15 inches high from the rear behind the driver, and just moments after the flame the whole car just exploded and was in flames; it was just engulfed in flames."

Another eyewitness, William J. Martin, a college English professor who once taught at Notre Dame University in South Bend, testified that the van "seemed to be traveling at a normal rate of speed on a highway," which he defined as being 50 miles per hour. The Pinto, he added, was moving "about 15 miles per hour, maybe slightly slower, maybe slightly faster." This would equal a closing speed of about 35 miles per hour. Martin, who had been driving in the opposite lane of traffic, said he saw the Pinto about two or three seconds before the impact.

Like Clark and his wife, Martin described a "bright flash of light" which came from the Pinto's rear on the driver's side. "Almost instantly, the Pinto just exploded," he said with horror, his eyes wide as if he were reliving the experience.

He said the Pinto exploded once more and that by the time he ran to the car and looked through the windshield, "all I could see was a solid mass of orange flame; there was absolutely no air space in the passenger compartment."

Outside the jury's presence, Martin described how he first saw Judy propping herself on her arms besides the Pinto. "She was incredibly burned," he said softly. "It astonished me, it shocked me that she could be so incredibly burned and still be alive."

Martin's wife, Honor, gave a similar description of the fireball which swallowed the Pinto. She said she agreed the Pinto was traveling about 15 miles per hour and the van was going "at a normal rate of speed." She added the Pinto's fire was so intense that she could feel the heat all the way across the five-lane highway.

A woman who was driving behind the van just before the accident, Vicki Shriner, testified the van was traveling at 50 miles per hour when it struck the Pinto, but she said she did not see the car before the crash.

Another eyewitness, an 18-year-old high school senior, said she had passed the van and the Pinto shortly before the crash and saw the accident in her rear-view mirror.

The van, she said, was going 40 to 45 miles per hour when she was next to it, and the Pinto was moving at 30 to 35 miles per hour when she went by. "It was still moving yet it was slowing down when it got hit," she said, estimating its speed at impact as being about 25 to 30 miles per hour. Like some of the other eyewitnesses, she said the Pinto's emergency flashers were operating before the collision.

When Neal asked her under cross-examination whether she had told two lawyers from his law firm during an interview that the Pinto could have been going "zero to five" miles per hour at impact, she said, "I told them I wasn't too sure."

Cosentino was satisfied with the evidence about the closing speed because all of the testimony established it well below the 45 miles per hour which Ford's own Capri showed it could withstand without gas leakage. That sort of design, he believed, would have saved the girls' lives if it had been used on the Pinto.

The prosecution had just one more eyewitness to describe the speed of the vehicles – the only survivor of the crash, Robert Duggar.

13

He looked child-like and timid sitting on the witness stand. His longish black hair was neatly parted down the middle. His slightly built frame was clad in a brown suit, a tan sweater underneath, a white shirt, and a solid dark-brown tie. He spoke in a meek, polite voice. He was 22 years old, and a freshman at a small college in Michigan.

Robert Duggar said his 1972 Chevrolet van was "a mess" on August 10,1978, and he was driving over to a friend's house in the evening to clean it out and get it tuned up for an upcoming vacation. The beer bottles in the van were from his brother's birthday party the previous weekend, he said. The marijuana under the seat consisted of burnt stubs from another day. The pills in the glove compartment were "speeders" which he used at work to increase his production. He testified he had not taken any drugs or alcohol that day.

Duggar said he knew his speed was 50 miles per hour as he was driving down U.S. Highway 33 near Goshen because he saw a police car with a radar unit and checked to make sure he was within the limit. Michael Cosentino asked him what happened next.

A. I reached for a cigaret, they had fallen on the floor, I reached down and picked them up and when I looked back on the road the Pinto was very close in front of me.

Q. *How close was it to you?*

A. I would estimate 10 feet or so.

Q. *Then what happened when you saw the Pinto?*

A. Well, I immediately went for the brakes and before anything I hit the rear end of the Pinto.

Q. *What did you feel when you hit the rear end of the Pinto?*

A. I -- I went up in my chair, I hit the steering wheel. . . .

Q. *All right. When you hit the rear end of the Pinto, what happened at that point?*

A. Well, I hit the Pinto and immediately I smelled gasoline and before I could even think, before I could even finish thinking about gasoline, the car was on fire. And right then, at that time, we were seperating.

Q. *Now, Bob, if you will, when you hit the Pinto, how long was it before the fire started?*

A. It was almost immediately, within a second. . . before I could even, you know, finish thinking about smelling gasoline, it was on fire.

Q. *Tell the court and the jury what the Pinto looked like when it caught on fire.*

A. It was – the whole car was on fire. It was just – the whole car was on fire. It was – the whole car was burning.

Q. *What happened then?*

A. Well, the Pinto turned in a clockwise position and ended up on the curb. And my van slid sideways across the righthand lane and stopped at the curb.

Q. *Now just before you hit the Pinto, did you have an idea the Pinto was moving or stopped?*

A. Yes, sir. The car was moving.

Q. *And do you have an opinion as to how fast the Pinto was moving?*

A. About 15 to 20 miles per hour.

Q. *And did you see any lights of any kind?*

A. Yes, sir. I seen lights.

Q. *Do you know what kind of lights they were?*

A. No, sir.

Q. *What did you do after your van came to a rest?*
A. Well, everything was on fire and I wanted to get out of my van, I thought my van was going to explode, too, so I got out of my van. . . .
Q. *Now, then, when you got out of the van, Bob, what did you do?*
A. The whole area where the Pinto was at, the grass and everything was on fire and I got outside my van and I ran clear around the car to the other side of the car. . . .
Q. *What did you do there?*
A. Well, sir, I wanted to help. And, well, I seen everything was burning, on fire, and, and I just fell on my knees. I froze. I don't know. I fell on my knees. A man and woman, they were right there. They came right up to me, and the woman put her arm around me and, you know, she was trying to comfort me, and I think the man had went for a fire extinguisher and tried to do some good with that fire extinguisher.
Q. *What do you mean — spray the Pinto?*
A. I think he was trying to spray the girl.
Q. *Now, can you tell me, will you ever forget that scene?*
A. No, sir. I can't.

Robert Duggar was sobbing.

A while later, after he became composed, Duggar testified that he was taken to the hospital with a scraped chin, bruised shins, and two cracked ribs. He said he was charged with possession of amphetamines and that, under an agreement worked out with Cosentino, he could plead guilty and the State of Indiana would not object to placing him on probation. The case was still pending even though the pills turned out to be made of legal caffein.

With Duggar and the jurors dismissed for a while, Neal told Judge Staffeldt he should have the right to bring up Duggar's driving record on cross-examination. He contended that Duggar "made a deal" with Cosentino in connection with his charges and "the deal is graver if the man has 10 convictions than an unblemished record."

Cosentino argued, though, that only prior convictions

dealing with a witness' veracity can be used against him in cross-examination. He said Neal was only trying to "prejudice the jury against Mr. Duggar."

"I think his driving record is an issue," Staffeldt ruled. "He was driving the van when this thing occurred."

Neal began his cross-examination of Duggar by reading a list of the young man's driving convictions – failure to yield in 1975; speeding and running a stop sign in 1976; speeding and his license suspended in 1977; cited for driving with a suspended license a month after that. He had received his license back 33 days before the Ulrich crash.

When asked about the force of the crash, Duggar replied: "Sir, the impact I didn't think was that great." Neal told him that, given his speed and distance from the Pinto, he would have had one-sixth of a second before impact to make a judgement as to the Pinto's speed. Duggar insisted, though, that his estimates were accurate. "I'm sure in my own mind that the Pinto was moving," he said.

Cosentino attempted to tell the jury about the statement by the grand jury which said Duggar may have been negligent but the grand jurors did not consider his actions to constitute a criminal act. Staffeldt told him, "You can't go into what the grand jury said."

Duggar marked the end of the prosecution's eyewitnesses, and Cosentino was confident that Duggar's estimate of the closing speed being 30 to 35 miles per hour, plus the similar and even lower estimates by other drivers, constituted powerful evidence that this was a moderate-speed collision in which fire was inexcusable. Just about the only way Neal could prove it was a high-speed crash would be to substantiate his claim that the Pinto had been stopped – a seemingly impossible task in face of the eyewitness accounts.

When it came time for him to meet the press that evening, Cosentino stared straight into the five television cameras and said defiantly as he shook his finger, "I defy Mr. Neal to *stop that Pinto.*"

Staffeldt became a little more liberal concerning testimony by Levi Hochstetler, the farmer who pulled Judy from the flaming wreckage, and Douglas Bechtel, a fireman, who both were allowed to tell the jury that Judy Ulrich had been alive, conscious, and speaking after the accident. "She spoke very coherently," Bechtel said.

That testimony, in the prosecution's estimation, helped establish that the crash was not as severe as Neal had claimed. "The higher the rate of collision," Berner told the judge, "the less likely the occupant will remain conscious afterward."

The next witness for the state, Dr. Sean Gunderson, a radiologist from Goshen, was intended to bolster the same sort of contention. He said that his analysis of x-rays showed that although Lyn Ulrich suffered a skull fracture. "it had to have resulted from fire or explosion, not from the impact."

Cosentino also used scientific evidence to support Graves' opinion that the mixture he found on the front floor of the Pinto contained gasoline and water. Graves had taken samples of the residue from the right front seat, rear seat, and console, as well as pieces of the left rear tire and what remained of the carpeting.

Michael T. Oliver, a sergeant in the state police laboratory in Indianapolis, testified that he analyzed the samples and they disclosed the presence of hydrocarbons like gasoline. He could not, he said, determine how long the gasoline had been inside the car.

Now that Cosentino was deep into his case, his already rocky relationship with the Ford lawyers became even more strained. Once when Neal motioned for Cosentino to come over to his table during a break, Cosentino walked only half way. Then Cosentino pointed straight down to the ground, silently insisting that Neal walk the rest of the way to him.

"Mr. Cosentino wants to make sure I come half way," Neal said to the judge in poking fun at his adversary. "I think you've come a little more than half way, Mr. Cosentino." With that, Cosentino took one step backward.

Neal saw no humor, though, in a controversial ruling later that day in which Judge Staffeldt dealt a serious blow to the Ford defense. Staffeldt decided he would take "a chance" and let the jury see a document he had not even read and which Neal considered extremely damaging to the automaker's case.

The sequence of events began when Kiely asked Staffeldt to let the jurors read a letter sent by NHTSA to then-Ford President Lee A. Iacocca on May 25,1978 – three months before the Ulrich crash. The letter informed Iacocca that NHTSA had finished its preliminary investigation of the 1971-76 Pintos and 1975-76 Mercury Bobcats and determined the cars had a safety-related defect.

The four-paragraph letter said that the Pinto's fuel tanks and filler pipes "are subject to failure when the vehicles are struck from the rear" and can result in fire. "Moreover, when impacted from the rear, the 1971-76 Pinto demonstrates a 'fire-threshhold' at closing speeds between 30 and 35 miles per hour."

The range of closing speeds, of course, was the same one which much of Cosentino's evidence indicated was involved in the Ulrich crash.

The letter also said that a public hearing would be held on June 14,1978, to give Ford a chance to rebut NHTSA's initial findings.

"You can't talk about the recall and not say why Ford did it," Kiely said. "They were forced to do it because the government had this information. . . . They recalled to avoid a public hearing and the possibility that (Ford's) knowledge (about the Pinto's fire-prone design) for nine years would be exposed to the public."

Kiely said the letter was being offered into evidence not to establish the truth of the statements it made, but to demonstrate to the jurors that Ford had been informed before the Ulrich crash the government believed the Pinto was dangerous.

Neal considered the possibility of the letter being read by the jurors damaging enough, but Kiely urged the judge to go one step further.

Sent to Iacocca along with the letter was a 17-page report summarizing the findings of NHTSA's eight-month investigation. Kiely told the judge the report should be shown to the jury because it provided the factual basis for what the letter told Iacocca. "You don't write a letter like this without some kind of report backing it up," he said.

"I can't see how all this (report) could possibly be admissible on any rational grounds," Neal protested.

His black-rimmed reading glasses perched on his nose, Neal stood behind his table and flipped through a copy of the report, pointing out to Staffeldt that it referred to the *Mother Jones* allegations, discussed the number of civil lawsuits pending in connection with Pinto crashes, and even talked about Pinto crashes in Canada. "It's triple and quadruple heresay," Neal insisted.

More significantly, it contained a summary of a Ford crash test of a 1971 Pinto conducted shortly after the car's introduction which showed massive gas leakage when it was backed into a wall at 21 miles per hour. So far, Ford had been successful in limiting the trial to 1973 Pintos only.

And the NHTSA report included a chart describing the crash tests of Pintos and Vegas conducted by the government. The results showed that two Pintos blew up when rammed from behind by a Chevrolet Impala at about 35 miles per hour, and seven others gushed gasoline at an average rate of two gallons per minute when hit at speeds between 30 and 35 miles per hour. A tenth Pinto, backed into a wall at 21½ miles per hour, lost 12 ounces of gas per minute. In comparable car-to-car crashes, two Vegas leaked virtually no gas, two leaked at rates of 7 and 17 ounces per minute, and the Vega backed into the wall lost none of its fuel.

The tested Pintos did not include any 1973 models, as the judge had preliminarily indicated would be the only ones discussed in the trial.

"This is outrageously prejudicial," Neal told the judge.

Staffeldt's comments seemed to indicate he was leaning against letting the report into evidence, but the bearded, bespectacled Kiely, who shed his low-key personality at the courtroom door became a forceful advocate before the bench, kept insisting the report was relevant and "extremely crucial" to the prosecution's case.

He said that, like the letter, the report was being offered into evidence not to prove the facts asserted, but only to show that Ford had knowledge before the Ulrich crash that the government believed the Pinto was defective.

Neal, however, was convinced the report was so powerful that the jury would be likely to give it more weight than that. "Mr. Kiely knows that if this goes (into evidence), no jury can look at this. . . and remember this is only offered as notice to Ford and not introduced as to the truth of the matter," he insisted.

"If you have no confidence in the jury to follow the court's instructions," Kiely retorted, "then what are we all doing here?"

Then Staffeldt, who did not hide the fact he had not read the report, issued a ruling which left Neal dazed.

Kiely: So again, we offer (the letter and report) into evidence in their entirety.

Staffeldt: Well. . . I am inclined at this point – and I guess there is nothing like taking a chance – to overrule Mr. Neal's objection and to admit it as you tendered it, for whatever it is worth, with the instruction to be given to the jury that it is not to be taken for the truth of any matters that are asserted in it, but simply that they may conclude that there was some knowledge of Ford Motor Company that there was someone's opinion that there may be a defect (in the Pinto).

Neal: Judge, there is a whole lot more (contained in the report than he had previously mentioned). I won't –

Staffeldt: I don't know. Maybe I should look at it.

Neal: I wish your honor would look at it.

Kiely: Is it accepted, your honor? I just believe you said it was accepted in its entirety. You said you were going to take a chance. If you are going to take one –

Staffeldt: I think I will, and we will admit it as it is.

. . . . Neal: Would your honor not want to look at this document? I know I am arguing after the ruling, but it is quite a document. It is quite a document.

Kiely: Judge, we just got a ruling that you are going to

take a chance on this one. We have got the copies (for the jurors to read). May I proceed? It is going to be a long day.

Staffeldt: I have ruled, and we will just leave it be as it is.

The prosecution team was ecstatic about getting the document into evidence. But their euphoria was short-lived because Staffeldt followed up his ruling by making another decision which was a potentially serious defeat for the prosecution's case.

The problem arose when Ford lawyers challenged the authenticity of the NHTSA report which Kiely had just successfully entered into evidence and was waiting to show the jury.

"How do we know it is what it purports to be?" Neal asked.

Kiely replied that the report was turned over to the prosecution from Ford's own files in response to a subpena and that it had "Property of Ford Motor Co." stamped on every page. This brought to the forefront the long-simmering issue of whether this would be enough to establish documents as being authentic.

"Production (of the document by Ford from its files) amounts to authentication of the document," Kiely contended. "Everyone knows this is a true copy. If this is a phony, where did Ford get it?"

Malcom Wheeler, who had earlier done research on the issue, stood up to argue against Kiely. It is up to the prosecutors, he said, to prove a document is authentic if the defendant does not admit it. "The fact that the document was turned over by Ford does concede that Ford had possession of it, but possession does not establish that it is what it purports to be," he said.

Then in an argument that sent chuckles through the press section, Wheeler said that a Ford janitor as a joke might sign Henry Ford II's name to a document and slip it into a filing cabinet at Ford's headquarters. If Ford lawyers then took this document from the file and turned it over to the prosecution under a subpena, this would not mean Henry Ford's signature was authentic.

"We've got musical documents here," Kiely commented. "They know this is a Ford document."

Staffeldt ruled, however, that "the party offering the evidence must prove its authenticity. We have to be careful not to open the door to all sorts of potential frauds."

"That's an impossible burden on the State of Indiana," Cosentino told the judge. "If it's a janitor's document, (Ford) has the people and the wherewithal" to rebut the document by demonstrating that.

When Wheeler contended that Ford lawyers had offered to concede authentication of numerous documents before trial, Cosentino snapped, "You offered (to agree) to the authenticity if we gave you our whole case in return."

Cosentino was not especially concerned about authenticating the NHTSA report. He knew he could get NHTSA officials to do that by giving him a certified copy of the study. His worry centered on the dozens and dozens of internal Ford documents he wanted to get into the jury's hands. Now he would have to fly witnesses to Indiana from around the country to testify that they recognized the signatures on these documents and that they were authentic, or bring in some other witnesses who could somehow attest that the documents were genuine. And that would take one thing he had little of – Money.

Cosentino complained to the press that evening that his case was "not in very good shape at all" because of Judge Staffeldt's decision.

"My budget is already committed," he said. "We may not have the money (to authenticate) all of the documents, but maybe we will have the wherewithal for some of them."

It was a defeat, but Cosentino was not defeated. "We're going to keep hammering away," he said. "I'm not a crybaby."

14

All was not well in Winamac.

Over at Rich's Cafe, a camera crew intruded on some early afternoon drinkers, trying to get some "man at the bar" impressions of the Pinto trial, and a tableful of bashful imbibers got up and left in a huff. Down the block, some merchants were getting peeved at the out-of-town reporters for filling up their prime parking spaces intended for customers.

"The locals' patience with the national media is wearing thin," Rick Sutton wrote in his weekly tabloid. "You haven't lived until you walk into Miller's Restaurant, sick of this national media jive, and have every bite filmed for national television. Now that is the last straw."

On top of that, a lot of people were still miffed about some of the cutesy stories in the national press which they thought poked fun at Winamac's rural personality. "We don't wear bib overalls to church," Sutton fumed.

Some of the other residents were perturbed because the heavy security at the courthouse made it difficult for them to get into an important meeting of the county commissioners which was being held on the same floor.

John Stombaugh, the outspoken corner druggist, was blunt as usual about the trial: "People just hope to hell this thing will get over with in a hurry."

Well, not everyone. At Matilda's Cafe, where the press corps guzzled its morning coffee before walking across the brick-lined street to the courthouse, ever-pleasant waitress Karen Hopkins was still enthusiastic about Winamac's sudden fame. "This is great," she exclaimed as she flitted from table to table with coffeepot in hand. "Usually it's pretty dull around here. At least *something's* going on."

Over in Staffeldt's courtroom, where an empty seat was still a rare sight, Cosentino was finishing his group of witnesses intended to bolster his contention that the crash involved a moderate impact which the girls would have survived if the Pinto's defective design had not sparked the fatal fireball. The next controversy came from Dr. Robert J. Stein, the flamboyant, husky-voiced chief medical examiner from the Chicago area who earlier gained noteriety when he directed the exhumation and identification of the victims of mass murderer John Wayne Gacy.

Dr. Stein had performed the autopsy of Judy Ulrich after her body was exhumed during the investigation of the crash. He testified that although she had burns over 95 per cent of her body, "there was no evidence of internal injuries."

"If there was no fire," Cosentino asked, "would Judy be alive today?"

"Yes," Dr. Stein replied.

After leaving the courtroom, Dr. Stein blasted Staffeldt for the order limiting him from discussing what might be considered "gruesome" details of his autopsy. "It was disgraceful, disgusting and unprecedented," he sputtered.

His testimony was followed by Dr. James A. Benz, chief of pathology at an Indianapolis hospital, who performed the autopsy on the exhumed body of Lyn Ulrich. He said that Lyn, who had been sitting in the Pinto's rear seat at the time of the impact, did not sustain the spinal cord injuries which he would have expected in a high-speed, rear-end crash.

She did, however, suffer a slight fracture of the thin part of the skull above the right eye, a minor bone separation in her thigh, and a broken leg. None of her traumatic injuries would have seriously incapacitated her if she had not been burned, the doctor said.

No autopsy was ever performed on Donna Ulrich. Cosentino did not seek to have her body exhumed because she was buried in Illinois.

In the meantime, Cosentino and Neal were in the midst of negotiating to see if they could reach an agreement, or "stipulation," as to the authenticity of the Ford documents which Cosentino wanted to introduce into evidence. Cosentino told reporters that he offered to drop about half of the 200 documents he intended to use if Ford would concede that the remaining documents were genuine.

The proposed deal, he said, "would chop (our case) down considerably, but there would still be enough evidence to present our story to the jury."

As it turned out, the two sides, which had been sending proposals and counterproposals via messengers between their offices on opposite sides of the downtown area, never could come to an agreement.

"We have offered to stipulate to (the authenticity of) the documents time and time again," Neal told the judge at one point.

"Your honor," Cosentino said, "their offer to stipulate says we cannot use the documents on cross-examination (of Ford's witnesses) and we give them a license to lie on the witness stand. And we cannot use them in rebuttal."

"That is a lie!" Neal shot back.

Whatever the truth of the matter, there would be no agreement reached, and Cosentino began making arrangements to fly witnesses to Indiana to testify that the documents – which had Ford letterheads, Ford logos, "Property of Ford Motor Company" stamped on each page, and were turned over from Ford's own files – were indeed Ford documents. That would be only the first step in getting them into evidence. After they were shown to be genuine, Cosentino would have to prove they were relevant to the issues in the case.

Cosentino conceded to reporters for the first time that he was being forced to spend some of his own money on the case to keep it afloat. When one reporter asked how much he and his law firm were spending, Cosentino snapped, "None of your business!" Sources said, however, that the final amount would be as much as $15,000 to $20,000.

As for Ford's overall defense expenditures, Jerry Sloan, the public relations representative, told reporters he would not deny stories that the automaker was spending $1 million. Before the trial was over, newsmen would be pegging the amount as high as $1.5 million or more. Sloan said he would not confirm any figures.

In wrapping up their case concerning the closing speed of the crash, prosecutors decided against using testimony by Fred Arndt, a Phoenix, Arizona, accident reconstruction expert who was hired by Cosentino to analyze the vehicles and physical evidence from the Ulrich crash. He concluded that the Pinto had been moving 5 to 10 miles per hour when it was hit, and that the closing speed was between 40 and 43 miles per hour.

The prosecutors believed that this would only tend to dilute the strength of the eyewitness accounts, which varied somewhat but which were consistent in establishing the impact speed at being below Arndt's estimate. In addition, Arndt had a schedule conflict with a civil trial being conducted in Miami, Florida.

One possibility discussed by the prosecutors was to use Arndt's testimony at the conclusion of the trial to rebut any accident reconstruction experts who might testify on behalf of Ford's defense.

Cosentino then moved into the second phase of his case, which would involve proving that the Pinto exploded because it was defectively designed and that Ford knew about the hazard for years yet failed to warn consumers. To do that, he was counting on two witnesses who had helped him from the outset of the investigation – Byron Bloch and Harley Copp.

Bloch was a long-time nemesis of the auto industry, having testified in dozens of product-liability lawsuits alleging hazardous fuel system designs in various makes of cars, including such Ford products as the Galaxie, Mustang, LTD, Thunderbird, Fairlane, pick-up truck, Comet, and Torino. He even participated in a case against one of Harley Copp's creations, the Falcon.

A 42-year-old native of Chicago who later moved to West Los Angeles, Bloch was a 6-foot, 2-inch, athletic-looking man with wiry hair the color of steel wool. He was former research editor of *Road Test* magazine, for which he wrote a column called, "On the Chopping Bloch," and had spent 15 years as an independent consultant in automobile safety design, earning fees of up to $300 a day.

As early as 1973, he warned a conference sponsored by an advisory council to the U.S. Department of Transportation that the Pinto's fuel system design was "very vulnerable. . .to even minor damage." Even before that, he held up a model of a Pinto on a national television show and pointed out its fuel system hazards. When Ford announced it was recalling the Pinto, Bloch urged the government to require a second recall to further improve the car's resistance to fire in rear-end crashes.

Bloch's most effective talent, which Cosentino intended to use as fully as possible, was as a teacher. A skilled artist and capable of reducing engineering concepts to everyday language, Bloch could be quite persuasive in using graphics and narration to go through, step by step, what he considered design flaws in a product. During three days of testimony before the grand jury that later indicted Ford, Bloch used color slides, drawings, and movies to illustrate the Pinto's lethal gas tank dangers.

Bloch had capitalized on his proficiency as a communicator by working as a technical advisor and on-camera expert for ABC-TV's investigative program, *20/20*, appearing on his own product-safety segment of a Los Angeles television news show; and speaking at more than 50 schools and seminars around the country (ranging from the Society of Automotive

Engineers to Miss Porter's School in Farmington, Connecticut).

His involvement in the Ulrich case came even before Trooper Graves could track him down and ask for his assistance. The day after the crash, Bloch noticed an article on the second page of the *Los Angeles Times* with the headline, "Pinto Hit, Tank Explodes; 3 Die," and then saw another article the following day which said the wreckage of the Ulrich car was being impounded for an investigation.

Bloch promptly called Cosentino and volunteered his services. "This was a needless tragedy," he told the prosecutor at the time. "Ford knew the Pinto's gas tank design was a disaster, they withheld ways to improve it, and it's wrong that these tragedies keep happening over and over." With all the news coverage the trial would attract, the publicity-conscious Bloch also knew the case could be a boon to his reputation and consulting business.

Cosentino accepted his offer and Bloch, who travelled to Elkhart several times in the following months at his own expense and became a major source of technical background and documents for the prosecutors.

In order to convince Staffeldt to certify Bloch as an expert witness who could give his opinions during testimony, Cosentino went through Bloch's educational and professional background. He emphasized Bloch's bachelor's degree in industrial design from the University of California at Los Angeles, his "A" average in the classroom work for a master's degree, his analysis of hundreds of experimental crash tests as part of his consulting work, and his testimony as an expert in dozens of civil lawsuits.

However, James Neal was ready for him. His aides carted into court box after box crammed with transcripts of previous testimony by Bloch in civil lawsuits, hoping to catch him in an inconsistency. His researchers had sifted through all of the transcripts and prepared an indexed catalogue of their contents so any topic could be instantly pinpointed among the 70-odd volumes, and then prepared folders bulging with other background information about the witness.

Neal knew he had little chance of preventing Bloch from being certified as an expert witness under Indiana's liberal rules. But he spent half a day in an aggressive, wide-ranging attack on Bloch's qualifications in an attempt to discredit him enough so that the jurors would give his opinions little weight. It was a masterfully executed assault which left a stain on the credibility of one of the prosecution's key witnesses.

Reaching back 23 years, Neal cited science courses which Bloch had failed while a student at Northwestern University, where he was dismissed for academic reasons. He pointed out that Bloch's resume listed, "Electrical Engineering, 1957-58, University of Kansas," even though Bloch took only one electrical engineering course at the school and failed it.

He produced another resume which said, "M.A., Industrial Design (1966)," although Bloch had never completed the thesis required to earn the degree. The same resume listed, "B.A., Industrial Design (Biotechnology), UCLA," and yet Bloch conceded he took only two courses in biotechnology at the school and failed one of them. He also went through Bloch's early employment record to highlight a few quick job changes after he graduated from college.

Neal poked fun at Bloch's walk-on part on the television show, "The Bold Ones," a program for which he served as technical advisor, and asked at one point, "I see you wrote an article called, 'Smog and Your Sex Life.' What does that concern? Oh, never mind, I withdraw the question."

Stressing that Bloch was not an engineer, Neal went through some of the products which Bloch had testified were dangerously designed, including coffee pots, garbage trucks, offshore drilling rigs, tractors, and various makes of cars. For each product, Neal elicited Bloch's response that he had never designed that sort of item for mass production. When he noted Bloch had testified in a case involving a safety exit on a train, Neal asked, "And have you ever designed a train door for mass production?"

An exasperated Cosentino sprang to his feet. "Why

don't you ask him if he's ever designed a banana cart?" he demanded, bringing chuckles from the jurors.

"No, but I bet he's testified about a defect in one," Neal replied, bringing more laughter.

Later Neal jabbed at Bloch by bringing up a "products liability rap session" he held at a fancy California disco and which featured, according to an advertisement, crash test movies "followed by mixing, libations, and dancing until 2 a.m." The ad invited lawyers to hear "how to expand 'accident' cases into products liability cases."

"His academic background is sadly lacking and I haven't found anything he's done since then except say he's an expert," Neal told Staffeldt in arguing against Bloch's recognition as an expert witness. "He has posed as a man on a white charger trying to improve the world. I say he's trying to improve his own resources."

Cosentino countered that Bloch's background of 15 years in a "get your hands dirty" approach to automotive design made him especially well-qualified to give his opinions about the Pinto.

Staffeldt agreed to let Bloch testify as an expert on auto safety design, but not on accident reconstruction or on the costs of various automotive design alternatives. By that time, though, Neal had already been effective in casting doubt on Bloch's expertise and credibility.

"I've heard all of that before," the self-assured Bloch told reporters in discussing Neal's assault on him. "The same questions come up in every case; it's like a broken record."

During breaks from the trial, Bloch demonstrated himself to be a zealous self-promoter, pummeling reporters with ideas for articles which would prominently feature him, passing out mimeographed lists of places where he had given safety presentations, and being followed around the courthouse by a photographer he had hired to capture him on videotape.

Kneeling at times in front of an easel and drawing with different colored markers, Bloch began his testimony with an energetic critique of the Pinto's fuel system design. The behind-the-axle location of its gas tank, he said, was "adverse or undesirable" because the tank was exposed to crushing in rear-end collisions. It would have been much safer to situate the tank either above or in front of the axle where it would be out of the "crush zone" and be protected by the car's structure, although he seemed to favor the forward-of-the-axle option.

The Pinto's filler tube yanked out and let gas escape during crashes because it was designed "the opposite" of how it should have been. And the Pinto also should have had body rails on both sides, not just a partial one on the left as in the 1973 model, as well as a frame across the back to create a protective perimeter around the tank, he said.

Bloch added that the manner in which the Pinto's gas tank was manufactured resulted in a thinning of the metal adjacent to the place where the two halves were joined, creating a weak spot where the tank could split open during a crash.

As he described each design flaw, Bloch drew a color-coded illustration on a large piece of white cardboard, creating an easy-to-understand display for the jury.

After a break for the weekend, Bloch resumed the witness stand on Monday, January 28. Cosentino asked him only a few preliminary questions and then startled the court by suddenly walking out into the hallway. A moment later he threw open the doors, revealing several muscular state troopers straining to carry the right rear-quarter of a dark blue 1973 Pinto.

Neal objected and the jury was dismissed, "We have no objection to the jury seeing demonstrative evidence – the *entire* 1973 Pinto," he told the judge. "Indeed, we will put a '73 on a hoist somewhere for the jury. But we do object to this; it is not reality."

"Your honor, we weren't able to show the jury anything about the homicide, nothing about the scene, how it looked," Cosentino said. "Now we aren't able to show the jury anything about how the car looked. He wants to stick it way up in the air someplace!"

"I assume Mr. Cosentino is talking for the press back there," Neal commented.

Staffeldt ruled that the two rear quarters of the 1973 Pinto were permissible as evidence and he allowed them to be brought into the courtroom opposite the jury box.

Cosentino, who had bought the Pinto for $100 at an Elkhart junkyard, wanted to use it as a visual aid for both Bloch and later Copp. His first concern was for Bloch to illustrate to the judge that the 1973 model of the Pinto was virtually identical to the 1971 and 1972 models of the car. He believed this would be sufficient to lay the foundation which was required before he could introduce into evidence any crash tests of those previous Pinto models.

His reasoning was simple: If the 1971 and 1972 models were virtually the same as the 1973 car, then the crash tests of those models would be relevant in discussing the defects of the 1973 model. And those same tests would demonstrate that Ford was aware of the fire danger of the Pinto even before the 1973 model was sold to the public. Despite this evidence, Ford failed to warn consumers of the hazard until pressured by the government into the recall in 1978.

Cosentino especially needed to have the jurors see the 1971 crash tests because he lacked any tests of the 1973 model which graphically demonstrated how the car fell apart and gushed gasoline in rear-end crashes. The tests of the 1973 Pinto were conducted at slower speeds than the earlier models and were below the car's breaking point at which massive gas spillage began.

In addition, he wanted to show the jury the powerful movies of the NHTSA crash tests in which a 1971 and 1972 Pinto were rear-ended by a full-sized car at 35 miles per hour and immediately exploded into a fireball. No 1973 models were tested by NHTSA.

He also hoped that once the 1971 crash tests were ruled admissible, he could use this as a stepping stone to get the Pinto prototype crash tests into evidence to show that the pattern of devastation in low-speed rear-end crashes went back as far as 1969.

As for the 1974-76 Pintos, Cosentino wanted to prove that these models were sufficiently similar to the 1973 so that their crash tests would be admissible as evidence. Many of these tests were conducted at speeds of around 30 miles per hour, which was faster than the 1973 tests, and they demonstrated that Ford knew serious fuel spillage continued to be a problem after the 1973 Pintos were on the road. Cosentino contended that these tests were admissible because, if anything, models after 1973 should be *stronger* than the 1973 model itself.

Bloch testified that the fuel system design of the 1971, 1972, and 1973 Pintos were "the same" except that the 1973 model had a 29-inch long, partial body rail along the left side. He said this rail was added "to keep the filler tube from coming out and also in meeting the 2½ mile-per-hour rear bumper standard" which was imposed that year to cut down on costly damage in fender-bender collisions.

"We are entitled to go into the 1971 and 1972 Pintos because they were the same cars (as the 1973)," Cosentino said to the judge. "Every automobile manufacturer has carryover models. You tool up and produce a new model, the 1971, and you carry over for at least a couple of years. That's what Ford did."

He pointed out that NHTSA had determined there were fuel system hazards in each Pinto through the 1976 model year. "All of this is very important, your honor, because a number of the crash tests we have involved the 1971 and 1972 Pintos. They did not crash test the 1973 Pinto as much as they did the previous ones," he said.

Neal was emphatic in stressing that the 1973 was different from the previous models because the partial body rail was added. He also contended, although Bloch disagreed, that there had been changes to the bumper of the 1973 model, too.

"Mr. Bloch acknowledges that (the 1973) was not the same (as the previous cars), that a rail was added to the '73. Now it wasn't put there because the horn didn't sound right. It was put there for fuel system integrity, and so it is different in an aspect essential to this case," Neal said. "They can testify about what they consider to be defects in the '73 Pinto. They do not have to go into a different car, which is the '71, and another different car, which is the '72."

The Tennessee lawyer also pointed out that the 1973 Pinto was the first model which had to comply with Ford's self-imposed requirement of being able to withstand a 20 mile-per-hour moving-barrier crash from behind without fuel spillage.

Bloch conceded there were "some slight revisions" between the 1973 and the 1974-76 models of the Pinto, such as an increased gas tank capacity; a little different position of the tank; a small lengthening of the filler tube's insertion into the tank; changes to the bumper; the addition of a rear "crossmember" or structural support across the back and a rail on the right side; and "very minor changes" to some sharp brackets situated near the tank.

In his ruling, Judge Staffeldt was steadfast in refusing to let Cosentino present documents or films concerning any Pinto models made before or after the 1973 car. "I think that this being a criminal case, the matter should be strictly construed," he said.

Neal repeatedly urged the judge to make his ruling final, but Staffeldt seemed to indicate he might give Cosentino another chance to get the other crash tests into evidence. Cosentino knew his last opportunity would be Harley Copp.

There was still another crucial area for Bloch to testify about – the "state of the art" of fuel system design for automobiles. This meant what engineering designs were available and feasible to use at the time that Ford engineers were deciding how to build or possibly modify the Pinto.

Cosentino wanted to demonstrate that Ford was aware through patents, articles, and competitive cars that there was a safer way to produce the Pinto, but they consciously chose a more hazardous design and then failed to warn consumers of the danger. Cosentino considered the state of the art to be an important standard of conduct with which Ford should have complied.

Bloch said that the "modern era" of fuel system safety began evolving during the 1950's. On April 21, 1959, for example, General Motors patented a fuel system design in which the tank was placed above the axle. The patent said that the design "enables the tank filler tube to be readily accessible and positions the tank beyond the danger of damage."

"I've never known a patent that didn't claim a lot of things," Neal sniffed.

Bloch also pointed out that in 1956, Ford applied for a patent, which was granted in 1961, for the "saddle-type" gas tank which was situated slightly above part of the rear axle and which was basically a forward-of-the-axle design. Ford used this sytem in building about 50,000 of its 1957-59 Skyliner models, which were hardtop cars with a roof that retracted into the area where the trunk normally would be located.

It was in the late 1950's, he said, when Saab, a Swedish automaker, introduced a car with its fuel tank located above the rear axle "and promoted that as a safety location." In 1961, Oldsmobile began selling cars with gas tanks positioned immediately behind the rear axle, away from the back edge of the car.

Rover introduced its Rover 2000 in England in late 1963, which was a front-engine, rear-wheel drive car with its tank located above the axle. At about the same time, the Triumph 2000 was introduced with a similar design.

In Japan during the mid-1960's, automakers began selling cars such as the Toyota Corolla and the Datsun 500, both of which were similar in size to the Pinto and had their gas tanks placed above the rear axle.

This was followed by Ford's introduction of the Capri in Europe, featuring an over-the-axle design as well as body rails on both sides. "This was a small car, very much akin to the Pinto," Bloch said. He described the Capri as being 3 or 4 inches longer than the Pinto, less than an inch higher, having a 6½-inch longer wheelbase, and weighing some 200 pounds less.

In Europe, General Motors introduced its Opel Kadett in the early 1970's, which employed the above-the-axle design like that patented by GM in 1959.

The next developement started in 1969 when some automakers began adopting the forward-of-the-axle gas tank position. For instance, he said, the Volkswagen K-70, a four-door economy sedan, was introduced in 1969, followed by the Honda Civic about 1972 and the Volkswagen Rabbit about 1975. Another example was the BMW 320i, which boasted in its advertising brochures that the gas tank "is in a protected position in front of the rear axle."

Later cars, such as the Dodge Omni, Plymouth Horizon, and Ford's own Fiesta, also incorporated the forward-of-the-axle configuration, Bloch said. In its European brochures for the Fiesta, Ford bragged under a section titled, "Safety," that the Fiesta's gas tank location would "avoid spillage in the event of a collision." Bloch said all of this language was absent from the brochures distributed in America when the car was later imported.

Then Bloch listed a potpourri of other cars featuring their tanks either above or forward of the axle, starting as early as 1969 including models of the Subaru, Peugeot, Rolls Royce, and Alfazud.

His conclusion was that the 1973 Ford Pinto sedan was a defective and unreasonably dangerous car.

"Did the corporation that designed and sold that car deviate substantially from acceptable standards of conduct?" Cosentino asked.

"Yes," Bloch replied. "Ford Motor Company did deviate."

Bloch testified that, in his opinion, the fire which killed the Ulrich girls would never have broken out if the Pinto had been equipped with a gas tank positioned either above or forward of the rear axle. In addition, he said that if Ford had placed the tank at the car's rear and used existing technology to better protect it from puncture and crushing, "it definitely would have reduced the likelihood of fuel leakage and fire" in the Ulrich collision.

He said that among the protection Ford should have provided for the tank were full body rails along both sides and a frame across the back to form a sturdy perimeter; double-strength fender panels; a protective shield to prevent puncture and encourage the tank to ramp over the rear axle when it was pushed forward; stronger metal for the tank itself; a shield or flak suit to protect against other puncture sources; and a filler pipe that was either inserted much farther into the tank or which was rigidly attached to the tank itself and designed to break off at the gas cap end in a crash.

Neal wasted no time during cross-examination in attacking Bloch's description of the "evolution" of fuel tank locations. "He went through a few selected cars and compared them to the Pinto," Neal charged. "I want to bring this into the real world."

When asked if it were true that the Capri, which was introduced with the above-the-axle design, later abandoned that system for a gas tank at the car's rear, Bloch replied, "It retrogressed, yes."

Neal also pointed out that the English firm that produced the Triumph 2000 with its above-the-axle configuration later came out with the GT-6 model with its tank at the car's rear. Bloch termed that another "retrogression with regard to location."

Bloch also conceded that in addition to having models with the above-the-axle design, Datsun, Honda, Toyota, Volkswagen, and Opel were among those carmakers also producing models with tanks at the rear of the vehicle.

At one point, Neal asked if Datsun came out with a "1200 coupe" in 1973, Bloch replied, "I'm not certain. I didn't memorize the 1200 coupe."

"You only memorized the ones with the tanks over the axle," Neal suggested sarcastically, and then apologized for the remark.

Bloch proved to be a difficult witness to handle at times. When Neal asked him to draw a Datsun 280Z to show that Datsun also produced cars with a tank behind the axle,

Bloch hesitated. "Should I indicate the frame rails, too?" he asked in a manner which stressed that the Pinto not only had its tank at its rear, but also lacked the structural protection which other cars featured.

"Can we have these extraneous remarks stricken?" Neal asked the judge, who agreed they should be disregarded by the jurors.

Bloch balked at Neal's persistent demands that he respond to many questions with a "yes" or "no." Bloch answered one inquiry by saying, "Partly yes, partly no, and partly maybe." Finally Bloch pleaded to the judge, "I thought an expert witness was entitled to explain his answer." Staffeldt, though, admonished him to follow Neal's directions and rely on Cosentino to seek out the explanations later.

Bloch griped to reporters that Neal was purposefully asking him questions which were impossible to answer in one word in an attempt to make him look evasive and cocky in front of the jury. If that was Neal's tactic, it worked.

Neal also highlighted a column Bloch wrote in 1968 for *Road Test* magazine in which he praised the Toyota Corolla for its quality and passenger safety, even though that car featured its gas tank behind the axle.

Then Neal asked whether Oldsmobile, starting in 1964, abandoned its design of putting its gas tanks directly behind the rear axle and away from the fender. "They abandoned it and Ford adopted it the same year," Bloch responded.

"Isn't it a fact," Neal asked after going through numerous car models, "that between 1968 and 1977, more than 90 per cent of all passenger cars sold in the United States had their fuel tanks behind the axle?"

"I think it would be somewhere in that range," he replied.

After that, Neal began eliciting testimony to support one of Ford's central contentions – that the Pinto was comparable to other 1973 subcompact cars.

For instance, Bloch agreed that the American Motors Gremlin, Chevrolet Vega, and Dodge Colt had their gas tanks behind the axle; that those cars had essentially the same bumpers ("I would say they were all bad," Bloch said); that the Vega had no body rails at all; that all four cars had somewhat similar distances from the tank to the rear bumper; that all of them had at least some sharp objects near the tank; and that the thickness of the gas tank metal on the Pinto was in the upper one-third of other 1973 (era) cars.

Neal asked if the Pinto's leaf-spring suspension would help strengthen the car's rear-end from crushing, and Bloch replied, "to a very minimum, inadequate degree." The Vega, Neal pointed out, had a coil suspension which did not contribute at all to rear-end strength.

Neal also asserted that the Pinto, unlike the other 1973 subcompacts, had steel plates in its trunk to add some rigid structure to the back of the car. Bloch insisted, though, that these were "in no way" the equivalent of body rails. He scoffed at them as being "hollow sheet metal panels."

In the end, Bloch said that he believed the Gremlin and Vega also should have been recalled to improve the safety of their fuel systems in rear-end crashes. He had no opinion as to whether similar action should have been taken with the Colt.

Neal's strategy was to emphasize that the Pinto was not much different, and in some ways better, than other subcompacts and therefore Ford could not be considered to have substantially deviated from acceptable standards of conduct by failing to warn consumers about the car. He was confident that no jury would consider the Pinto defective if its design was merely the norm among American automakers.

Cosentino told reporters, though, that the Pinto's performance in actual crashes proved the car was "in a class by itself" concerning fire danger. He said although the Vega "performed poorly" in the NHTSA crash tests, the Pinto "was far worse" and was the only car that the government pressured an automaker to recall.

"It's typical for a defendant to say, 'Everybody else is doing it, so why can't I?'" Cosentino said.

Neal also had Bloch show the jurors the small hole

made in the Ulrich tank when it was shoved into the sharp edges of the differential housing during the crash. "Can everyone see that?" Neal asked the jury as Bloch pointed to the hole. "It's difficult."

"It sure isn't difficult to see the other hole!" Cosentino called out angrily, referring to the gaping hole in the side of the tank. Bloch testified that this larger hole was caused by a combination of the tank being crushed and the build-up of hydraulic pressure inside which caused a bursting effect.

When Cosentino got another chance to question Bloch, he tried using a crash test of a prototype Pinto to illustrate the Pinto's "crashworthiness" in actual collisions but Judge Staffeldt blocked him.

Prosecutors believed that Bloch had accomplished what he set out to do – "educate" the jurors about the basics of fuel system design and the particular problems with the Pinto. They were concerned, however, about how much Neal's probing cross-examination and Bloch's smart-aleck demeanor on the witness stand crippled his credibility, and with it the credibility of the entire prosecution. Indeed, some jurors would comment after the trial that they ended up giving Bloch's testimony less weight than other witnesses.

All of this meant that Harley Copp, always considered the prosecution's main witness, would be even more important than originally anticipated.

15

At the prosecution camp, Mike Cosentino came up with a new idea for how to authenticate the internal Ford documents he wanted to try to introduce into evidence. He discarded his earlier plan of having witnesses attest to the signatures on the papers because that would involve too many people, cost too much money, and some of the most important documents lacked any signatures. Instead, his new approach would be to bring in lawyers involved with civil lawsuits in which the same documents had been turned over by Ford and in which Ford never contested that they were genuine. Because some of the lawyers would donate their time, Cosentino's expenses would be cut down, although their testimony would be certain to drag out the trial's length.

Across town at Ford's headquarters, lawyers were coming to believe that while they were winning the courtroom battle over the authentication of documents, they might be losing ground in the arena of public opinion. There was a growing feeling that Ford was looking absurd by playing coy about the authenticity of documents which no one doubted were genuine.

When Cosentino arrived at court on Monday, February 4, he brought with him two civil lawyers from Chicago and New Orleans who were prepared to testify about the authenticity of two dozen documents. Before he could begin, though, Neal stood and made an announcement.

He said that Ford Motor Company would concede the authenticity of any document specifically relating to the 1973 Pinto, which he believed were the only documents which should be allowed into evidence anyway. The authenticity and admissibility of all the other documents, the ones which Cosentino considered crucial to his case, would still be opposed.

To Cosentino, who had spent dozens of hours and part of his already-ailing budget to line up witnesses to testify the documents were genuine, Neal's offer was too little, too late.

"If this is such a sincere, honest effort on the part of Ford, it could have done this a long time ago," Cosentino charged in his usual tone of outrage. "I submit this is not good faith at all; it's an attempt to confuse and castrate the state's case, to keep evidence from the jury, to prolong this trial until March or April, and nothing more."

Neal began pushing Judge Staffeldt for a final ruling that all documents except ones specifically concerning the 1973 car would be barred from the trial. "It's got to be resolved," he told the judge. "We're up in the air."

Actually, Neal was well-prepared for two types of defenses – one if only 1973 documents were allowed into evidence, and the other if the judge was more liberal and admitted documents concerning prior and later years. Perhaps his highest priority in the case, though, was to win a decision severely limiting the number of documents which would get into the hands of the jurors.

Neal urged Judge Staffeldt to hold a hearing outside the jury's presence to consider whatever evidence Cosentino wanted to present and then issue his final ruling.

Cosentino was furious. "I've never been so thwarted and interferred with and so shoved and kicked and pushed around in my case-in-chief in my life by a defendant who plays by

Judy Ulrich

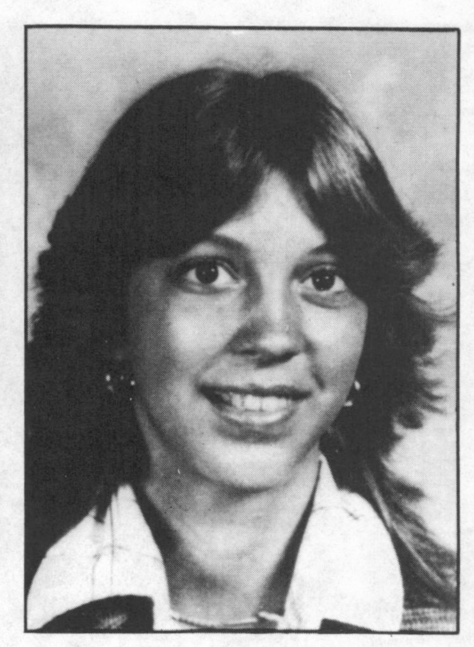

Lyn Ulrich

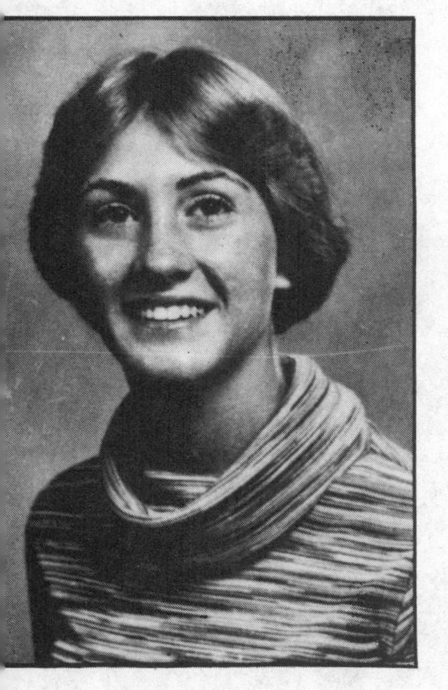

Donna Ulrich

Following three pages: Photographs depict accident scene, showing the scorched, devastated Pinto in which the Ulrich girls were riding and the van which sustained limited front-end damage.

chevyvan

PEACE
TWP
FIRE

Prosecutor Michael Cosentino

Chief Ford defense lawyer James F.

Judge Harold Staffeldt
of Pulaski County.

Lawyers meet the press in courthouse lobby.

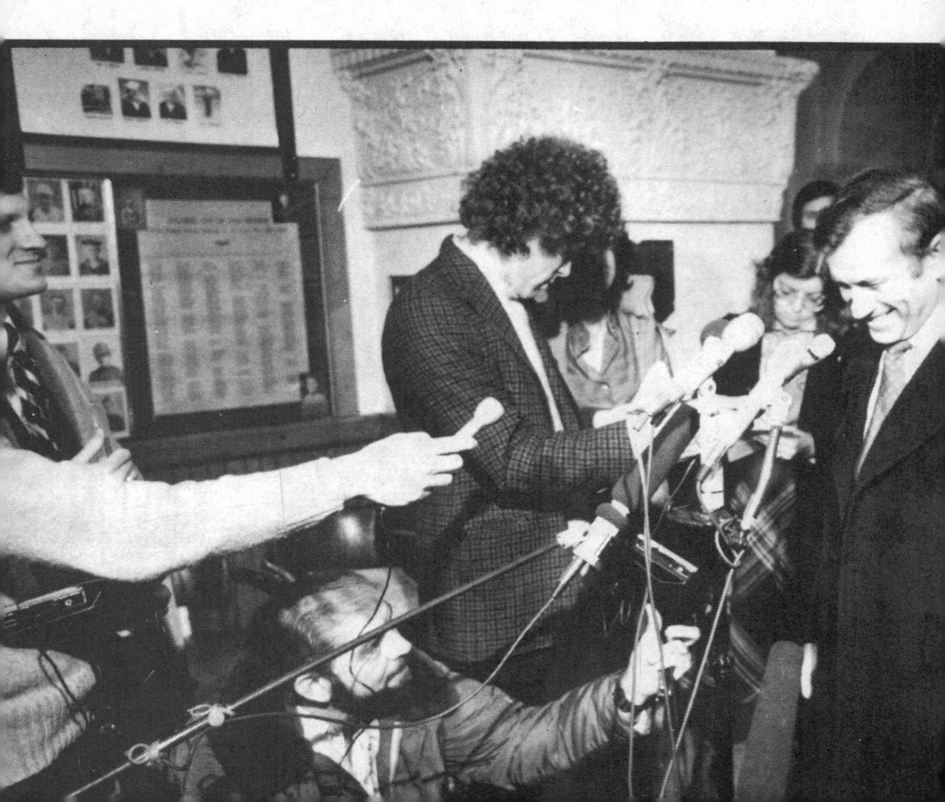

Winamac lawyer Lester Wilson, far left, leaves court with defense attorney James F. Neal, center, and other Ford team members.

Following page: Mrs. Mattie Ulrich, mother of Judy and Lyn, departs courthouse with investigator Billy Campbell after her testimony.

Law student Donald Seberger carries documents from court.

Chevrolet Impala rams Pinto in crash test run by

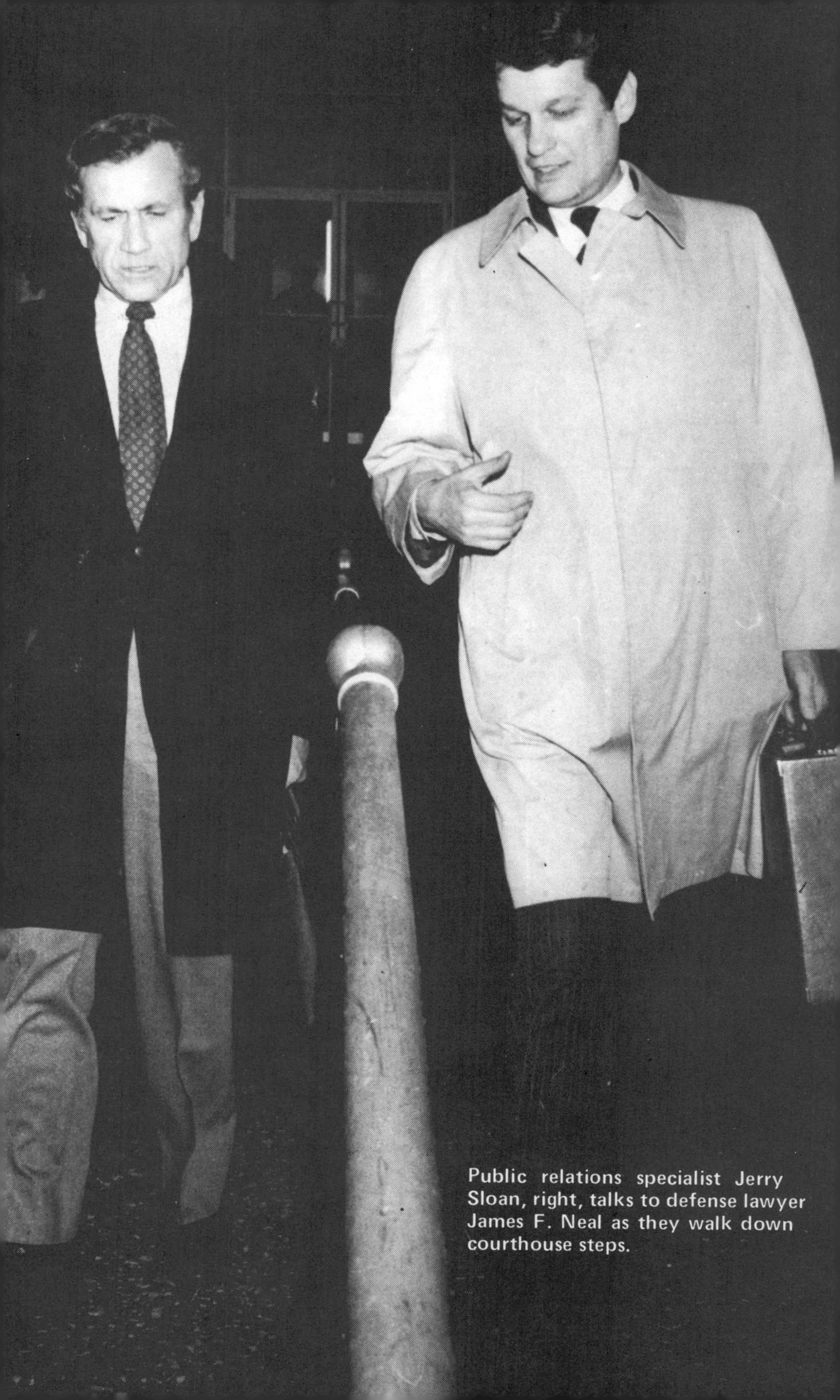

Public relations specialist Jerry Sloan, right, talks to defense lawyer James F. Neal as they walk down courthouse steps.

Levi Woodard, a hospital orderly who gave surprise testimony about his conversation with Judy Ulrich before she died, reads newspaper account of the trial.

Facing page: Jurors leave courthouse for lunch during break in deliberations.

Following page: Ford team member carries boxes of papers away from 84-year-old Pulaski County Courthouse.

one set of rules – his own!" Cosentino, his face reddening with anger, said as he stood and pointed at Neal. "This is a defendant who fought like a tiger not to be here, who files protective orders so no one knows about the documents, and a defendant who maintains that janitors put documents into its files. Well, the State of Indiana is not going to collapse!"

What Ford was seeking, Cosentino said, was a chance to hold two trials – one outside the jury's presence "where they can do and say what they want" and then, after that rehearsal, another in front of the jury. "I've never seen a trial where we have a mini-trial and a trial," he declared.

The soft-spoken Staffeldt leaned back in his padded leather chair and ran his fingers through his thinning silver-gray hair. "The court is mainly interested in the search for truth in this matter," he stated. "I do think we probably will take a recess when it comes to the question of how the court should rule and see if a foundation can or can't be laid."

Cosentino proceeded to present testimony by Tony Job of New Orleans and Charles Reed of Chicago, two lawyers involved in a civil lawsuit against Ford on behalf of a girl grotesquely burned in an explosion of a 1975 Mercury Bobcat.

They identified each document as being the same one turned over to them by Ford lawyers in their case. Asked if Ford ever denied the authenticity of those documents, Job replied, "There's never been any problem." Asked if Ford lawyers ever suggested or implied the signatures were not authentic, he said, "They never said anything like that." Reed's testimony was similar.

Aware that Cosentino had lined up more attorneys with similar accounts, Neal and Ford Motor Company suddenly stopped raising the issue of authentication. They began to rely exclusively on their next line of defense against the documents, which was that they were irrelevant and inappropriate unless they dealt with the specific model involved in the crash.

Neal also launched a renewed and hard-fought effort to convince Staffeldt to reverse his earlier decision to let the jurors see the controversial NHTSA report on the Pinto investigation. The report, of course, contained a lot of information about Pintos other than the 1973 model, including a chart summarizing the NHTSA crash tests. But the judge refused to change his mind. He let Cosentino, who had obtained certification from NHTSA that the report was authentic, give copies to the jurors to read.

"The significance of this is that we've got our first set of documents into evidence so far, and hopefully we're on the right track," Cosentino told reporters.

Cosentino's hopes of getting any more documents into evidence would rest solely on the 59 year-old Harley Copp, who would be Cosentino's final witness before closing his main case against Ford.

Copp's neatly combed gray hair, his dark-rimmed glasses, his conservative dark blue suit and white shirt, and his sincere, easy-going smile gave him a grandfatherly appearance as he sat on the witness stand. Despite the poised pens of the national news media and a courtroom full of curious spectators, Copp appeared to be at ease. His hand was steady as he poured water from a silver pitcher into his drinking glass.

Cosentino spent more than an hour leading Copp through a description of his career at Ford, starting with his summer work as a teenager at an experimental Ford soybean farm and his 50-cent-an-hour job as a guide in a Ford museum. The automaker paid his way through the Edison Institute of Technology where he studied engineering, and then after World War II and a short stint with his own manufacturing company, he rejoined Ford as a designer-trainee in June, 1946.

One by one, Copp described his rapid promotions within the company. His first supervisory position came in 1950 when he had 25 employees working for him in basic engine research. He helped design engines for military vehicles for a while, became head of the special military vehicles section, then worked with William Clay Ford on the Continental Mark II project, a high-priority undertaking to develop "a worthy successor to the original Continental." His efforts culminated in the introduction of the 1956 model of the Mark II.

From there he became director of Lincoln and Continental engineering, reporting directly to William Clay Ford, and then he was named assistant chief engineer of the Ford division. When it came time to design and introduce a new car called the Falcon, Copp was put in charge.

"Was the Falcon your car?" Cosentino asked.

"Well, no one person does a motor car, but I was the executive in charge and the can would have been tied to my tail if it wasn't done right. At least, that's the way it was put to me," Copp said.

The car, a much-praised compact with a six-cylinder engine, was a major success, and Copp's career continued to zoom. He was promoted to director of engineering for Ford of England at a time when the company was putting a new emphasis on its international operation. At that time, he had 2,600 employees under him, and was involved with putting out a British car called the Escourt and then the Capri, which was introduced as a 1969 model.

After being named a member of the board of directors of Ford Motor Company Ltd., Copp was appointed director of engineering for Ford of Europe and was responsible for 4,000 employees.

A year later, Copp was brought back to the United States and an 11th floor office at Ford's World Headquarters to handle "the complete reprogramming of the new 1972 Ford products – the Fairlane, Montego, Thunderbird, and Mark IV." His title was assistant chief research engineer. His later tasks involved organizing a new engineering and technical services office to work on emissions, safety testing and computer science, and then he became executive engineer of testing services.

Copp said he was forced into early retirement two days before Christmas, 1976. The letter notifying him of his termination, which the jury was allowed to read, said: "Your extended and unauthorized absences from work and consequential failure to carry out your assigned responsibilities in a satisfactory manner have led to this action."

Cosentino told the television cameras, though, that Ford's real motivation in getting rid of Copp was because he was too outspoken about the need for increasing the safety of cars. And even before he was forced out of Ford Copp had been giving speeches to plaintiffs' lawyers on the topic, "The Secret of Obtaining Corporate Secrets."

Neal blocked Copp from testifying about his highest salary while at Ford. Cosentino told reporters the amount topped $250,000. Asked how he was earning a living while on his Ford pension, Copp had a simple answer. "I'm an expert witness."

Copp began talking about the Pinto by saying it was designed on a 10-year cycle plan, which meant it would be produced for 10 years until 1980. This was considered a particularly long cycle. The Falcon's was six years and the Model A's was five. As a general rule, he added, the fuel system of a car remained the same throughout the cycle, "although very often there would be an increase in tank capacity."

Q. And during the planning and approval of the Pinto sedan, for how long was it planned by Ford that the fuel system design, location, and packaging would remain the same?

A. I believe for the life of the vehicle, which was 10 years.

Cosentino then began eliciting testimony to establish that the 1971 and 1972 Pintos were the same cars (although Copp did note that the thickness in the upper half of the Pinto's fuel tank was actually *reduced* by 27 per cent during the 1971 model year). Cosentino was doing this as a prelude to establishing the similarities between those two cars and the 1973 model so he could lay the fundamental requirements to get the much-needed earlier crash tests into evidence.

When Neal realized what Cosentino was doing, he objected and asked for the jury to be dismissed. Then Neal, with the judge's permission, began questioning Copp about the *differences* between the 1973 Pinto and the two earlier models, even though Cosentino had not yet started to establish their similarities. Cosentino objected.

"What troubles the court," Staffeldt interrupted, "is just exactly what does the 1971 and 1972 Pinto have to do with the '73 Pinto that was involved in this accident?"

Cosentino: Because they can't crash test a '73, your honor, before they know how to build it. They have to crash test something before they know how to build a '73.

Staffeldt: This has something to do with product liability rather than the reckless omission (to warn about the car) which Ford is charged with.

Cosentino: The state must prove, as the state has charged in the indictment, everything a civil products liability plaintiff would have to prove and more. . . .The point is, this is a products liability case, only it goes one step beyond, with the burden of proof being beyond a reasonable doubt, and the showing of the recklessness of the defendant. But we have to show the design of the Pinto was reckless to begin with, then that Ford knew about the recklessness and had a duty to warn about the product. . . We are trying to show, your honor, that a crash test of a '71 tells us about the '73.

Staffeldt: I think it would be error to go back that far, just the same as it would be to go forward after the (1973) vehicle. After all, we are concerned with the vehicle that was involved here. . . .It's the same thing if you are trying a murder case, you are concerned with the weapon involved, not all the other guns a fellow might have in his gun rack.

Cosentino: They built a bomb in 1971 and 1972 and that's why they don't want us to get into it, and they know it. And they are trying to say, 'We've got a little less of a bomb in '73.' And besides that, your honor, we don't have the documentation of the '73 model.

Staffeldt: I have ruled one time that these things would not be admissible unless there was a proper foundation laid.

Cosentino: I haven't been able to show the court, your honor. I have been cut off! I was stopped (by Neal's questioning of Copp) when I was comparing the '71 and '72. I was completely stopped!

Neal then suggested that Cosentino resume his

questioning of the witness in order to establish the similarities between the 1973 and earlier models.

"*Now* I can?" Cosentino replied bitterly. "Why couldn't I do it before? Because you've got the court's ruling now, that's why."

Under Cosentino's questioning, Copp then said the fuel system location, filler pipe design, fuel system packaging, fuel system design, fuel tank attachment, spare tire package, differential cover, rear overhang, tank capacity, and length of insertion of the filler tube were all the same for 1971 through 1973 models.

He testified that the 1971 and 1972 Pintos could only withstand up to an 18 mile-per-hour rear-end crash by a moving barrier without gas spillage. Because of the partial body rail on the left side of the 1973 model, the safety level was raised by four or five miles per hour, he said.

The prosecutors considered it significant that Copp could quantify the difference between the models because the jurors could take this into account in considering the earlier crash tests.

"What we are saying," Berner said to Staffeldt, "is that the '71 and '72 vehicles were tested by Ford for the purpose of determining how the '73 would perform, which goes to the question of the '73 design. . . .If the purpose of the test is to figure out how to build a '73, you can't crash test a '73."

Neal interjected that there were a few tests of specific prototypes of the 1973 model, although these tests were conducted at speeds below the car's breaking point.

Judge Staffeldt reiterated that he would not let crash tests of other models into evidence. "It is a criminal case; strict construction is involved," he said.

The ruling was a serious loss for the prosecution. Outside the courtroom, Cosentino looked grim as he leaned against the stairway railing and chain-smoked cigarets. "It hurts like hell," he said of Staffeldt's decision. "This forecloses the bulk of our evidence."

He was not, however, willing to concede defeat. "Maybe," he wondered aloud, "if we go into the evidence about the '73 car first, then he'll let us go into the others. . . ."

One of the reporters talking to Cosentino rolled his eyes. "Is he kidding?" he whispered to a colleague. "He's crazy if he thinks Staffeldt's gonna let that stuff in."

Cosentino began thinking of various possibilities. Maybe Harley Copp, with his inside knowledge of Ford, would be able to provide oral testimony which would be similar to the contents of some of the excluded documents. And maybe, just maybe, there were enough loopholes left which would give him a chance to slip into evidence at least a few of the most important ones. After 18 months of grueling work and overcoming many other setbacks, Cosentino was not going to stop now.

One of the most bizarre incidents of the trial occurred before the jury entered the courtroom to being hearing Copp's testimony. Cosentino commented that Ford had forced Copp to fly to California for a five-minute court appearance on a civil lawsuit pending against the automaker. As a result, Copp was "exhausted" because he had just returned in time for his testimony in Indiana.

Neal accused the prosecutor of "making reckless statements" and added, "How can a man stand up there and make statements to the court like that unless he knows what he's talking about?"

Feeling his Southern honor being soiled, Neal arranged for a lawyer in the California case to fly to Winamac, and then Neal interrupted the trial so the attorney could testify that Cosentino had been mistaken about Ford's role in Copp's trip.

16

Harley Copp, speaking in a conversational tone as if over the dinner table, began describing how the Ford Pinto developed from an idea in the late 1960's into perhaps the most controversial automobile ever built.

It was in 1967 or 1968, he said, when Ford management started thinking about building an American-made small car to fight against the Volkswagen Beetle and the increasing number of Japanese subcompacts which were seizing a significant portion of the domestic market. "Lee Iacocca was the promulgator of the whole concept," Copp said, referring to Ford's tough-talking executive vice president of North American Automotive Operations. Iacocca was later named one of three presidents of Ford's operations, was elected the sole president shortly after the Pinto's introduction, was forced out in 1978, and became the high-profile head of the financially floundering Chrysler Corporation.

The $2,000/2,000-pound objectives for the Pinto were "set early on," as was the car's basic low roofline and general sporty appearance, Copp said. In the summer of 1968, Iacocca showed the proposed Pinto to Henry Ford II and

Semon E. "Bunkie" Knudsen, who at the time was president of the corporation.

Copp said he was told several times by persons who were at the meeting that Knudsen "strongly opposed Ford-U.S. doing a subcompact car. . . .He wanted to do it overseas where they knew how to do these kinds of cars." Staffeldt, however, refused to let the jurors hear that statement after Neal branded it "intramural heresay."

When asked about the time guidelines for the Pinto's development, Copp told the prosecutor, "As soon as possible; it was a rushed project." The car's styling, with its long front hood and short rear deck, was "frozen" in September, 1968, which Copp termed "unusual."

"The car was frozen before the engineers could package all the components," he said. "The engineers were left with a minimum amount of space in which to put the spare tire, the fuel tank, the muffler, the suspension, and provide luggage space. And if you don't believe it, just look at the weird shape of that fuel tank."

Copp recalled a conversation in late 1968 or early 1969 with a frustrated assistant chief research engineer who was working on the project:

A. He essentially said that the car was styled, that he was locked in, and that he was not happy with the spare tire – fuel tank arrangement that he had on the car.

Q. What did you tell him, if anything?

A. Well, I agreed with him because I had done subcompact cars previously. . .He said, 'You know how it is, Harley.' The fact that the car was styled and evidently locked in, essentially that was the conversation.

Q. Now, normally, Mr. Copp, would there be some give-and-take between styling and engineering feasibility?

A. Yes. That is the normal manner in which a car evolves.

Q. With regard to the Pinto, in that period of time, was there any give-and-take?

A. I'm sure there was, but there wasn't enough in this area because the (short) rear overhang and the style of the car had been set.

At that point, Cosentino handed Copp a copy of the 1969 internal Ford report which disclosed that the engineers considered putting the Pinto's gas tank above the axle and abandoned the idea because it would have cut into luggage space. Neal demanded to see the document, saying this was "just plain common courtesy," and Cosentino reluctantly showed it to him.

Neal glanced over the report. "I don't know how many times the court has to rule on this," he said angrily, referring to the fact that the document dealt with a design considered by Ford before the introduction of the original 1971 model.

"I sustain the objection," Staffeldt said. "It's too remote in time from the '73."

"Mr. Cosentino is trying to push the court and push the court until the court finally gives up in frustration and reverses itself in its rulings," Neal warned the judge. "At least, that's his strategy."

Cosentino considered the 1969 memo a key document to his case, and he saw Staffeldt's quick rejection of it as a sign that he was going to continue cracking down on the amount of evidence he would rule admissible. With the memo excluded from the jury, Cosentino's only alternative was to elicit Copp's own opinions about the above-the-axle tank design.

Copp testified that Ford engineers could have designed "a kidney-shaped tank and mounted it over the axle," although he said there "would have been some compromise in luggage space because of the spare tire storage arrangement."

He said, however, that in order to create an equal amount or even more luggage space with the above-the-axle design, all the engineers had to do was take 1½ to 2 inches off the car's front and add it to the rear so the spare tire could be stowed lower.

Q. *Would adding that two inches, and putting the gas tank over the axle, have increased the cost of the Pinto?*

A. In aggregate, no, I don't think so. In aggregate, as over the (10-year) cycle that we are talking about here.

Shifting the two inches, however, would "change the

styling proportions" of the car, and the styling was frozen early in the developmental stage, he said.

As for the Capri, which used the above-the-axle system, Copp called it "a very good handling car" and that he knew of no performance or maintenance problems the design created for Capri owners.

Copp testified that the Pinto received approval of Ford's board of directors in January or February of 1969. Yet, at that time there had been no rear-end crash tests performed to determine whether the car's design would survive without dangerous gas spillage. "Either they didn't have the time or didn't place importance on it," he said.

Kiely interrupted the questioning of Copp and began offering into evidence several internal Ford documents dating back to 1970. These documents included ones that demonstrated, he said, that Ford management was aware through engineering reports that the safety of the Pinto in rear-end crashes could be substantially improved to meet the government's proposed standard, which was equal to a 44 mile-per-hour car-to-car crash from behind. Included were such engineering suggestions as putting the tank above the axle, adding rear-end structure such as body rails, improving the filler pipe, adding shields or flak suits, changing the spare tire arrangement, and other design alternatives.

"They had this information in hand, considered it, and rejected it," Kiely told the judge. "Ford decided that (its internal) 20 mile-per-hour moving-barrier requirement for 1973 would be tops. As far as the state is concerned, that is horrendous."

Neal moved quickly to exclude the documents from evidence. "The issue," he insisted as he stood and used both hands to gesture toward the cut-up Pinto at the side of the courtroom, "is how *this* car was built, not how it *might* have been built. What we might have done is irrelevant; it's *this* vehicle we are accused of recklessly failing to warn about."

He said that the prosecutors only had to prove that the 1973 Pinto, as it was sold to the public, was defective and dangerous, not that it was recklessly built. The alleged recklessness involved Ford's failure to warn about the danger. "We could have built a Lincoln," he said. "This car might have been a horse, but it's a 1973 Pinto built in a certain way."

"It could have been a horse, but it also could have been a car that didn't incinerate three children," Kiely retorted. "We're not talking about what they *could* have done —although that is a necessary part of the background—but the issue is, what did they *know?*

"The reason Mrs. Ulrich lost her daughters is because this company did not warn that family that at 30 miles per hour that car was going to blow up like a bomb. These documents prove that Ford Motor Company had that knowledge for years and kept it from the public and eventually tried to keep it from the federal government until they were pressed into recalling that car. . . .These documents state the Pinto cannot meet a normal highway-speed collision without leakage, that Ford was aware of that back in 1970 and was aware of alternate designs, and that highlights Ford's recklessness."

"We knew what that thing was," Neal said, again motioning toward the cut-up Pinto. "And either we should have warned or shouldn't have warned. . . .If you hit this thing in the rear by a vehicle weighing 4,000 pounds at somewhere over 30 miles per hour, we knew that this vehicle would leak. I can't say the floor pan would tear up, I can't say how it would leak. I simply say that it is not our contention, it never has been our contention, and it will never be our contention that this vehicle would not leak if hit by a car weighing some 4,000 pounds at speeds somewhere over 30 miles per hour."

"He doesn't want to admit," Kiely asserted, "that at 30 or 35 miles per hour, the floor pan rips open, or that the gasoline seam welds split open and that the gas tank on many occasions hits the ground. These documents show that the Ford Motor Company was aware when they put this car on the street that there was not just a *little* leakage problem, but *serious* leakage problems and that is what this case is all about."

After the arguments, Judge Staffeldt agreed with Neal that the case involved "not a matter of what could have been done, but what Ford *did* do." He excluded from evidence every document to which Neal objected – including ones describing various ways Ford engineers suggested to make the Pinto safer from fire in rear-end crashes – and thus narrowed the scope of permissible evidence even further than before.

Cosentino, Kiely, and the rest of the prosecutors were angry and bitter over another major portion of their case being barred from the jury. Cosentino tossed his papers into his briefcase and slammed the lid. Some of his assistants started making snide comments about the judge to reporters. The usually even-tempered Trooper Graves smashed his fist into his hand.

Looking weary and depressed, Cosentino told reporters as he left for lunch, "I think we still have a case, but it's like fighting a battle with one arm tied behind your back."

Later that day, Cosentino tried another legal maneuver in an attempt to get some of the previously excluded crash tests into evidence.

He elicited Copp's testimony that the 1973 Pinto would have started leaking gasoline in rear-end crashes above 22 to 25 miles per hour. When Cosentino asked the basis for his opinion, Copp said that he had relied on crash tests of the 1973 Pinto as well as crashes of the 1971 and prototypes of the 1974 model. Because these tests were the basis for Copp's expert opinion, Cosentino tried to have him amplify on the contents of those tests.

"Mr. Cosentino pays no attention to the rulings of this court," Neal complained after the jury was dismissed at his request. "He's going to push us to the point where we'll have to move for a mistrial because of misconduct of counsel."

"Mr. Neal is impugning the character of the state's team and I have to take offense at that," Cosentino's volunteer assistant, John Ulmer, told the judge. "We've tried to abide by the court's rulings. It was our belief that an expert could testify about what was the basis for his opinions. Maybe we were wrong."

Staffeldt agreed they were wrong, and ruled that Copp could not discuss the contents of the excluded crash tests even if they did help him reach his opinions about the 1973 car. It was clear there would be no way Cosentino could maneuver around the judge's rulings or change his mind. Cosentino reluctantly resigned himself to the probablity that the crucial crash tests, which made up an integral part of the story he was trying to tell, would never be seen by the jury.

Then Staffeldt, after five weeks of trial, astonished the court with a disarmingly sincere and troubling admission. "It's difficult to narrow the issue to where it really should be, to avoid injecting products liability into this," he remarked. "I do feel there has been a lot of evidence already admitted that probably should not have been admitted and that might be the basis for reversible error."

The comment startled the prosecutors because they were convinced he had been letting in *too little* evidence. Did this mean his increasingly severe limits on the amount of admissible evidence would become even more stringent? And was he correct that, even if the prosecutors succeeded in convicting Ford, an appellate court would negate all their work by reversing the conviction?

At the same time, the Ford lawyers wondered exactly what sort of evidence Staffeldt was having second thoughts about. Many believed he meant the controversial NHTSA report.

Cosentino plunged ahead anyway, trying to get Staffeldt to let him show the jurors some movies of the crash tests run by NHTSA during its investigation. Neal was quick to point out that the tests involved just about every model except the 1973. "I say bring in a crash test of a '73," Neal said.

"If we had it, we'd bring it in," Cosentino snapped.

The parade of documents continued, and each time Staffeldt ruled against attempts to get them to the jury. Kiely thought for sure he could get a document titled, "1973 Pinto Fuel System Integrity" into evidence because its very inscription indicated it dealt with the car in dispute. "This directly relates to the 1973 Pinto; that's why the title is on top," he said.

But Neal was able to block it from evidence on grounds it discussed the development of the rubber bladder and how it had been successful in a crash test involving a 1971 Pinto.

"It talks about things that might be done," Staffeldt said. "I don't see the relevance to the '73."

Kiely argued that "they don't make cars over the weekend" and that Ford had to test earlier models of the Pinto to develop designs which could then be adopted in later models, such as the 1973. Staffeldt reiterated his ruling.

The depression among the prosecutors deepened after this series of losses. "I have well over 200 documents; I've been able to put in 10 or 12 of them. I guess you know how I feel," Cosentino told the news media.

"Our story is not being told. We should have been able to get more evidence in than we have. There's a lot more to this story in our files that what the jury has."

Neal was ebullient. He told reporters that Staffeldt was only doing what was proper – preventing the case from becoming a wide-ranging examination of how to build an automobile or a civil product-liability case in which the rules of evidence were more relaxed. That evening, the champagne flowed at Ford's makeshift headquarters.

There was still some hope among the prosecutors that at least part of the contents of the excluded documents might get to the jury through Harley Copp's testimony. There was always the question, though, of whether this would be as persuasive as the jury actually seeing internal Ford documents which were stamped "confidential" and which had been wrested from the automaker's own files.

In resuming his testimony, Harley Copp called the Pinto's design "grossly inadequate and the weakest I've seen in cars the last 10 or 12 years." He said the car lacked a "balanced design," which meant that since the 1973 Pinto could withstand a 40 or 50 mile per hour rear-end crash without its passengers being killed by impact injuries, it should also protect them from fire at those speeds. Otherwise, the passengers would survive the impact only to be burned to death because of fuel leakage.

Copp said that at a meeting in August, 1969, at which Iacocca was present, Ford management decided that the 1973 Pinto would be built to withstand a 30 mile-per-hour rear-end crash without fuel leakage. He said this plan was later watered-down to a 20 mile-per-hour requirement "because of costs and ensuing profits." However, Copp conceded that the higher standard apparently was never officially adopted by Ford.

With his most vital documentary evidence excluded, Cosentino had to rely on Copp to tell the jurors that Ford had been aware of the Pinto's hazardous design and yet failed to fix it or warn the public. In perhaps the most effective testimony of the prosecution's case, Copp went through, one by one, seven design defects of the 1973 Pinto, described each one as dangerous, said that Ford knew about the problem, and that Ford failed to do anything because it would have cut into profits.

Q. *What was Ford's knowledge relative to the inadequacy of the crush space forward and behind the fuel tank?*

A. They knew it.

Q. *And what did Ford do about it?*

A. Nothing. They didn't do anything.

Q. *And why didn't Ford do anything about it?*

A. I think the costs, the tooling costs and piece costs and so forth, and the effect it would have had on profitability.

Copp pointed out that the car's floor and no reinforcements to strengthen it, resulting in increased crushing and damage to the car and fuel system in rear-end crashes. He said Ford knew about the problem, and only added one partial body rail to the 1973 car, which did not fix the flaw. Asked why Ford did not do anything more, Copp said it was because "it would have cost more. . . .and would have affected profitability.

Q. *What was Ford's knowledge relative to filler tube pull-out in the '73 Pinto?*

A. They were aware of it.

Q. *And what did Ford do about this problem?*

A. On the '73 Pinto, nothing I am aware of.

Q. *And why didn't Ford do anything about it?*

A. Well, again, it would have taken some retooling and added piece costs; to make profits.

Copp said that the welding between the car's floor and body was spaced too far apart, causing the floor to "unzip" in a crash and let flaming gasoline spray into the passenger compartment. Copp said Ford knew about this problem and did nothing about it on the 1973 model. "Again," he said, "it would have required a considerable re-design and re-tooling and that adds costs and affects profitability."

He testified that the shape of the Pinto's gas tank itself was fairly high in relation to its length, and this allowed a build-up of hydraulic pressure inside the tank when it was crushed, leading to leakage or bursting. Copp showed jurors a tank from a 1973 Vega, which he said was shaped flatter and made with a low-carbon steel. "The very purpose of it is to allow the tank to contort and balloon without bursting when these hydraulic pressures are generating," he said.

Q. *What was Ford's knowledge relative to the increased hydraulic pressures due to the shape of the tank?*

A. Well, they knew it. It was a basic engineering principle.

Q. *What did Ford do about this problem?*

A. Nothing.

Q. *And why didn't they do anything about it?*

A. Well, they would have had to repackage the rear end of the vehicle, which would mean a complete testup and retooling of the vehicle, which would have cost money.

Copp cited the sharp edges and bolts close to the gas tank as being potential puncture points during crashes, and said that the gas tank retaining straps were not properly designed to hold the tank during a collision. He said Ford had been aware of the problems and failed to do anything because "again, it would have added cost."

One kind of documentary evidence which the jurors had not been allowed to consider was how inexpensive it would have been for Ford to increase the fire safety level of its Pinto. The internal Ford documents about the cost of the bladder, shield, and flak suit were among those already excluded from evidence, even though Cosentino considered this information important in illustrating Ford's recklessness in failing to fix or warn about the car.

Cosentino tried once more, this time attempting to convince Staffeldt that the jurors should be allowed to see an April 22, 1971 internal memo which discussed the cost of making the Pinto safer. As with the other documents, Staffeldt refused to let it into evidence.

Cosentino persisted in trying to elicit from Copp the same information that was contained in the excluded document. "If the document is inadmissible, then testimony about the document is inadmissible," Neal protested.

But surprisingly, Judge Staffeldt decided to let Copp testify about the cost. The ruling kept alive a spark of optimism among the prosecutors that they would be able to recoup at least a bit of what they had lost in his prior decisions.

Copp testified that Ford Motor Company decided against spending a design cost of $6.65 per car to increase the fire safety level of the 1973 Pinto from a 20 mile-per-hour moving-barrier standard to 30 miles per hour. "This," he said, "improved the profitability of the vehicle."

In order to make certain the Pinto would consistently meet a 30 mile-per-hour standard if one had been adopted by Ford, the car probably would have been built strong enough to withstand a crash of several miles per hour faster. Based on the eyewitness accounts of the closing speed in the Ulrich crash, this left the ominous suggestion that making this inexpensive improvement to the Pinto would have saved the lives of the three young girls.

That evening at the regular press conference, a television reporter tried playing a joke by sticking $6.65 into James Neal's hand. Neal, who was upset that his virtually solid wall against Cosentino's documentary evidence had been breached by Copp's testimony, did not consider it very funny.

Cosentino was also successful in introducing into evidence an actual recall kit which Copp said Ford started sending out a month after the Ulrich crash. Included was the lengthened filler pipe and the two polyethylene shields which protected against punctures and helped the gas tank ramp up over the axle instead of being crushed in a crash. The pieces were passed among the jurors, some of whom flexed the larger of the two shields and frowned.

Also during Copp's testimony, Kiely was able to get into evidence two studies on fires in car accidents. One was a 68-page report released in April, 1974 by the University of Michigan Highway Safety Research Institute and reported that 180 to 260 annual fatalities in car fires could be eliminated by 1984 if all vehicles complied with the proposed federal safety standards.

Another was a Ford Motor Company report dated October 18, 1968, which said that 600 to 2,200 persons were fatally burned in car fires each year. Kiely wanted to demonstrate to the jurors that there was an awareness in the automotive industry that car fires were claiming lives and were a problem in need of a solution.

The animosity between Consentino and Neal continued to escalate during this hard-fought part of the trial. As Cosentino was sulking in the hallway outside court after being repeatedly rebuffed in trying to get documents into evidence, Neal pranced by and taunted him by saying in a sing-song voice, "Don't lose your cool, don't lose your cool!"

During Copp's testimony, Cosentino showed the witness a picture of the Ulrich Pinto with an above-the-axle gas tank superimposed on it to illustrate its position in relation to the car's damage. Neal objected because Cosentino did not show him the picture first.

"I will be glad to (show it to you) as soon as I finish a couple of more questions," Cosentino said.

"I think cousel is entitled to see the picture before testimony about them is admitted, okay?" Staffeldt said.

With that, Cosentino strode over to Neal. "Here," he said sharply as he handed him the picture. Then Cosentino whined to the judge, "Is he entitled to go 'phew' and make those faces when he looks at my evidence?"

"I don't know," Staffeldt replied.

Although he did not make a 'phew' sound himself, Staffeldt nevertheless barred the photograph from the trial after Neal said that "anyone would know that fuel tank is not going to look like that after this accident." Staffeldt said that "what we have here is speculation as to what might have happened."

"But, your honor, this man is an engineer and certainly can testify about what he believed would have happened had there been a different fuel tank on this particular vehicle," Cosentino said. Staffeldt did not change his ruling.

However, Cosentino was able to ask Copp if he believed the Ulrich fire would have occurred if the Pinto had employed an above-the-axle design like that used in Ford's Capri.

"I believe that the risk of fire would have been minimal. The escape time of the passengers in the vehicle would have been sufficient to prevent serious burns," he said.

When Cosentino tried getting into the cost of moving the Pinto's tank to the above-the-axle position, Staffeldt blocked him by saying, "This isn't product liability."

Copp also testified that if a 1973 Pinto were hit by a moving barrier at 30 miles per hour, "the floor pan welds would have separated, the filler pipe would have been di-engaged, fuel would have exited from the tank, and there would have been a high probability of fire." The floor pan would begin ripping open at speeds as low as 21 miles per hour, he added.

Q. *And what would have been the risk to the occupants of the vehicle?*

A. Well, because the doors would jam, they would be pinned within the vehicle until they could get the doors open or the windows open and the risk of fire is high.

Q. *Mr. Copp, did any 1973 subcompact produced by Ford and sold in the United States have the capability of withstanding a 50 mile-per-hour rear impact without risk of fire?*

A. Yes. Without risk of fire, yes. I believe that. . .was the Ford Capri.

Q. Did Ford apply this knowledge and information to the 1973 Pinto sedan?

A. No.

Copp's conclusion was that the Pinto was "unreasonably dangerous" in low-to-moderate speed rear impacts and that owners of the car should have been warned.

Q. And who, in your opinion, was responsible for warning owners of the 1973 Pinto sedan of the serious fire hazard in low-to-moderate speed rear-end impacts?

A. That would have been Lee Iacocca, the president.

Q. And was he aware of the Pinto itself?

A. Yes. He was the father of the Pinto.

Kiely and Cosentino attempted to get more of their documents into evidence, but Staffeldt ruled them inadmissible as he had done with previous internal memos. "The closer a document gets to actual relevance, the more agitated Mr. Neal gets," Kiely commented.

After a while, Staffeldt would not even wait for Neal to offer an objection to some of Cosentino's questions. "I expect you have an objection, Mr. Neal," the judge would observe, and Neal would acknowledge that, indeed, he did have one. One Indiana newpaper noted that Staffeldt had a tendency to lean forward and smile whenever he was addressed by the nationally famous Neal, and to divert his eyes and frown when Cosentino talked to him. That stopped after the article was published. A member of the Ford team defended the judge by remarking, "Who'd want to smile at Cosentino? He doesn't even smile back like Jim (Neal) does."

Reporters James Warren and Brian Kelly commented in one column that the judge "has clearly shown an unusual deference toward Neal" and that "when he's not looking toward Neal, the judge seems to be seeking guidance from Lester (Wilson)."

Neal's cross-examination of Harley Copp was not as intense as his questioning of Bloch, but Neal was able to bring out several points helpful to the defense.

For instance, Copp was forced into conceding that the 1969 Capri, for which he was largely responsible, was never subjected to rear-end crash tests before Ford's board of directors approved the design.

Q. *And isn't it a fact, Mr. Copp, that when you (put the gas tank above the axle in the Capri), you didn't do that for safety, you did it to increase the luggage space?*

A. That is true.

Q. *And that was the only reason, isn't that true?*

A. That was the only reason.

Copp also made the damaging admission that it was not until 1977 when he came to his final conclusion that the above-the-axle gas tank design was safer than putting the tank at the car's rear.

Q. *Isn't it a fact that, in your opinion, no small car made in America in 1973 could withstand a 40 to 50 mile-per-hour rear-end impact without fuel leakage?*

A. That I am quite sure of.

Q. *And as a matter of fact, Mr. Copp, isn't it your opinion that every car made in America from 1966 through 1976 was defective from the standpoint of fuel system integrity in rear impact?*

A. Yes, sir.

As for the $2,000/2,000-pound criteria for the Pinto, Copp said that it was not uncommon for a car to have weight and price goals during its development.

Copp also testified that he believed Harold MacDonald, the engineer in charge of the Pinto's design, and two other main Pinto engineers were safety-conscious individuals.

When Cosentino got his second chance to question Copp, he brought up the names of those same three engineers and asked if he believed they were free to exercise their best judgment with reference to fuel tank location and fuel system integrity.

A. No, I do not.

Q. *And why was that?*

A. Because they were locked in style, and they were locked-in in terms of total vehicle cost.

Q. *And who locked them in?*

A. Mr. Iacocca.

Q. *Mr. Copp, do you believe Mr. Iacocca to be a good engineer, and a thorough, responsible and conservative man?*

A. No.

Q. *And why not?*

A. I believe that his ambitions overbalanced his sense of morality, if you want my honest opinion.

At the end of Copp's six days on the witness stand, Cosentino announced the state was resting its main case. His attempts to get his most powerful documents into the hands of the jurors had been a disaster. Indeed, except for the important NHTSA report, his main success came in submitting a series of correspondence between Ford and NHTSA which, he contended, showed that Ford delayed and tried to frustrate the NHTSA investigation into the Pinto controversy. Given the complexity of the letters, it was doubtful the jurors gleaned much from them.

The few other documents he was able to get to the jury consisted of evidence which was not opposed by Ford and therefore not particularly damaging; which was partially masked to hide portions which Ford opposed; or which made up only a few random pieces of a giant jigsaw puzzle which made little sense without the surrounding elements.

He was able to make gains through Copp's oral testimony, even though the tangible Ford documents would have been much more powerful. And the NHTSA report, although it was not supposed to be considered for the truth of its contents, did convey to the jurors a sense of some of the information which was otherwise excluded.

In addition, the case was far from over. Cosentino had more evidence he intended to bring out during Ford's defense case, and he also hoped there would be some opportunities for him to try to get more documents accepted. While disappointed that his case was so diluted, Cosentino believed there was still a chance for conviction.

"We got in a lot less evidence than I'd hoped for," he told a reporter. "But I still think we've told a story. Whether it's enough of the story, I don't know. I've just got to hope we can build on it during (Ford's defense) case."

Ford lawyers from Neal's office and the New York and Los Angeles branches of giant Hughes, Hubbard & Reed prepared a 32-page request that Staffeldt dismiss the charges at mid-trial. After hearing oral arguments, the judge said: "I agree with (the prosecution) that there is a question for the jury, and where there is a question for the jury it would be error to do anything other than deny the motion."

Neal presented his client with three options – present no defense case and gamble that Cosentino's weakened case would lead to an acquittal; present only the core of the evidence Ford had planned; or go all out with the entire defense that had been developed during the previous year.

Realizing there were two juries in the case – one in Winamac plus public opinion – Ford management decided to present its full case. After all, when else would Ford have the national news media's captive attention while it told its side of the Pinto story?

17

When Michael Cosentino heard through the Winamac grapevine that James Neal intended to launch his defense "with a big bang," he was not surprised. Neal had a reputation for starting his cases with a strong, dramatic piece of evidence to grab the attention of the jurors and then finishing the same way to impress them just before they started their deliberations. But Cosentino had no idea of what Neal was planning until court was called into session on Wednesday, February 13.

Neal rose and told the court that his first witness would be a 29-year-old Michigan man named Levi Woodard, who would testify that Judy Ulrich told him on her deathbed why she turned her car around and that she had been stopped on the highway at the time of the crash.

Cosentino, who had confidently defied Neal to "stop that Pinto," was shocked. "There was a massive state investigation at the scene and afterwards," he declared, a hint of panic in his voice. "This Woodard now comes out of the woodwork; he never came forward to the police. It's very difficult to understand how this man suddenly appears at the scene."

Despite Cosentino's surprise, the name of Levi Woodard was contained in a report buried in the mountain of evidence gathered by the prosecutor's office during the investigation. Almost 17 months earlier, Wanda Lumpkin, the nurse who quoted Bible verses to Judy during the trip to the Fort Wayne burn center, told one of Cosentino's investigators that a hospital orderly named Levi Woodard had been inside Treatment Room 5 with Judy at Elkhart General Hospital. Yet no one ever bothered to track down Woodard to find out if Judy told him anything important about the accident.

Aubrey Harwell had been more thorough. During his investigation for Ford, he heard persistent rumors about someone at the hospital knowing a key bit of information about the crash. At first, Harwell knew nothing about this mysterious person or what he might know, but Ford lawyers kept pressing hospital workers for details. The only lead they got was that his first name could be Levi.

Finally Harwell located Miss Lumpkin in Costa Rica, where she was beginning her new career as a missionary. In a telephone interview, she said she remembered a black orderly being in the room with Judy, although she could not recall his name. She did, however, provide Harwell with the name of still another person who was finally able to provide a full identification of Woodard.

There were still more roadblocks. Woodard had left the Elkhart area in April, 1979, and taken a job at another hospital. When the hospital was pinpointed as being in the town of Petoskey, Michigan, and there was no telephone listing for Woodard in that area, Harwell sent two of his associates by private plane to find Woodard and get his story.

They found him living with his wife and two children on a 25-acre piece of land near Levering, Michigan, and he told them the story of his conversation with Judy. He agreed to testify if Ford needed him, and the day before his court appearance a private plane was dispatched to bring him to

Winamac. "It was a much bigger thing that I thought it would be," Woodard said later about his role in the case.

Indeed, it was a big thing for Cosentino. It meant Neal could meet his pledge to provide some solid evidence that the Pinto had been stopped on the highway and therefore the closing speed could have been substantially higher than Cosentino's claim. And more than that, it meant that the riddle of why Judy turned around would be solved by a defense witness, thus creating some doubt in the jury's mind as to the completeness of the state's investigation.

Woodard was a shy, soft-spoken man with black-rimmed glasses and a closely cropped beard. He recalled that "it was traumatic to see the sight of Judy" the night she was wheeled into the emergency room, begging for someone to talk to her about Jesus. Because of Staffeldt's rulings, Woodard could not describe how Judy's features were virtually melted, her nose was burned off, and her lips were gone.

A Seventh Day Adventist who had studied the Bible since he was a child, Woodard said he talked about Jesus to her for five or ten minutes. During that time, "she said she and her sister and cousin were on their way to Goshen, to a volleyball game, and they stopped to get gasoline at a self-service station and one of them put gas in the car.

"And she said that they failed to replace the cap, they put it on the roof of the car. And as they continued toward Goshen, they looked and saw the cap roll across the highway. So she put her flashers on and she said she made a U-turn to go back and pick up the cap. . . .and she said she was stopped beside the cap to get it."

"Stopped?" Neal asked sharply, squinting at the witness over the top of his glasses.

"To get it," Woodard continued. "And she looked in the rearview mirror, she said, and she saw a van coming but it didn't look like it was going to stop, and then it hit her.

"And so I asked her if anyone was able to get out to get the cap – to see if anyone was not injured, you know – and she said that they didn't have time to get the cap."

Woodard said he told Judy's story to a sheriff's deputy

stationed in the emergency room. He recalled the officer taking his name but not copying down any other information.

Cosentino almost jumped out of his chair when it came time to cross-examine the witness. He knew it was vital for him to challenge Woodard's story or his credibility. "You never came forward to tell me or anyone from my office?" Cosentino asked in a skeptical voice.

"No, I didn't," Woodard said. "I felt that after telling the sheriff. . . if they wanted me to testify, they would come and find me." He added that he made no secret of the conversation, having recounted it to several people at the hospital as well as many of his relatives.

Cosentino's questioning was unable to shake Woodard's sincere demeanor. Immediately after he finished, Cosentino ordered an investigator to return to the Elkhart hospital and "turn the place upside down" to find someone who might have been told a different story by Woodard.

Neal had lived up to his reputation. Woodard's testimony was a sensation, impressing the usually cynical press corps and making the front pages of several major newspapers. Reporters badgered the self-satisfied Neal and Harwell for details about how they pulled off the coup. "He challenged me to stop the Pinto," Neal said proudly. "Well, I did it, didn't I?"

As for Cosentino, the questions by reporters were tough and humiliating: If your investigation was so thorough, why didn't you know about Levi Woodard's account? And did this mean that other crucial facts slipped through your supposedly tightly woven net?

Cosentino tried to play down the significance of Woodard's testimony. "I don't think it was damaging when you compare it to seven eyewitnesses," he said. "If necessary, we'll bring in more eyewitnesses on the speed."

Privately, most of Cosentino's assistants believed that Woodard's account of the gas cap rolling across the road was probably what happened because it fit the physical evidence perfectly. They also believed that while Woodard was telling the truth, a girl as horribly burned as Judy, who was so apprehensive about the fate of herself and her passengers, would probably not be very precise in telling her story to an orderly. Maybe she meant she intended to stop, or wanted to stop, or was trying to stop, and that she had not actually come to a halt on the road.

They believed that the unanimous eyewitness accounts that the Pinto was moving would overshadow one man's story about a conversation with a dying girl who might have been under the influence of pain-killers. However, this did not erase the disturbing implication that Cosentino's investigation had been sloppy and that potentially vital leads had never been pursued.

Woodard was not the only embarrassment for the prosecution that day. Neal's second witness was Dr. Galen Miller, a surgeon in the emergency room of the Goshen hospital where Duggar was treated after the accident.

"In taking his history," the doctor said, "I asked what happened and he said he was traveling in a van and dropped a smoke on the floor, took his eyes off the road, and when he looked up there was a car immediately in front of him. And there was no way to avoid an accident."

Then came the devastating part of his testimony: "He told me the car was stopped."

Dr. Miller added that Duggar told him he had not been drinking. "I asked him if what he was smoking was marijuana, or a joint, and he didn't answer. I asked him a second time and he didn't answer," Dr. Miller said.

Cosentino knew about the doctor before his appearance in court but the part concerning the Pinto being stopped was not uncovered during the investigation. It was another direct attack on the credibility of the prosecution.

All of this was just the beginning of Ford's rapid-fire defense. Neal told Judge Staffeldt that he wanted to move into the courthouse basement some cut-up 1973 subcompact cars – a Vega, Gremlin, and Colt, all of which featured their gas tanks at their rear like the Pinto, and a Toyota Corolla, which had the above-the-axle design favored by the prosecution.

"Mr. Neal banged on that Pinto (in the courtroom) the other day and said that *this* is the car we're concerned with, not others," Berner said in opposing Neal's move.

"In determining whether the Pinto was defective," contended the defense attorney, "the jury can consider comparable 1973 cars. I'm literally astounded that the prosecution. . .contends we can't let the jury see 1973 cars to let them decide what acceptable standards of conduct were for the manufacturer of subcompacts in 1973."

Staffeldt ruled that the cars would be permissible. "When the State of Indiana went into the state of the art, that opened the door for this," he said. "This would be to show what the industry was doing at the time (the 1973 Pinto) was manufactured."

With the judge's blessing, Ford workers then hauled the partially dissected cars into the cramped, dingy, and poorly lit courthouse basement. It was immediately evident that both sides were using subtle psychological factors in their car displays. The Pinto which the prosecutors introduced into evidence had its gas tank painted a bright, fiery red; the cars offered by the defense had their tanks painted a cool and tranquil blue.

Ford's next witness was Douglas W. Toms, the president of a recreational vehicle company based in Elkhart and who headed the National Highway Traffic Safety Administration from 1969 through 1973. A former college professor of traffic administration, Toms testified there were no standards for rear-end crashes when he took over the agency. At that time, however, there was a pending proposal that a 20 mile-per-hour moving-barrier standard be imposed on the industry. "We thought that was a good proposal and reasonable," he said.

This proposal never became law. Instead, it was supplanted by a more stringent fixed-barrier proposal which was disclosed at about the time the Pinto was introduced. This would have required cars to survive a 20 mile-per-hour rear crash into a fixed cement wall in 1972 and 30 miles per hour for 1973. That 1973 standard, of course, was equal to a 44 mile-per-hour car-to-car crash from behind.

"We were remarkably naive and there was still a great deal of information to be learned about barrier testing at that time," Toms said, "We speculated that the fixed-barrier tests were severe but we didn't know exactly how much." He said they announced the intention of adopting the fixed-barrier standards "because we wanted to get feedback" on the suggestion.

Asked if the agency did get feedback, Toms replied, "We really did. . . .It became clear to us there were significant disadvantages to fixed rear barriers."

As a result, the fixed-barrier proposal was dropped and the 30 mile-per-hour moving-barrier standard became effective for the 1977 model year. "We thought that was reasonable and appropriate," he testified, adding that there were no requirements that earlier models be recalled and improved to comply with the new rule.

The agency, he said, never forced automakers to put the gas tank above the axle in any cars. "The fuel tank may be anywhere in the car. The important thing is how it performs, not where the tank was located," he testified.

Then Ford lawyer Malcolm Wheeler asked Toms specifically about the 1973 Pinto sedan. "My opinion is that it was a very conventional automobile and was designed and constructed comparably with most other cars of its type at the time," Toms said.

When Wheeler asked if Ford had deviated from acceptable standards of conduct in designing the car, Toms replied: "No, (Ford) did not substantially deviate. . . .The information I've seen involving the number of Pintos in rear-end crash fires is about equal to the (number of) Pintos in the automobile universe. I was amazed (Ford recalled the Pinto) based on that data."

Toms added that the 20 mile-per-hour moving-barrier requirement for the 1973 Pinto, which was the internal standard that Ford voluntarily imposed upon itself, was a "reasonable and acceptable standard" for that time period.

Under cross-examination by Kiely, Toms said that the 44 mile-per-hour car-to-car standard would "not necessarily" have been beneficial to consumers if it had been adopted by NHTSA. Asked if thought that standard would have made cars safer in rear-end crashes, Toms said, "Maybe not."

Later, Toms explained that when a car's rear-end structure was beefed up to make the car capable of withstanding a 44 mile-per-hour rear crash, "you have to make changes elsewhere in the car, and maybe this would cause a problem with front and lateral collisions. Less than 5 per cent are killed in rear-end crashes and that is the safest type of crash. So you like to have the resources put in frontal (protection)."

Adding more rigid structure to the Pinto "may or may not" increase the likelihood of severe whiplash injuries to the Pinto occupants when the car was hit from behind. "It depends on the kind of structure added," he said.

Kiely asked if Ford had lobbied against the fixed-barrier proposals and Toms replied only, "There was a considerable amount of opposition." He said he was "not personally aware" that Ford's own Capri was capable of meeting even the strictest proposed requirement.

Toms added that Ford "responded favorably" to the less stringent moving-barrier standard which was adopted as of 1977, although some manufacurers opposed it, including American Motors, Chrysler, Triumph and Volkswagen.

As for the frequency of fire deaths in rear-end crashes, Toms testified there were 2,000 to 3,000 fire-associated fatalities annually but only 125 to 250 a year involving rear-end crashes. And most of those fatal collisions, he said, occurred at "very high speeds."

Was it true, Kiely inquired, that Toms' company did $1 million in business with Ford Motor Company the previous year? Toms said he could not remember the exact amount but conceded it was "substantial."

As part of Toms' testimony, the jurors, court personnel, and news media were herded into the crowded and musty basement so he could testify about the various subcompact cars offered into evidence by Ford. "In my view, most of these vehicles are comparable; they're all in the same league,"

Toms said as he stood with a pointer next to the torn-up Gremlin. "And some of the structural characteristics of the Pinto are superior." He specifically noted the metal supports inside the Pinto's trunk, which added rigidity and reinforced the corner of the car in side crashes, and the leaf-spring suspension "which provides some resistance to crush."

Comparing the features of the various subcompacts, though, proved confusing and contradictory. Kiely first went through each car and had Toms point out characteristics which could make the car safer than the Pinto in rear-end crashes. After that, Wheeler went through the same cars and elicited Toms' description of the features he considered worse than the Pinto. It was, in sum, a courthouse version of the old joke, "I've got some good news and some bad news."

For instance, the Colt had body rails on both sides; featured a flat-type gas tank; had a smooth differential instead of one with sharp protruding bolts which can puncture the tank. All of that went in Kiely's "plus" column. Then under Wheeler's questioning, Toms described what he considered the car's deficiencies – the suspension was less substantial than the Pinto's, the filler pipe was exposed in the trunk; and the car lacked the Pinto's metal braces inside the trunk.

As for the Gremlin, it also had body rails on each side; the tank was a little farther from the rear bumper than the Pinto's; and the filler tube was rigidly affixed at the gas cap end as recommended by Byron Bloch. On the negative side, Toms said the filler tube was vulnerable to being cut in half and allowing fuel to spill into the passenger compartment.

The Vega got good marks for having a muffler as a sort of shield between the gas tank and the sharp bolts on the differential; having the flat gas tank praised by Copp; and being designed so the tank might ramp over the rear axle instead of getting crushed in a crash. The demerits came because it lacked any body rails; the muffler straps could puncture the gas tank; and the car had a coil suspension which did not contribute at all to rear-end strength.

The Toyota, being the only one of the cars with its

tank situated above its rear axle, provided almost 30 inches of crush space between the bumper and the tank. Also, Toms said the spare tire would absorb some energy during a crash and that the car had a protective rail across its back. Then, of course, came the bad news. Toms said the Corolla's tank could actually be shoved into the passenger compartment in a massive crash; the car's center of gravity could be raised and thus adversely affect handling; part of the filler tube was inside the passenger compartment just 15 inches away from where a passenger would sit; there were no body rails; the tank could be punctured by items in the trunk; and the car might be more vulnerable in rollover or lateral collisions.

No one seemed certain how all of these pluses and minuses added up. If anything, Toms' testimony bolstered Cosentino's earlier contention that the best way to really find out how a car will perform in rear-end crashes was to conduct a experimental crash test.

"The only thing I can figure from all of this," one reporter commented, "is to buy a van, not a subcompact."

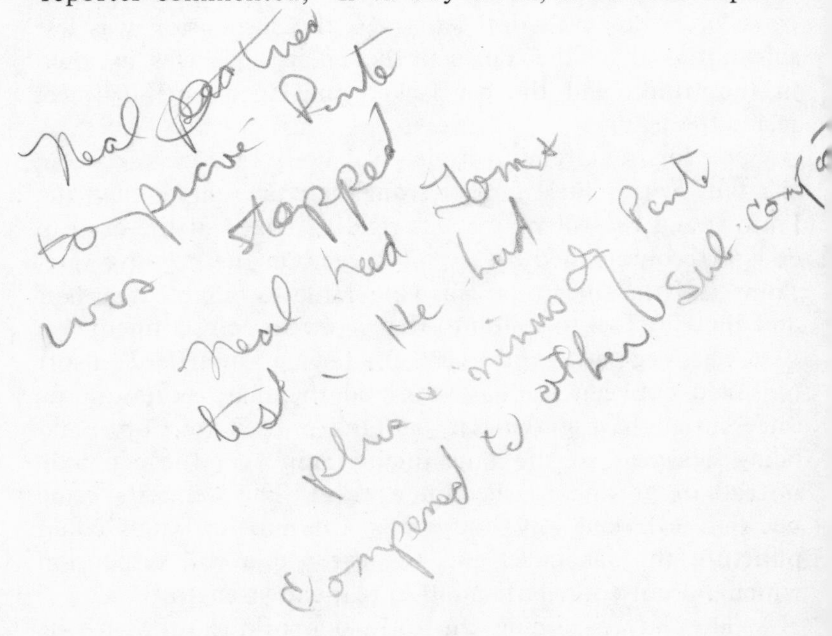

18

The throng of reporters covering the Ford Pinto trial quickly discovered two things after arriving in Winamac – first, Winamac wasn't New York, Chicago, Detroit, or even Elkhart. And second, that wasn't such a bad thing.

After covering the four-day-a-week trial for more than a month, most of the press corps came to appreciate the slow-paced and sociable atmosphere of the amiable town. They were amazed when they would go to interview a local pharmacist or merchant about the trial, only to have him suddenly produce a "Closed" sign, stick it in the window, and invite the newsman down to Rudy's Roost for a leisurely conversation over an afternoon drink. They were surprised, and perhaps a little nervous, when the homeowners they were living with would leave their front door unlocked all night.

There were no qualms about leaving an expensive coat hanging on the rack outside the courtroom. The two local newspapers were quick to offer the free use of typewriters and telephones. And when one reporter's car got stuck in a deep snow drift, several teenagers materialized from nowhere to push him out. The only thing they would accept in return was a "thank you."

Dennis Royalty, the *Indianapolis Star* reporter who dressed better than the lawyers, was treated so much like a son by the owners of a motel in nearby Francesville that he had to let them know when he would be home later than 8 p.m. so they wouldn't worry.

Some reporters tried fitting into the local scene by buying those John Deere, baseball-type hats that farmers always wear. The townspeople appreciated the gesture, although they snickered a little at the combination of a farm hat and a beige trenchcoat.

The number of reporters at the trial varied, with the ranks swelling at the beginning, end, and during key testimony. Usually there was a hard-core group of about 25 regulars, representing newspapers in Chicago, New York, Detroit, and elsewhere, as well as an equal number of technicians, cameramen, and producers. If the importance of a trial can be gauged by the amount of network news coverage, the Pinto case ranked among the top. Camera crews stayed for each day of the trial, lurking in the cavernous courthouse lobby and filming the same things over and over - a station wagon pulling up at 9 a.m. to unload boxes full of Ford documents; Neal leading the Ford troupe up the stairway; and Cosentino and his clan walking down the sidewalk from Tankersley's office.

One smooth-talking reporter named Reginald Stuart of the *New York Times,* who introduced himself to the locals as being from "a little paper you've never heard of," became such a popular figure around town that there was talk among the press of running him for mayor (until it was discovered there was no such office in Winamac). Stuart even had a local printer make up some stationery with the inscription: "The Winamac News Team – Reporting to America on the Ford Pinto Trial – 1980."

Alan Lenhoff, whose articles for the *Detroit Free Press* were among the most perceptive written about the trial, used his wry sense of humor to enliven the most routine aspects of the trial coverage. After the twice-a-day press conferences in the courthouse lobby degenerated into predictable banter, Lenhoff suddenly asked Neal one day, "What's Dolly Parton *really* like?"

Neal's expressive eyebrows shot up as he commented about his client, "I don't know; I haven't been able to get close enough to find out."

At another press briefing, when Neal was especially angry at Cosentino, Neal quipped, "I suppose we don't have to guess what the "A" stands for in Michael A. Cosentino."

"What does the "F" stand for in James F. Neal?" Lenhoff shot back.

"Why, 'Flash,' of course," the indignant attorney replied.

While reporters were peppering the lawyers with questions during the press conferences, Ford was doing its own intelligence gathering. A former Federal Bureau of Investigation agent working as a Ford investigator would inconspicuously tape record Cosentino's question-and-answer session and a secretary would provide Neal with a typed transcript within an hour. There were several times when Cosentino would make comments to the press in which he would try to punch holes in Ford's defense, only to discover that Neal took note of those criticisms and promptly plugged the holes with later testimony.

One reporter, David Schreiber of the *Elkhart Truth*, tangled with Neal a few times at the trial's outset after Neal learned the newsman was living with the prosecutors in one of their cottages. "Are you asking that question for yourself or your roommates?" Neal would reply when Schreiber made an inquiry. The defense attorney said near the end of the case, though, that he thought Schreiber's coverage had been exceptionally fair.

Schreiber's biggest problem was that his newspaper had an insatiable appetite for news about the trial because of its local angle. Schreiber, who resembled comedian Dan Ackroyd and who was dubbed the "senior correspondent" because he had covered the case since the crash, was assigned to write a news story as well as a full-fledged feature article each day. After six or seven weeks, feature material was getting a bit scarce. When one reporter glanced out his breakfast window and saw the first snowflakes of the trial, he knew immediately what it meant: "Schreiber'll be out there in five minutes interviewing the flakes for a feature."

Three big-city reporters became honorary Winamacians by living in the home of a local couple and their twin teenage sons. They spent the evenings talking around the blazing fireplace, playing a friendly game of billiards, challenging each other to video games, or having a home-cooked meal of spaghetti or lasagna complete with too much wine. "My own home isn't this homey," one of them cracked.

One way reporters passed the time during the frequent breaks from testimony was to perfect their imitations of the trial participants. Lenhoff did an excellent rendition of Neal stepping before the microphones each day, being asked a difficult question, and then flicking the ashes off his giant cigar, chuckling, and saying slowly, "Now, y'boys all know ah can't answer that." Others preferred to parody one of Cosentino's violent outbursts: "I've never been so kicked and mauled and destroyed and crushed and mutilated and demolished and maimed and butchered and mangled and smashed by a defendant in my life!" Another popular pastime was to update the ever-changing list of the "Five Jerkiest Witnesses."

When reporters started getting a little restless after five weeks or so, Lenhoff organized the "First (And Last) Annual Ford Pinto Trial Bowling Festival" at the community's just-opened bowling alley. "The only rule," Lenhoff announced, "is that anyone who's got their own ball is considered a professional and can't play."

The occasion attracted a flock of reporters and several Ford attorneys, each person earning a fancy certificate titled "Victory Over Boredom" which was signed by Judge Staffeldt. The tournament was described in a *National Law Journal* article and was featured in a photospread in the society pages of the *Pulaski County Journal.* That was followed by the impressively titled "First Annual Bo Derek Film Festival," which was nothing more than a group of half-drunken reporters who headed over to the local Isis Theater to see the movie "10."

For the most part, the news media were well-behaved, although they fell far short of the angelic behavior exhibited by the Ford workers who were imported to Winamac. Under special instructions not to ruffle any local feathers, Ford paralegals and secretaries could be seen scurrying from their headquarters at 1 a.m. to feed their parking meters, despite the fact the the rest of the town ignored the meters even during business hours.

Some genuine affection seemed to develop between the press corps and the townspeople. At the conclusion of the trial, the regular reporters chipped in $4 each and bought a large ad in the *Pulaski County Journal* to say, "Thank You, Winamac."

A few of the local residents were impressed when a big-name television reporter like Carl Stern of NBC News would show up for a day or two, but that reaction was nothing compared to the star-struck greeting given to Ford's next witness. Instead of a calling in a dull Ford engineer to testify about the disadvantages of the above-the-axle gas tank location and the rubber bladder system of preventing gas leakage, Ford called on famous champion racecar driver Tom Sneva.

The jurors, who were getting weary of the dry testimony, perked up when the good-looking Sneva strolled up to the witness stand. Giggling schoolchildren, who heard in advance of his arrival, came to court for his appearance and then followed him outside for an autograph session.

Sneva testified that he preferred the Pinto's gas tank location to an above-the-axle design. "I would definitely (favor putting the tank) down low and as far from the driver as possible," he said. "Anytime you move a mass of weight up (in a car), you affect the handling characteristics of a car adversely."

He also said that the rubber bladders used to contain gas in racing cars cost about $3,700 each, are difficult to install, must be oiled each year to keep them pliable, and last only a few years before they need replacement. The lowest price he had seen for a bladder was $685 - a far cry from the $6 per bladder price quote given to Ford in 1971 by the Goodyear Tire & Rubber Co.

Under cross-examination by Shewmaker, Sneva conceded that the weight of the gas tank in the above-the-axle position could be counterbalanced by putting body rails and the spare tire lower in the car. He also said that the Chevrolet Corvette once used a bladder in its gas tank.

In an unsuccessful attempt to get the contents of an internal Ford document into evidence, Shewmaker asked Sneva if it were true that Ford rejected the bladder approach because it was a costly safety measure even though Ford had been given a $6 per bladder cost estimate. Staffeldt sustained Wheeler's objection to the inquiry.

After the court session, Cosentino told the television cameras that calling Sneva to the witness stand had been "a grandstand play" by Ford. What he did not reveal, however, was that the prosecutors attempted to get actor and racecar driver Paul Newman to testify for them, but were unsuccessful. "Those blue eyes would've made that jury forget all about Sneva," one prosecutor said.

Sneva's testimony came on Valentine's Day and the usually obstinate Cosentino said he would not object to the court being dismissed a little early so that Neal could catch a private jet to Nashville for the weekend. Neal was so overcome with gratitude that he rushed over to Cosentino's table and pinned a rose on the straight-laced, unsmiling prosecutor. "There," Neal said. "Now you have a heart."

Ford led off the trial's seventh week with testimony by Donald Huelke, a professor of anatomy at the University of Michigan Medical School and a former consultant to Ford. His task had been to deliver up to 10 lectures a year to Ford engineers from 1965 to 1973 on the topic of "what was happening in the real world of automobile crashes."

Huelke said he never lectured on the topics of injury or death from fire in rear-impact crashes during that time period. "It was my opinion at that time that there were much more important areas to be lectured on," he testified. "Fires are an extremely rare event in terms of injury-producing accidents."

During cross-examination, Cosentino showed Huelke copies of a 1968 study from the University of California at Los Angeles which said that relatively inexpensive design changes could make cars safer from fire in rear-end crashes, and a 1972 University of Texas report which called car fires "a catastrophic occurrence" that claimed 3,500 lives a year. Huelke said the UCLA report "doesn't ring a bell" and he may have read the University of Texas study.

"Isn't it true that more people are burned to death in automobile collisions than are killed in airplane accidents?" Cosentino asked.

"I don't know," Huelke replied.

Cosentino also emphasized that Huelke was a frequent defense witness for Volkswagen, General Motors, and Ford in civil lawsuits, charging $50 an hour to testify.

Neal said later that the point he was trying to establish with Huelke's testimony was that "it wasn't until recently that anyone considered rear-impact fires to be a serious problem."

One difficulty Neal faced in representing Ford was the same problem encountered by other defense attorneys whose task is to stand up for a corporation in court – How can the corporation be personalized for the jurors? Defense lawyers fear that jurors will find it much easier to return a guilty verdict against a faceless paper entity rather than an individual defendant who sits in the courtroom each day and looks them in the eye.

Neal tried providing personality to Ford Motor Company during his opening statements by talking about the corporation's heritage, dating back to its founding by Henry Ford in June, 1903.

"Ford Motor Company is a corporation. I guess, in a sense you can say it is bloodless, a piece of paper," Neal said to the jurors. But he added that the jury would actually be trying the individuals who constituted the corporation and who were "decent people with families, who do their best in a difficult world that is getting more difficult each day."

Still, Neal felt he had to go beyond that in order to help the jurors empathize with Ford. He rejected the tactic used by some lawyers in which an officer of the corporation sits in the courtroom during the trial as if he personally were the defendant. "That's too phony," Neal said. "The jury would be insulted."

Instead, Neal chose to focus the case on one individual – Harold C. MacDonald – who would proudly stand up and say he was responsible for producing the 1973 Pinto. Neal wanted the jurors to see this one man as representing Ford Motor Company so that when they talked about the defendant in the jury room, they would visualize Harold C. MacDonald instead of some amorphous paper giant. At one point, Neal even said in open court that "Mr. MacDonald is here very much in the nature of a defendant."

Harold MacDonald had the perfect image that Ford was trying to project to the jurors. He was a 62-year-old, pink-faced man with fluffy white hair, silver glasses, and a frail-looking build (although this was deceptive because he jogged two miles every morning before breakfast). He was the father of two sons and two daughters, a grandfather of three young children, a Navy veteran who served in the South Pacific during World War II, a deacon in his church, active in a Christian day school, and was on the verge of being installed as national president of the 40,000-member Society of Automotive Engineers.

He looked so unassuming that it was difficult to imagine that he received $395,000 in salary and bonuses the previous year and owned almost $450,000 in Ford stock.

"Did you see that man?" Neal whispered to a reporter during a break. "Does he look like a reckless killer to you?" Neal said he was hoping to convey to the jurors that "nice, kind, decent men" like MacDonald were in charge of producing the Pinto.

During his 32-year career at Ford, which began after short stints at the Packard Motor Company and General

Motors, MacDonald worked his way up to the position of vice-president of the engineering and research staff. From 1965 to 1975, he was the top Ford engineer responsible for all the passenger cars produced in the United States. Among his former employes was Harley Copp, who was working for him at the time that the Ulrich Pinto was shipped from Ford's New Jersey plant on June 23, 1973. If Copp's rise within Ford's hierarchy was rapid, MacDonald's was nothing less than spectacular.

"You are the official at Ford Motor Company responsible for the 1973 Pinto?" Neal asked him.

"Yes, sir," MacDonald replied in a crisp voice. "I am."

"Was that car a reasonably safe automobile at that time from the standpoint of fuel system integrity?"

"Yes, sir, it was."

When Neal asked the basis for that opinion, Cosentino objected, observing that Harley Copp had been precluded from discussing the crash tests which formed the basis for his conclusion that the 1973 Pinto was a dangerous car.

"I have some recollection of Byron Bloch spending days on his opinions and how he reached them," Neal said. Staffeldt ruled that MacDonald could continue.

MacDonald said his opinion was based on three facts. First, the 1973 Pinto met all federal fuel system safety requirements in force at the time, as well as Ford's internal standard that the car not leak when hit from behind by a moving barrier at 20 miles per hour.

"Did any other American manufacturer other than Ford have *any* standard in rear-end crashes at that time?" Neal asked.

"I have good reason to believe none did," MacDonald replied.

MacDonald said he believed this internal standard was "quite reasonable" because it was the same one recommended at that time by the federal General Services Administration; the Canadian equivalent of the GSA; the Society of Automotive Engineers; and a private consulting firm hired by NHTSA to investigate fires in accidents. In addition, it was the same as the standard proposed by NHTSA in January,1969.

MacDonald testified that his second reason for believing the 1973 Pinto was reasonably safe was that he compared it with other subcompacts of it era and concluded the Pinto was "fully equal" to them.

His third reason was that when he became concerned about how the Pinto was performing on the road, he turned to available statistics and discovered the Pinto's record was equal to other cars. MacDonald said he got these statistics in September, 1977, and they showed that in 1975-76 the Pinto made up 1.9 per cent of the cars on the road and was involved in 1.9 per cent of the fatal accidents accompanied by some fire.

As for NHTSA's strict fixed-barrier proposals which came out at the same time as the Pinto's introduction, MacDonald called them "too severe" and said that the deadline for their imposition was too short. "The literature suggested that fatal fires in rear-end crashes were rare and when they did occur, they were at high speeds and at severe conditions," he said.

Neal tried introducing into evidence a 1969 report by a task force of the Society of Automotive Engineers which he said concluded that "fire on rear-impact is not a high risk problem," but Cosentino blocked him.

That objection by Cosentino was one of the few he was successful in asserting during MacDonald's testimony. After being repeatedly overruled, Cosentino cut short his arguments on another objection by saying, "I realize I'm going to be overruled, so I'll sit down." When the judge continued ruling against Cosentino's objections, the prosecutor sighed and told the witness: "Mr. MacDonald, testify to whatever you want to – you're free."

MacDonald said he felt "very strongly" that the above-the-axle gas tank design like that employed on the Toyota Corolla was "less safe. . . than the 1973 Pinto." His reason for what he called his "strong personal concern" against the above-the-axle design provided one of the strangest ironies of the entire case.

MacDonald explained that when he was a teenager in

1932, his father, a traveling salesman, was driving his Model A Ford through Southern Michigan on his way home. That particular car featured its gas tank at its front, close to the driver. MacDonald said that his father's car went off the road, smashed into a tree, the gas tank erupted into flames, and his father was burned to death.

"So I've been very sensitive about fuel tank placement," he said. "I feel very strongly it should be as far from the engine and passenger compartment as possible."

"Do you think the 1973 Capri (with the above-the-axle design) was safer in terms of fuel tank location than the 1973 Pinto?" Neal inquired.

"No, sir, I do not."

Neal showed him a Ford advertisement bragging that the Capri's gas tank was "safely cradled between the rear wheels and protected on both sides."

"Are you saying you are in disagreement with that ad?" he asked. "Yes, sir, I am," MacDonald said firmly. "I was not responsible for the Capri because it was built in Britain."

MacDonald scoffed at Ford's own test which showed the Capri could withstand a 31 mile-per-hour rear-end crash into a cement wall, which was equivalent to about a 45 mile-per-hour car-to-car collision. "If you use a flat barrier as the sole criterion for positioning the fuel tank, then the over-the-axle is safer," he said. "But there is a lot more involved than the barrier test."

He said that in cars with the above-the-axle design, loose items in the trunk can puncture the tank. The Capri test was not an accurate reflection of a real-world collision because the car's trunk was empty at the time, he added.

MacDonald also criticized the Capri-like design for having its filler pipe positioned higher so that "the cap can come off in a rollover and spray gas around the car." In addition, he said the gas tank's weight could harm the car's handling and that the design precluded the building of the popular station wagon or hatchback models.

Q. *Did you, for the 1973 Pinto, consider yourself locked-in by weight or monetary considerations?*
A. No, sir, I did not.
Q. *Did the styling of the 1973 Pinto dictate the location of the fuel tank?*
A. No, sir, it did not.
Q. *Did the 1973 Pinto substantially deviate from acceptable standards of conduct?*
A. No, sir.
Q. *Did you act in conscious, unjustifiable disregard of harm?*
A. I did not.

Then came a tidbit of information which Neal believed to be potent evidence that the 1973 Pinto was a reasonably safe automobile. MacDonald testified that he drove a 1973 Pinto himself and that he also bought one for his own son to drive.

When Cosentino began his cross-examination, which was perhaps his most effective of the trial, he was able to introduce into evidence without opposition the Capri crash test in which the car withstood the equivalent of a 45 mile-per-hour car-to-car crash. Cosentino also argued that MacDonald's opinions about the safety of the Pinto "opened the door" for him to submit into evidence the previously excluded crash tests as well as other internal Ford memos and reports which the judge had barred earlier.

Each time Cosentino attempted to get one of the documents into evidence, though, Judge Staffeldt reiterated his ruling that they were inadmissible. The judge even blocked Cosentino from trying to use MacDonald's testimony to lay a foundation to prove that the documents were relevant to the case.

"The state is obviously wasting the court's time," Cosentino finally said in a bitter tone after Staffeldt rejected a stack of internal Ford memos. It appeared the prosecutor's hope of being able to introduce his vital documents into evidence during Ford's defense case had been only wishful thinking.

One by one, Cosentino then went through what the prosecution considered hazardous design characteristics of the Pinto – the gas tank location, its short distance to the bumper and differential, the sharp edges and bolts near the tank, the filler tube's short insertion into the tank, and the welding that could come "unzipped" in a crash. For each one, Cosentino asked which Ford executive made the decision to build the 1973 Pinto in that manner. And for each one, Harold MacDonald replied, "I did, sir."

When asked if it were true that safety was not considered when each one of those design decisions was made, MacDonald said curtly, "No, sir."

"Is it true that the welds in the floor pan will split in a 21 mile-per-hour moving-barrier crash?" Cosentino asked.

"They may," MacDonald said. "One time they will and the next time they won't." He added that he had never heard of the term "zipper effect" to describe how the floor pan would rip up and allow gasoline to flood the passenger compartment. And he said the spacing between the welding on the 1973 Pinto was comparable to the 1973 Vega, Colt, and Gremlin.

Cosentino handed MacDonald the recall kit for the Pinto and asked him to examine it. "You still maintain that without these improvements, that car still would have been safe?" Cosentino asked.

"Yes, sir," MacDonald replied, his voice conveying an underlying hostility.

"If," Cosentino said, "an automobile manufacturer designed a car with an inherently dangerous fuel system with a high tendency to burn when hit from behind at low to moderate speeds, would that be a bad practice or undesirable?"

"I don't know how to answer that; I have no answer," MacDonald sputtered. Cosentino repeated the question. "I can't answer it," MacDonald replied, explaining later that he considered the question "complex" and was not certain what Cosentino meant by "low to moderate speed."

Q. *Is it true that Lee Iacocca had the original idea for the subcompact car which ultimately became the Pinto?*
A. That's not an accurate statement of what took place.
Q. *Is it true that Lee Iacocca approved every major design change you made?*
A. That's not accurate.
Q. *Is it true that Lee Iacocca was fired from Ford after the Pinto was recalled?*
A. I think 'fired' is the wrong word; I don't know exactly how to describe it.
Q. *Did he leave after the recall?*
A. I guess yes; I'm not sure of the date.

Cosentino tried asking MacDonald about a cover article on Henry Ford II published in *Fortune* magazine a month after the Ulrich crash, but Staffeldt precluded the inquiry. In the article, Ford was quoted as saying about the Pinto: "The lawyers would shoot me for this, but I think there's some cause for the concern about the car. I don't even listen to the cost figures – we've got to fix it."

Cosentino also attacked the statistics cited by MacDonald which indicated that the Pinto's involvement in fire-accompanied fatal crashes was consistent with the number of Pintos on the road. Cosentino produced his own data, taken from a government computer printout in 1978, which showed that the Pinto was involved in *twice* as many fatal *rear-end* collisions involving fire that would be statistically expected. Rear-end impact fires are commonly fuel-fed.

For instance, Cosentino said that although the Pinto represented 1.9 per cent of the cars on the highway, the Pinto accounted for 4.1 per cent of the fires with fatalities resulting from rear-end collisions. For the 1973 Pinto alone, the car accounted for .8 per cent of the number of fires with fatalities in rear-end crashes, even though the 1973 Pinto model made up only .4 per cent of the cars on the highway.

When comparing the 1973 Pinto with all other 1973 cars, the Pinto was involved in 7 per cent of the explosions or fires with fatalities in rear-end crashes, although only 3.5 per cent of the 1973 cars on the road were Pintos.

"I don't recognize that data," MacDonald said.

Cosentino was vague during his questioning as to the time span covered by the statistics, and Ford executives complained privately to reporters that this information was not available at the time MacDonald sought his statistics in 1977.

Cosentino maintained at the daily press conference that "Lee Iacocca was more responsible (for the Pinto) than this witness because he had the final say-so on the go-ahead for the car, according to our information." Then he added as an afterthought: "I personally would not want to take credit for the '73 Pinto."

Neal, however, seemed confident that MacDonald had given the jurors a concrete image of the people behind the Pinto. "It's easy to criticize big corporations." he said to the reporters. "But they're made up of good, decent people just like Harold MacDonald."

A few of the reporters had a somewhat cynical view of MacDonald's testimony, and battled the boredom of frequent lulls by composing some new verses for an old children's song:

Old MacDonald built a car
P - I - N - T - O
And on that car he place a tank
P - I - N - T - O
With a sharp bolt here, a bracket there
Here a shock, there a bracket
Everywhere a puncture point
Old MacDonald built a car
P - I - N - T - O

And when he was done Ford gave him a bonus
M - O - N - E - Y
With a half-mil in stock
And more cash on the block
Lots of thrills; no more bills
Soon a home in Bloomfield Hills
Old MacDonald made his dough
P - I - N - T - O

Now Ford sales are really low
P - I - N - T - O
No one wants a great big blow
P - I - N - T - O
With a lawsuit here and a lawsuit there
Here a Bloch, there a Copp
Everywhere a chop-chop
Chrysler soon will be on top
P - I - N - T - O

Neal lead [illegible] Sneva test & MacDonald – men responsible for Pinto – He felt they were safe enough for his family

19

Harold MacDonald was followed to the witness stand by two more Pinto engineers whose message was simple: If the 1973 Pinto was safe enough for their families, it was safe enough for everyone else.

Frank G. Olsen, a 33-year Ford employee who was paid $154,000 in 1978 for his work as assistant chief engineer, testified he was among those involved with the production of the 1973 Pinto. "I certainly did," he replied when asked if he thought the car was reasonably safe. It was so safe, he said, that he gave one to his own daughter to drive. At the time, she was 18 year old, which was the same age as Judy Ulrich at her death.

Howard P. Freers, who was paid $267,000 in 1978 in his position as Ford's chief body and electrical engineer, said the 1973 Pinto was safe enough for him to drive and to give another to his son, who owned it for two years.

James Neal emphasized during his opening remarks that this was strong evidence that the Pinto's design was not dangerous. He compared it to Air Force drills in which paratroopers had to pack their parachutes, mix them in a pile, and pick one at random to use on a jump. "The best evidence that you are not going to be reckless is when you have to pick out a parachute and jump with it," he said. "And the best evidence that you are not reckless is that when you design a car, you drive it for yourself, your wives, and your children."

Just about all Cosentino could accomplish on cross-examination of these witnesses was to stress their lucrative salaries and annual bonuses, which were based on the level of Ford's profits. Cosentino was hoping that the generally blue-collar jury might be skeptical of testimony from high-paid executives who had much to lose if Ford were convicted. Cosentino had expected that Olsen and Freers would appear, but he was taken off guard by the brevity of their limited testimony. He wasted 10 hours preparing for the cross-examination of one of them because he anticipated a much wider area to be covered by Neal in his questioning.

Then Ford brought in another engineer expert, James J. Schultz, of Palo Verde, California, who worked on truck designs during most of his 24 years with the Chrysler Corporation. After comparing the Pinto with the Vega, Colt, Gremlin, and Corolla, Schultz said the the 1973 Pinto "is certainly comparable and in some respects it would be superior" to its competitors.

A solemn, self-confident research engineer who was paid $41 per hour as a professional witness in lawsuits, Schultz pointed out the Pinto's positive features and made some points which directly contradicted testimony by the prosecution witnesses. For example, although Harley Copp said the shape of the Pinto's gas tank encouraged the build-up of dangerous inner pressure during a crash, Schultz said the shape was a positive characteristic. The tank had the ability to "reconfigure" and "reshape" itself without reducing its volume and creating pressure during a collision, he testified.

He also praised the Pinto for having its entire fuel system outside the passenger compartment, unlike some other cars; having a spare tire well above the gas tank to stiffen the area; providing the metal plates in the trunk; and having the leaf-spring suspension "which can resist crush."

Schultz added that he experimented with the bladder concept while at Chrysler in 1975 and discovered "a plethora of problems," including durability, insertion of the bladder into the tank, abrasion between the tank and the rubber, and how to attach the bladder to the gas tank opening through which fuel was poured.

As for the spacing between the welds which attached the Pinto's floor and body, Schultz said it was "typical" of 1973 cars. "You're limited by technology as to how close one can place those spot welds and be consistent with the state of the art," he testified.

In addition, Schultz said that the Pinto's gas tank location would fare better in rollover crashes than the Capri's, and that the Capri's tank would be more vulnerable to rupture in rear-end crashes in which the striking vehicle climbed up onto the back of the car.

Cosentino thought Schultz' testimony strayed too much into irrelevant areas, and he objected when the witness started discussing rollover crashes. Frustrated by being repeatedly overruled, Cosentino finally huffed, "Let him testify all he wants."

Schultz was never asked his opinion of the closing speed in the Ulrich crash until he commented on cross-examination that he believed the Ulrich Pinto "did quite well for this particular accident considering the speeds involved."

"Oh?" Cosentino said. "And what speeds were involved, in you opinion?"

Schultz said he believed the Pinto was stopped on the highway and the van was going 60 miles per hour when it smashed into the car's rear. This estimate was even higher than the 50 mile-per-hour closing speed Neal had claimed during his opening remarks.

"Assume that all of the eyewitnesses testified that the speed difference could have been as little as 15 miles per hour and as high as 35 miles per hour," Cosentino said.

"With the damage on the car," Schultz replied without hesitation, "I cannot conceive of anyone saying it was a 15 or 35 mile-per-hour closing speed."

The damage to the van, he added, "can be" consistent with a 60 mile-per-hour collision because the front of this model was very tightly packed with the radiator, battery, master cylinder, and engine immediately behind the grill. "It has a very stiff front end; it will not show the damage as one would expect," he testified.

"Assume that the driver, Judy Ulrich, would have walked away from the collision without a scratch if there had been no fire," Cosentino said. "Do you still say the closing speed was 60 miles per hour?"

"Yes, I do," he said.

"Assume the other girls would be relatively uninjured if there was no fire. Do you still say the closing speed was 60?"

"Yes, I do."

Schultz conceded he did not know at what speed the 1973 Pinto began leaking gasoline or its floor pan split open except that it was somewhere between 20 and 60 miles per hour.

Neal considered the next defense witness particularly important in combating the allegation that Ford acted recklessly by failing to repair or warn about its 1973 Pinto sooner than it did. The witness was Thomas J. Feaheny, the $385,000-a-year vice-president for car engineering who joined the automaker's ranks in 1957. Feaheny testified he had given some statistics in March, 1978, to Ford's board of directors because of increasing concern about the NHTSA investigation into the Pinto's vulnerability to fire in rear-end crashes.

The statistics were intended to demonstrate to the directors how the Pinto was performing in actual use. As a visual aid for the jurors, the data were reproduced on giant pieces of cardboard.

The first chart showed that, based on information from the federal Fatal Accident Reporting System (FARS), the Pinto performed about as well as all cars in 1975-76 based on the number of fatal accidents accompanied by some fire. The Pinto and the Vega were involved at a rate of 7 per million cars, compared to 9.7 for the Datsun; 9.3 for Volkswagen; 5 for the Toyota; and 6.8 for all cars.

For small cars the rate of fatal accidents accompanied by some fire in 1975-76 was 7 per million for the Pinto and Vega compared to 7.3 for all compacts and subcompacts. The Pinto ranked better than the Honda, Gremlin, Datsun, Volkswagen, and Opel, and not quite as good as the Colt and Toyota.

Other statistics, gathered by the State of Washington for the years 1972-76, concerned the number of collision-induced fires per million vehicles. The Pinto performed better than the Honda, Opel, Gremlin, Volkswagen, and Vega, and worse than the Toyota, Datsun, and Colt.

Cosentino vigorously objected to the statistics being admitted into evidence, calling them "self-serving." Judge Staffeldt ruled that the jury could consider them not for their truth or accuracy, but for the purpose of determining what Ford's knowledge was at that time.

Neal believed that the jury would not find Ford guilty of acting in "plain, conscious, and unjustifiable disregard of harm" by failing to recall the cars sooner if Ford had been convinced by the statistics that the Pintos were not dangerous.

But why, then, did Ford proceed to recall the 1971-76 Pintos three months later if it believed the car was performing better than many other subcompacts? The real reason, Feaheny said, was not safety, it was public relations.

"The corporation had been subjected to allegations of a problem unique to the Pinto, and this obviously was damaging our corporate reputation and the attitude of the public," Feaheny testified. "It had become a critical problem for the company, a reputational problem resulting from allegations of a defect in the Pinto . . . On balance, it was felt that if we could reach an agreement with NHTSA (on a recall), it would reassure the owners and public of the company's good intentions on the matter."

"And that was the basis for the recall?" Neal asked.

"Yes," Feaheny said.

Like the other witnesses, Feaheny noted that his own wife drove a 1973 Pinto. "We were kind of proud of the Pinto," he said of himself and his fellow engineers. "We bragged about it to our wives and friends."

Cosentino attacked Feaheny's data because they were not concerned with *rear-end* collisions, which was the kind of crash in which the Pinto was most vulnerable. And he said the small samplings from the State of Washington made its figures subject to distortion.

Again, Cosentino produced his statistics which showed the Pinto was twice as likely to be involved in rear-end fatal crashes involving fire than would be statistically expected.

The prosecutor also elicited Feaheny's admission that the board of directors was not shown any of the Pinto crash tests dating back eight years which showed the car's design was susceptible to serious gas leakage in low-speed crashes. Feaheny said he did not even know the threshhold of gas leakage for the 1973 Pinto, but said he still considered the car safe because it met Ford's internal 20 mile-per-hour moving-barrier requirement.

And he conceded that although the purpose of the recall was to "restore our reputation," the improvements made to the cars under the recall would reduce the risk of gas leakage in at least some kinds of collisions.

It was during Feaheny's testimony that Cosentino stunned the Ford lawyers by offering into evidence an exhibit showing that Ford Motor Company was convicted of 350 counts of violating the Clean Air Act in 1973. "Ford knowingly made false and fictitious statements for certification of the 1973 model vehicles – and that is *that* car," Cosentino said, pointing to the Pinto in the courtroom.

Cosentino said the convictions, for which Ford was fined a total of $7 million, were admissible to challenge the credibility of the defendant. "This man (Feaheny) is speaking for Ford Motor Company; we're entitled to impeach the corporation through him because that's the way corporations act – through individuals," Cosentino said.

"It's hard to believe Mr. Cosentino would attempt to do that," Neal said, shaking his head.

"It's hard to believe Ford was convicted of that," Cosentino remarked.

Cosentino wanted the jury to hear about the convictions in order to cast doubt on the veracity of the testimony by various Ford executives during the trial. He hoped the jurors would conclude that if the corporation lied to the government, it would not hesitate to lie during its defense of an important criminal case.

Neal told the judge that it would be improper to use a conviction against a corporate defendant in an attempt to challenge the credibility of individual witnesses. Neal, who believed the issue had serious implications for Ford's defense, would comment later that, "If I could have prostrated myself in front of the bench (to prevent the convictions from being admitted into evidence), I would have."

Judge Staffeldt gave both sides time to research the law on this vague question and then surprised everyone – especially the prosecutors – by deciding to let Cosentino inform the jurors about the convictions.

Neal immediately seized the offensive by calling Herbert Misch, a Ford vice-president of the environmental and safety staff, to the witness stand to explain the events leading up to the convictions. Misch said he learned on Thursday, May 11, 1972, that a false accounting system had been established by some employees concerning emissions testing.

"I went to see Mr. Henry Ford II as soon as he got out of the stockholder's meeting," Misch testified. "Mr. Ford said, 'Herb, do whatever is necessary and right.' "

Misch said he promptly informed the federal Environmental Protection Agency of the matter and asked the agency to return Ford's application for approval of its engines. Ford was charged and when the case came up in federal court, the automaker entered a "no contest" plea. As for the four employees who devised the false accounting system, Misch said they were demoted, reprimanded, transferred, or docked pay. No one was fired.

Neal also called to the witness stand a former EPA official who confirmed that Ford provided information to the government concerning the case.

That day, the usually coy Neal became a fist-shaking advocate in front of the television cameras, proclaiming that the convictions "may have been Ford Motor Company's finest hour" because the automaker "took the transgressions to the government and blew the whistle on itself."

Despite the fact that Cosentino intended to offer evidence disputing Ford's version of the events, Neal asked Judge Staffeldt for a ruling that "this matter is over." Without hearing Cosentino's evidence, Staffeldt agreed that "we've gone into (the matter) sufficiently" and then he shut the door on any further evidence about the convictions.

Neal was uncertain how much the evidence about the convictions may have damaged the credibility of his witnesses. There was little question, though, that the impact had been considerably softened by Ford painting itself as a whistle-blower and then preventing Cosentino from challenging that account.

Neal resumed his evidence about the recall by bringing Misch back to the witness stand. He described how he first learned on May 8, 1978, that NHTSA had reached an initial determination that the 1971-76 Pintos and 1975-76 Mercury Bobcats were defective because they leaked gasoline in rear-end collisions. Misch said he called in MacDonald and Feaheny to discuss Ford's two options – Either fight the allegation "because we didn't think it was just," or find a way to reach a settlement with the government.

They decided to work out an agreement to recall the cars. "The adverse publicity was seriously damaging our company's reputation," he explained. "And we just decided, though in our opinion the government was wrong, that it's a difficult thing to win when you carry on that kind of fight (with NHTSA)."

"Did you think then that the 1973 Pinto was unsafe with regard to its fuel system?" Neal asked.

"I did not and I do not," Misch declared.

After working out some details with the government, Ford announced the recall on June 9, 1978, which was two months before the Ulrich tragedy. This headed off a public hearing which would have exposed the Pinto's defects, although Misch maintained this had nothing to do with Ford's decision to recall the cars. The press release reporting the recall "was a very newsworthy item," Misch added.

The release, which stressed that Ford disagreed with NHTSA's initial finding that the Pintos were an unreasonable risk to safety, said that Ford dealers would be expected to process the first requests for modifications in September, 1978.

Misch, who authored the recall announcement as well as the earlier 8-page denunciation of the *Mother Jones* charges, said he never recommended that Ford buy newspaper advertisements or broadcast commercials to warn the public about the alleged dangers of the Pinto.

"I think such a recommendation would be a ridiculous recommendation. You'd be asking a million and a half people not to drive their vehicles. . . and to get in another vehicle no more safe than the Pinto."

Calling such advertisements "unnecessary" and possibly "counterproductive," Misch said that "there was no reason to tell (Pinto owners) not to drive their cars."

Misch testified that from the date of the recall announcement until the date of the Ulrich accident, Ford was working with NHTSA on the recall kit, which was finally approved on August 15,1978, five days after the Ulrich crash. The first letters notifying owners of the recall were mailed during the week of August 21,1978.

Misch emphasized that during the time between the recall announcement and the Ulrich crash, NHTSA was regulating the recall. Neal considered this a crucial fact in the case. Ford was accused of acting recklessly by failing to warn consumers or repair the car during the 41-day time period before the Ulrich deaths. But if NHTSA was regulating Ford's actions concerning the recall during that time period, how could Ford be said to have acted recklessly?

The beefy, gray-haired Misch demonstrated on cross-examination that his temper can be as volatile as Cosentino's. "Is it true," Cosentino asked, "that you are of the opinion that the public will not pay any more for safety?"

"I am *not,*" Misch answered.

When Cosentino suggested that Misch's response to a question on the television program *60 Minutes* indicated that this was his viewpoint, Misch exploded. "The total interview was cut and spliced!" he charged as he pounded his fist on the wooden railing around the witness stand. "My total answer did not appear on television! I did not give that answer to that question!"

The exchanges between Cosentino and the witness continued to be heated, with Misch insisting at one point, "I've got to elaborate to explain my answer." Cosentino snapped: "You don't *got* to do anything but answer my questions!" And after Misch used a polyethylene shield to illustrate on the courtroom Pinto where it was installed on the recalled cars, he jabbed it hard into Cosentino's hand as he gave it back.

Misch conceded that the longer filler pipe installed on the recalled Pintos and Bobcats did provide "an incremental improvement" in the safety of the Pinto. He also admitted that Ford originally did not intend to crash test the proposed recall modifications. As it turned out, the final recall parts were not successfully crash-tested by Ford until after the Ulrich collision.

Cosentino also asked whether part of Misch's job as vice-president of Ford's "environmental and safety engineering staff" involved lobbying to soften proposed government regulations. "I don't recognize the term 'lobby,'" he replied indignantly. He said he merely tried persuading various regulatory agencies to Ford's position, usually at their request.

Was it true, Cosentino inquired, that Ford would never have modified the Pinto unless NHTSA had pressured the automaker into the recall? "I'm not certain of that. The adverse publicity was going on. . . and we may very well have come out in the same place," he said.

Neal also presented testimony intended to establish that

once Ford decided to recall the car, the company acted as quickly as possible to get the recall kits put together and shipped to dealers so installation could begin. This was intended to prove that during that crucial 41-day period before the Ulrich crash, Ford was diligently at work on the recall and therefore could not have acted recklessly in failing to warn about the car or repair it.

Cosentino's contention was that Ford knew from its own crash tests dating back some eight years before the crash that the Pinto was vulnerable to gas spillage and fire in low-to-moderate speed rear-end collisions. He believed Ford should have acted years before the Ulrich deaths to modify the car or warn about it instead of waiting until NHTSA discovered the defect and pressured Ford into the recall. This way, the recall and warning would already have been in effect when the 41-day period began.

However, the internal Ford crash tests which proved the company was aware of the car's leakage problems even during its development stages were already barred from the jury by Judge Staffeldt.

Perhaps the most boring testimony of the trial came from Ronald L. Hoffman, a 32-year-old supervisor in Ford's parts and service department, whose dry account of the recall process put at least one juror to sleep. In the end, though, his testimony proved vital in supporting Ford's contentions that the company worked as fast as it could on the recall after the government announced its initial finding that the cars were defective.

Hoffman, who was involved in coordinating Ford's recall campaigns, explained several intricate charts which were intended to show the complexity of recalling 1.5 million cars. He said he began developing plans for the recall even before its public announcement. "My boss told me to drop what I was doing and put this information together as quickly as possible," he said.

The persons involved with the Pinto recall program worked "around the clock, seven days a week, at whatever cost, to do whatever was necessary to get the job done,"

Hoffman said. The company authorized unlimited overtime and chartered airplanes to fly in parts from distant suppliers, he added.

"Was there anything that could have been done to expedite the recall before August 10,1978 (the date of the Ulrich crash)?" Neal asked.

"No," Hoffman said, shaking his head.

"Was there any way to get a (recall) kit to Elkhart, Indiana, prior to August 10,1978?"

"No, sir."

Hoffman said it was not desirable to send out letters to Pinto owners informing them of the recall before the parts were ready for installation on their cars. "It's not in the best interest of the customer; it's bad customer service" to tell them to bring in their cars for modifications if no parts were there. "They'd get upset," he said.

More testimony about the recall came from Roy P. Vasher, a "vehicle information systems manager" for Ford whose staff began writing the necessary computer programs for the recall in early June, 1978. "I told the employes to work whatever overtime was necessary to get the job done as quickly as possible," he testified.

Vasher's job was to provide a company called R. L. Polk with a list of the serial numbers of the cars being recalled, and on July 17 Polk sent back the names and addresses of most of the Pinto owners. Added to these were the names of 16,000 Pinto owners who had sent in their addresses when they heard about the recall. As for the Ulrich car, the first recall letter was sent out about August 22,1978, to a man in Atlanta, Georgia, who was the car's first owner.

The bulk of the notices were sent out in two mailings – one in late August and early September, 1978, and the other in late January and early February, 1979. "We did all that was possible to get the notices out as quickly as we could," Vasher said.

During cross-examination, Cosentino pointed out that Ford "made no effort" to contact the Indiana Bureau of Motor Vehicles to get the current Pinto registrations; instead it waited to get Polk's information which was a year old. But Vasher said that instead of using the services of Polk, Ford would have had to go to all 50 states, many with different computer systems, and run all of the 1.5 million serial numbers through each of them. He said it usually took two to three months to get a response from a state.

With just one more legal hurdle to overcome, James Neal was ready to launch the big finale to his case. At least, he *thought* it would be the climax. He would only find out later that this would be just a prelude to a dramatic conclusion which no one had anticipated.

20

When mechanical engineer John Habberstad took the witness stand in the Ford Pinto trial, he brought with him several bronze-colored canisters containing Ford's most powerful evidence that the Ulrich collision occurred at such high speed that virtually any car would have exploded.

Inside the metal cans were 16mm films of experimental crash tests in which Habberstad, using Ford's own facilities, smashed a 1972 Chevrolet van like Duggar's into the rear of a 1973 Pinto sedan like Judy Ulrich's. The impact speed was 50.26 miles per hour. Then he used identical vans, each outfitted with the same sort of wooden bumper used on Duggar's vehicle, to crash into the rear of 1973 models of the Vega, Colt, Gremlin, Corolla, and even a full-sized Chevrolet Impala, all at impact speeds of about 50.5 miles per hour.

For Habberstad, an $80-an-hour consultant with 10 years of experience in analyzing accidents, it was the most elaborate preparation he had ever seen for a court case. Crash tests usually cost $8,000 to $9,000 each, and he ran nine of them for a total cost of about four times Cosentino's budget for the entire case. On top of that, Ford was paying Habberstad at least $22,000 for his analysis and testimony.

But before Habberstad could show the films and disclose the results of the crash tests, Ford lawyers had to convince Judge Staffeldt that they were relevant and permissible. Aware that the movies were a cornerstone of Ford's defense case, Cosentino sent his evidence professor, Bruce Berner, into battle to fight against the judge allowing the jurors to see them.

Berner pointed out that Judge Staffeldt had limited the prosecution in its case by excluding evidence about 1971 and 1972 Pintos on grounds they were too dissimilar to the 1973 model. "But certainly," he urged, "the 1973 Pinto is much more similar to the 1971 and 1972 Pintos than to a Colt, a Vega, and a full-sized Impala."

Besides, he added, Neal himself said earlier that each crash was different. "There's a 'signature' to every accident," Berner told the Judge. "Unless the crash tests are *identical* to the Ulrich accident, they could mislead or prejudice the jury." To duplicate the Ulrich collision, Habberstad would have to provide the same asphalt roadway, replicate the same gouges the Pinto made on the highway, and account for the Pinto's bumping against the curbing and sliding on spilled gasoline after the impact, he said.

"If you have eyewitnesses to a crash," he added, "you don't need to reconstruct the accident."

In addition, Berner said that "all of the dangers inherent in a simulation are magnified by the fact" that the defendant itself conducted the crash tests, making the results "suspect."

Malcolm Wheeler, Hughes, Hubbard & Reed's expert on the Pinto, conceded that the crash tests were not identical to the Ulrich collision. "But that's not what's required by the law. They must be substantially similar in relevant respects," he said.

As it turned out, Wheeler added, the test involving the Pinto was "almost incredible" in its reproduction of the Ulrich crash. In a sarcastic attack on Duggar, Wheeler commented that "our van was exactly like Mr. Duggar's van, although we didn't put any marijuana or beer bottles in it."

Harley Copp and Byron Bloch could only speculate as to what happened in the crash, and these films would help rebut their opinions as being "unfounded in fact," Wheeler asserted.

"Bloch said that if the car had its tank over the axle, there wouldn't have been a fire. Well, Bloch's contention is quite literally nonsense," Wheeler claimed. "The true cause of this fire had nothing to do with the Pinto's fuel system; it had to do with a van weighing 4,000 pounds smashing into the rear of a Pinto at more than 50 miles per hour."

Berner stood again to plead with the judge. "Mr. Copp was prevented by Ford from going into the crash tests which backed his opinion; now Ford says his opinion was unsupported and speculation. And now they want their witness to be allowed to use films as a basis for his conclusion," he said.

"The issue," he concluded, "is not what might or could have happened that evening on U.S. Highway 33. It was what did happen."

Judge Staffeldt ruled that "any scientific demonstrative evidence is encouraged by the court and I would choose to follow that rule." Habberstad would be allowed to proceed if he could prove the tests were relevant by laying a foundation.

Habberstad had a doctorate in engineering, studied accident reconstruction for eight years, analyzed 1,200 accidents, authored a book on the subject, and worked for both plaintiffs and defendants as an expert in litigation. He grew up on a farm in the Northwest ("I was the chief resident mechanic") and still owned a farm near Spokane, Washington. He wore his dark brown hair combed over to the side, his sideburns a little long, and he appeared uncomfortable in his ill-fitting suit. After court, he looked more relaxed in his blue jeans, pointed leather boots, lumberjack shirt, and a sheepskin vest. He spoke with the drawl of a rancher, often answering questions on the witness stand by saying, "Sure do," "sure will," or "sure can."

About 10 percent of Habberstad's business activity was for Ford Motor Company, which translated into about 15 cases a year. As for working for both plaintiffs and defendants, he remarked, "I'll talk to the first person who calls."

Outside the jury's presence, Habberstad testified that he calculated the closing speed of the Ulrich crash to be 50 to 55 miles per hour, based on the amount of energy required to crush the metal on the Pinto. Using that conclusion, he arranged for a 1973 Pinto to be rear-ended at 50.26 miles per hour to test his estimate.

"I was not simulating the accident," Habberstad cautioned. "I simulated only the actual crush (of the Pinto) at the time the metal deformation took place." There was no attempt to duplicate the "rollout" or behavior of the Pinto as it careened down the highway after the actual collision.

Staffeldt gave permission for Habberstad to show the court a movie of Ford Crash Test Number 4382, in which the Pinto was rear-ended at 50.26 miles per hour at Ford's Dearborn test facility on October 16,1979.

The press corps crowded into the jury box to view the film, which was projected onto a screen directly in front of where the jurors would sit. The scene of the test looked like a giant garage. The first shots showed the stationary Pinto and van, with the camera briefly peering inside to reveal dummies positioned where the Ulrich girls and Duggar had been sitting. The anticipation was heightened by the soundtrack, which included an eerie, muffled buzzer which sounded every five seconds or so to warn the personnel at the test site that a crash was imminent.

The first view of the crash was taken through the front windshield of the van as it sped down a darkened tunnel toward a lit area where the Pinto sat. The driver's view caused the audience to wince at the moment before the van plowed into the back of the car with a sickening thud, propelling it in a slow arc down the track until the brakes were applied by remote control.

A side view of the collision was recorded on film by slow-motion cameras operating at speeds of up to 1,000 frames per second. With time drawn out, these movies showed in ballet-like detail how the van merged with the Pinto, the van's front wheels lifting off the ground like a stallion rearing back, and the Pinto's sheet metal buckling almost to the rear axle even before it was shoved down the roadway. A spray of glass hung in the air, glistening in the bright lights, until it sprinkled to the ground after the two vehicles moved out of the picture.

The test Pinto sustained a smaller rip in its gas tank due to a build-up of inner pressure than the Ulrich Pinto. But more significantly, the test Pinto's rear crushed an average of 33.2 inches, compared to an average of 37.9 on the Ulrich car. The structural damage to the van, Habberstad said, was "very close, although there was less distortion on the test vehicle than in the actual accident."

Based on this information, Habberstad said, he concluded that the Duggar van plowed into the Ulrich Pinto "at a minimum of 55 miles per hour."

"There has been a sufficient foundation laid," Staffeldt said in ruling that the jurors could view the film.

Then Wheeler asked the witness: "Did you form any opinion regarding whether other 1973 vehicles could have survived a crash by an identical van with a closing speed at 55 miles per hour without substantial leakage of fuel?"

"They would not," Habberstad said.

To back up his assertion, Habberstad then showed films of similar crash tests of a Vega, Gremlin, and Colt, each one being hit at about 50 miles per hour. In each instance, the car was crushed almost to the rear axle and the gas tanks gushed stoddard solvent, which was a substitute used for gasoline because it was less flammable.

After that, Habberstad showed a film of a 1973 Toyota Corolla, a car featuring the above-the-axle gas tank design like that favored by Copp and Bloch. In a rear impact with a van at 50.8 miles per hour, the Corolla spattered red stoddard solvent on the windshield of the striking van. The camera zoomed in as more solvent flowed from the rear of the car after it came to a stop, the liquid forming a giant pool on the test track.

Next, Habberstad showed the film of a 1973 Impala being rear-ended by a van at 50.24 miles per hour. Again, the car was severely crushed and solvent gushed out.

"They're not comparable vehicles," Cosentino complained about the Impala in relation to the 1973 Pinto. "Why don't you bring in a bus or a truck next and crack it up at eight or nine thousand a pop?"

Wheeler said these films were being offered into evidence for two purposes. The first was to illustrate the custom and practice within the industry in 1973, which was that manufacturers were not building cars to withstand the severity of crash which he contended was involved in the Ulrich collision. The second reason was causation. Kiely, he said, had used Douglas Toms' testimony to point out the better features of the Pinto's competitors, implying they would have performed better in the collision. Wheeler said these films indicated the cars do not perform any better than the Pinto in this kind of high-speed crash.

But when it came time to rule whether these other tests would be admitted into evidence, Judge Staffeldt could not even remember the basis for his decision.

Staffeldt: I would overrule the objection and admit them. I understand that they are offered for the purposes of causation, and I have forgotten the other.

Wheeler: Industry custom and practice, you honor.

Staffeldt: That's right. It's the industry custom and practice.

Cosentino: Can we put our crash tests (of 1971 and 1972 Pintos conducted by NHTSA) into evidence under the same reasons? For causation and practice in the industry?

Staffeldt: If you can get someone to authenticate them for that purpose –

Cosentino: Ours are authenticated.

Staffeldt: Not as far as I am concerned.

Cosentino: Dynamic Science has authenticated them, your honor, on the front and back sides with the proper ribbons.

Staffeldt: I don't think that is sufficient, but we are not going to get into any arguments here. I have ruled and that's it.

The consensus among the press corps was that the films

were potentially devastating to the prosecution unless Cosentino could somehow cast doubt on them or Habberstad. Ford, however, virtually invited suspicion by conducting the tests at its own facility instead of contracting with a neutral company to run them.

Cosentino told reporters that if the jurors accepted the closing speed as being 50 miles per hour, "I haven't lost my case but it makes it much more difficult." Indeed, the higher the closing speed, the more likely the jurors would conclude that it was not a defect in the Pinto, but the natural consequence of a massive collision which was responsible for the fatal fire.

The topic at the daily press conference, though, was money. "What we are seeing here in Winamac is a test of the criminal justice system because we are talking about money," said Cosentino in echoing a complaint of the sort usually reserved for penniless defendants locked in combat with the well-financed government. "It's a test of whether a defendant can pour enough money into a case and win the case. . . . I'm not saying we're impoverished. What I'm saying is that it's difficult to understand the number of dollars the defendant has poured into this case compared to what we had available."

Neal discounted the suggestion he was overpowering Cosentino with Ford's resources. "I wish you knew the resources available to Mr. Cosentino," he told the television cameras. "I've always said we're the David and he's the Goliath."

In a darkened courtroom with light peeking in through gaps in the blinds, the jurors were shown the series of five crash test movies the following day. Several of them flinched and one woman held her hand over her mouth as the camera inside the van provided the dramatic driver's view of the test Pinto being battered from behind. When the above-the-axle Toyota splashed stoddard solvent on the windshield of the van, one woman juror nudged the person sitting next to her and motioned to the screen.

Then Wheeler surprised the prosecution by offering into evidence still another film, this one of a Pinto being rear-ended by a van at slightly more than 35 miles per hour. Habberstad had conducted this test just five days earlier at Ford's Dearborn test facility. "I wanted to find out if there was any possibility I was wrong about the closing speed," he explained. "The result was definitely consistent with the opinions I've previously expressed."

Although he had not seen the film, Cosentino strongly objected and Wheeler withdrew his request for permission to show it. "I know when the other side wants to put something into evidence, it isn't going to help me," Cosentino said later. "It probably showed the bumper was dented or something."

In another important area, Habberstad testified that even if the Ulrich car had been modified under the recall, "there would have been a fuel loss. . . . A hydrostatic rupture still would have occurred in the gas tank." He added that the fire also would have broken out if the filler pipe stayed inside the tank, if the tank had been protected on all sides by shields, or if a body rail had been added to the right side.

"Would the fire occur if the Pinto had been recalled so the fuel tank could be relocated above the axle?" Wheeler asked.

"It wouldn't have made any difference," Habberstad said as he shook his head. The crush of the metal extended beyond where the above-the-axle tank would have been located, and putting a protective metal shield around the tank only would have "increased the possibility it would have ruptured."

Asked if the fire would have entered the passenger compartment if the seam welds holding the floor to the body had not split open, Habberstad testified, "It most definitely would because the windows broke out and there was no way to keep the fire out."

Habberstad added that in his opinion, the Pinto "was most likely stopped" on the highway at the time of the crash. He noted that the metal deformation on the right side of the Pinto indicated the door had been ajar when the accident occurred. With the point of impact being adjacent to where the gas cap was found, Habberstad concluded that someone was trying to step out of the car to get the cap when the van struck.

In what amounted to a 20-minute, graduate-level lecture on physics, Habberstad used a drawing board to try to explain the scientific principles he used in coming up with his initial estimate of the closing speed of the Ulrich crash. The presentation left the courtroom dozing, except for Malcolm Wheeler, who was a physics buff ever since growing up in the Canal Zone where his favorite teacher launched him on a path toward becoming a physicist (a career he abandoned for law after he whizzed through MIT).

Cosentino's cross-examination was aggressive, almost desperate, as he tried challenging the reliability of the films and the credibility of Habberstad. Cosentino began by claiming that when the Impala crash test was shown to the lawyers, he could hear someone in the background exclaim, "It's a good one!" at the time of the impact. But he said the sound was turned down so this was inaudible when the film was shown to the jurors.

Cosentino asked for the film to be replayed, and this time the jury and audience strained to hear the faint voice. "You've got mighty fine ears," Habberstad remarked.

Cosentino was implying that Ford may have kept repeating the tests until it got the fuel spillage it was seeking. However, Habberstad said the probable reason for the comment on the film was that an earlier test had to be aborted because the van's speed was not fast enough just before the collision.

"Is it true," Cosentino asked, "that these tests could have been done at an independent facility where (the vehicles) would not have to be braked after impact?"

"We probably could have found one, yes," Habberstad said. He explained later that he thought Ford's facilities were the best he had ever used.

"Assuming that every eyewitness has the Pinto moving at 15 miles per hour, at a minimum, and every eyewitness has the van at 50, does that change your opinion of the speed differential being 55?" Cosentino asked.

"The answer is no," Habberstad said.

Cosentino complained at another point that Habberstad was "not being responsive" to his questions, and Cosentino prefaced one inquiry with the remark, "As a scientist you tell this jury you allegedly are. . . ." But nothing flustered the witness or undermined his appearance of quiet competence. "He's a tough nut to crack," Cosentino sighed during a break.

Cosentino tried asking Habberstad whether passengers in a Pinto hit at 55 miles per hour would have suffered severe injuries if no fire had broken out. The judge, however, appeared to block this inquiry, even though Cosentino considered it extremely important because the Ulrich sisters lacked serious traumatic injuries.

"There's no issue of injuries in this case," Staffeldt said.

"The issue is speed," Cosentino insisted.

"That may well be true," the judge remarked.

Later, Staffeldt relented somewhat, and Cosentino was able to ask if dummies would be thrown violently around in a collision such as Ford's 31 mile-per-hour fixed-barrier test crash involving the Capri.

"They would be thrown around quite violently," Habberstad said.

Then Cosentino attempted to introduce into evidence a Ford film of the Capri test, believing this would be a simple matter because the judge had already let the written report of the test into evidence. Unlike the tests conducted for this case, the Capri film showed the dummies being extremely battered in the crash, and Cosentino wanted to suggest that if this happened in the equivalent of a 45 mile-per-hour car-to-car crash, the results of a 55 mile-per-hour collision would be even more devastating. But Wheeler objected to the film as being "irrelevant" and Staffeldt ruled, "I sustain the objection."

Habberstad conceded that there were no internal cameras on his test Pinto to record the body movements of the dummies in the 50 mile-per-hour crash. He said there were some sensors on the dummies, but he could not interpret the data.

Habberstad added that the minor injuries sustained by Duggar "would be consistent" with a 55 mile-per-hour collision. This was because the rear-end of the Pinto pushed forward 37.9 inches "like a big shock absorber, a big cushion that allows the occupant to withstand the change in velocity. . . . I've seen it happen time and time again," he said.

In what Cosentino considered an important point, Habberstad testified that if a car were in motion when it was hit from behind, the underbody debris which was knocked loose and the shattered glass would end up somewhere down the roadway. If the car were stopped on the highway, the debris and glass would fall around at the impact point.

Cosentino pointed out that the underbody debris from the Ulrich Pinto was found 32 to 113 feet down the highway, and the glass was found 24 to 98 feet from the point of impact, implying this meant that the Pinto had been moving when it was struck. Habberstad said, though, that 24 feet was "not a real long way down the road" and maintained that he could see a few glass particles in a picture of the impact point.

In another bit of intriguing testimony, Habberstad divulged that wooden blocks had been added to the test Pinto's suspension so that the van would strike it at the same spot as the Ulrich car was hit. Habberstad maintained that these blocks, which were also used on the Gremlin and Colt, had no effect on the crushing of the test cars. He indicated, though, that he would have kept running tests until the impact points matched those on the Ulrich car. Films of two other Pinto crash tests which were conducted at a 50 mile-per-hour closing speed were never shown to the jurors.

Cosentino produced a 1971 report by Habberstad on the topic of vehicle fires in which he warned that "fuel tanks located near the perimeter of a vehicle are particularly susceptible to damage during an impact. . . . When, however, the fuel tank is properly located, accidents of this type can be significantly reduced. One of the better methods of limiting the possibility of tank cave-in or collapse during an accident would be to position it where considerable crushing of the vehicle structure would have to occur before the fuel tank would be deformed. One such choice is between the main frame members and a considerable distance ahead of the rear bumper, or behind the front bumper of the vehicle."

The report cautioned that there must be adequate structure around the tank as well as an absence of sharp objects nearby.

When Cosentino asked if Habberstad believed an above-the-axle design would be much safer than putting the tank behind the axle, Habberstad replied, "No, not when everything is considered."

The crash tests appeared to be an impressive and effective defense strategy, although the decision to conduct them at Ford's own facility gave Cosentino ammunition in implying they were untrustworthy. Still, even if the jurors did not accept Habberstad's interpretation that the closing speed in the Ulrich crash was 55 miles per hour or faster, the dramatic crash tests might at least convince them that the impact was as a higher speed than Cosentino claimed.

For sheer showmanship, Neal's decision to conclude his case with the spectacular, attention-grabbing films was an excellent decision. But Neal's plan to wrap up the defense case was changed at the last minute due to a fortuitous incident which, thanks largely to Cosentino himself, Neal came up with a show-stopping final witness.

Ironically, Cosentino's unwitting assistance in helping Neal uncover the witness began when the prosecutor dispatched an investigator to try to find someone at Elkhart General Hospital who might discredit Levi Woodard's account. As a precaution, Aubrey Harwell sent a South Bend lawyer to the hospital. "Hang around, find out what's going on, make your presence known," Harwell told the attorney.

Talk of the Ulrich accident had died down a long time earlier at the hospital. But the frantic questioning of hospital workers by Cosentino's agent generated a renewed interest and the accident became a major topic of discussion around the hospital. Because memories were jogged, the identity of another potential defense witness was pushed to the surface, and the Ford lawyer tracked her down for an interview on Friday 29. On Sunday, March 1, James Neal decided to put her on the witness stand the following day at the completion of Habberstad's testimony, thus ending his case with a witness that was as much of a surprise to him as to Cosentino.

Her name was Nancy Ellen Fogo, a Goshen resident who was the mother of three children and had just been named assistant director of the hospital. A graduate of Michigan State University with a nursing degree, she was a prim, business-like woman with straight, dark-brown hair that fell to her waist.

On the night of the Ulrich accident, Mrs. Fogo was the house supervisor in charge of all nursing activities at the hospital. She recalled talking to Dr. Donald Miller, who treated Judy, and agreeing that a nurse should be sent with Judy when she was transferred to the burn center. In preparation for sending nurse Wanda Lumpkin on the assignment, Mrs. Fogo walked toward Treatment Room 5 to tell Judy about the plans. She indicated that she encountered Levi Woodard, who told her that Judy had been stopped on the highway.

Judy, who was still blind, heard Mrs. Fogo's voice in the hallway and apparently thought it was her sister Lyn. "No, that's the nursing supervisor," a nurse told her.

Mrs. Fogo testified that she walked over to Judy's bed. "I said, 'I understand you had a bad situation out there on (Highway) 33 tonight,' and she said, 'Yes.' Then I said, 'I understand you stopped out there on 33; did you have car trouble?' And Judy said, 'Yes, I stopped,' and she said something about the gas cap, something about checking the gas cap. And I asked her if she saw a vehicle coming, and she said, 'Yes, I thought it would stop.' "

Cosentino's cross-examination bordered on being angry. Why didn't she tell the police about her conversation? "I believe I did discuss this conversation with the officers," she replied, mentioning the name of a specific Elkhart policeman.

She repeated that the precise words Judy said were, "Yes, I stopped." Cosentino demanded to know how Judy could say the word "stopped" when her lips had been burned off.

"She was using her teeth," Mrs. Fogo explained. "Her lips were very fixed." Cosentino told her to try saying the word "stopped" without using her lips, which she tried doing several times. The word was distorted but recognizable.

She added that although Judy had been given some medicine for pain, she was still coherent enough at that time to provide the telephone numbers of her parents, her aunt, and a church camp south of Elkhart where her parents might be found.

Outside the courtroom, Neal was ecstatic. "Cosentino challenged us to stop that Pinto," he said, stifling a chuckle. "Well, now we've stopped it *twice*."

Levi Woodard's testimony was damaging enough to the prosecution, but Cosentino hoped he would be able to somehow explain it away. Now, however, Mrs. Fogo's testimony re-enforced Woodard's account and bolstered its credibility, virtually putting it out of the reach of any challenges. And at the same time, the credibility of Cosentino's own investigation of the case was again being battered.

In the same report in which Wanda Lumpkin provided Cosentino's office with Woodard's name 17 months earlier, she also gave the name of Mrs. Fogo as the supervisor who explained to her about the accident and assigned her to accompany Judy to the burn center. Although there was no indication from Miss Lumpkin that Mrs. Fogo had talked to Judy, Cosentino's investigators failed to interview Mrs. Fogo to find out if she knew anything important about Judy or the crash.

In a closed-door session which was held in Staffeldt's chambers and was protested by the press, Neal raised the extremely serious question of whether Cosentino had violated the law by withholding from the defense some information which would tend to aid the defendant. Under a United States Supreme Court case called *Brady vs. Maryland*, prosecutors are obligated to disclose to the defense any evidence they encounter which might tend to exculpate the defendant.

Clearly, Cosentino should have turned over any evidence he obtained which indicated the Pinto had been stopped on the highway, especially since Neal had specifically sought this sort of information prior to the trial. Why then, Neal wanted to know, did Cosentino fail to provide him with information about Woodard and Mrs. Fogo, whose names the prosecution had in its possession since September 25,1978?

"The state had the names of Levi Woodard and Mrs. Fogo. . . and it was my understanding that after Woodard testified, a state investigator went to Elkhart and Mrs. Fogo's name was mentioned," Neal said after the private session was moved into the courtroom. Neal wanted to know whether anyone from the prosecution had interviewed Mrs. Fogo or Woodard, or had heard from anyone about the information these two witnesses possessed.

"Nobody knew anything about them; they came out of the blue to us," Cosentino said. "Nobody knew anything about what they would testify to." As a result, he concluded, he had no exculpatory information to turn over to Ford.

Cosentino had just one more chance to present evidence to the jurors – his rebuttal case – and he knew he needed some powerful testimony to counteract Ford's vigorous 11-day defense case. One possibility was to put accident reconstruction expert Fred Arndt on the witness stand. His estimate that the closing speed was between 40 and 43 miles per hour looked much better at this point than it did at the beginning of the case. True, it was higher than the eyewitnesses believed, but it was substantially lower than Habberstad's calculations and Schultz' opinion. In addition, Arndt would testify that the fact that the van overrode the rear of the Ulrich Pinto resulted in extreme metal deformation which made the Pinto look like it was struck at a much higher speed than it actually was.

Cosentino planned to present more testimony by Trooper Graves and Dr. Stein to help rebut Ford's contentions that the Pinto had been stopped and the closing speed was 55 miles per hour or faster. Also waiting to testify was a statistician who would challenge the Pinto accident data cited by MacDonald and Feaheny.

Cosentino knew it was vital that he attack the spectacular crash test films which formed an essential part of Ford's defense case. To do that, he brought in Frank Camps, a former Ford employe with first-hand knowledge of how Ford had "rigged" its safety-related crash tests in the past. Cosentino was counting on Camps' testimony to create a considerable amount of skepticism about the reliability of the crash tests conducted for this case.

But why, the reporters wanted to know at the evening press encounter, were Woodard and Mrs. Fogo never questioned? "Perhaps you're right, perhaps they should have been checked out," Cosentino replied. But he became defensive when someone suggested this meant his investigation had been careless. "Not at all," he insisted. "I think it was as complete as any investigation I've ever been involved in. . . . If you checked out every person who appeared on every page (of the police reports), well, unfortunately we're not Chicago, we're not New York, we don't have that kind of manpower. As far as Elkhart County, Indiana, is concerned, I am very proud of the job the investigators did."

Then Cosentino charged Neal's true motive in bringing up the issue was to disrupt the prosecution as it was trying to prepare for its rebuttal case.

"That is outrageous," Neal exclaimed when told of that accusation. "He knows that's an outrageous statement, but if he wants to make those kind of statements, that's the way he does things." He added that he was satisfied with Cosentino's answer that he had no prior knowledge of what Woodard and Mrs. Fogo knew about the case, but he sidestepped the question of whether this meant Cosentino's investigation had been sloppy. "You'll have to put your own characterization on it," he said.

Taken together, Cosentino figured his planned rebuttal would be a persuasive counterattack which would diminish the impact of Ford's high-priced defense. At least, that's what he hoped. He wasn't aware that Ford was planning an all-out assault in an attempt to prevent Cosentino from presenting any rebuttal case at all.

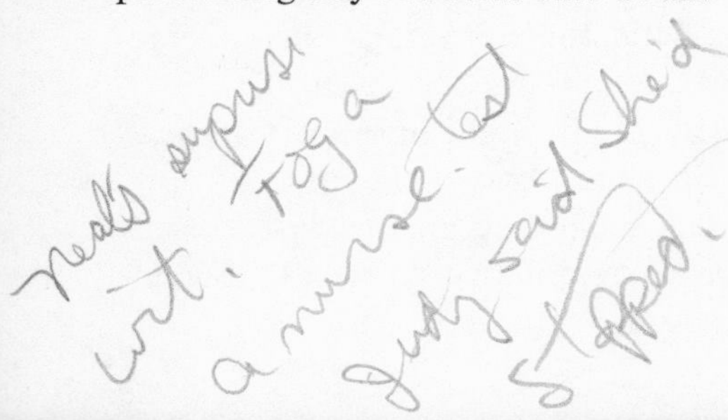

21

The Ford Pinto trial was more than eight weeks old and James Neal was anxious for it to end, especially with the vivid crash test films and Mrs. Fogo's critical testimony fresh on the minds of the jurors. When he walked into the courtroom on the morning of Tuesday, March 4, he immediately launched his offensive to bring the trial to a quick end by preventing Cosentino from presenting his rebuttal case.

"I believe the prosecution will seek during rebuttal to offer testimony concerning the closing speed," he told Judge Staffeldt. "In my judgment that would be improper rebuttal. . . . It's improper to hold back on a portion of your case for rebuttal. They've made their case (concerning the closing speed) and we've made ours." Neal added that Cosentino "has a reputation" for saving part of his evidence until the end of the trial and then presenting it with a flourish after the defense case.

Neal's explanation for the press was a little more colorful. "It's an old trick to hold back part of your case and hope to sandbag the defendant after he rests his case. Well, I'm an old dodger of sandbags."

"It's difficult to understand," Cosentino told the judge, "how Mr. Neal can put on two witnesses saying the Pinto was stopped and now says the state is prevented from going forward with evidence to rebut that. . . . They've made more of an issue (of the closing speed) than it was when the state rested its case."

When Neal repeated that "it's unfair to hold back on part of your case," Cosentino retorted, "That's right! Anything that hurts you is unfair!" He urged the judge for some time to research the law on the issue.

"I can give you time but my understanding of rebuttal is that you rebut that which is new. There is nothing new. . . as far as the closing speed is concerned," Staffeldt said.

"All of the evidence of the car being stopped is new," the prosecutor insisted.

Staffeldt said he would give Cosentino and his staff 30 minutes to research the law before trying to convince him that the rebuttal evidence would be proper. The prosecution team almost ran down the block to Tankersley's office. Law students Don Seberger, Tom McGarry, Susan Zander and others dashed to the law library, one of them calling out case numbers from a digest as the rest grabbed books from the shelves at a frenzied pace, glancing over the cases before handing them to Berner. He sat at a long wooden conference table, the stack of opened books getting bigger and bigger in front of him as he scribbled notes on a yellow legal pad.

Half an hour later, Berner stood before Staffeldt. "What the defendant is trying to do," he said, "is to get any particular issue in the posture they want it, and then cut off anybody else from going into it." He cited how Ford had previously succeeded in preventing the prosecutors from rebutting its version of how the 350 convictions for violating the Clean Air Act came about.

Berner quoted from a 1975 Indiana Supreme Court case in which a defendant claimed that rebuttal testimony must be limited to refuting new issues raised during the defense case. "No authority is cited for this proposition," the case said. "Rebuttal evidence may be *any* competent evidence which explains, contradicts, or disproves the adversary's proof."

Berner described another Indiana Supreme Court case which said that expert testimony can be used to rebut other testimony by expert witnesses. The key, he said, is that while the state cannot repeat previous testimony, it should be allowed to rebut evidence presented by the defendant during its case.

Although he provided the judge with the wrong name for the case, Neal cited a 1959 Indiana Supreme Court opinion which said that "orderly procedure requires that a party not divide his evidence. . . . If he goes into a subject originally, he should present all of his evidence upon that point, and if he does not do so, he cannot complain that he is not permitted to present such evidence out of order."

Neal said Graves and Dr. Stein had testified previously and Arndt and Camps were available to the prosecution at the beginning of the trial, so that the prosecution should have presented their full testimony during its main case, which is called the "case-in-chief."

As for the defense evidence that the Pinto had been stopped, Neal said the only reason this was significant was that it meant the closing speed could have been higher. And the prosecution already had a "clear, open shot" at presenting all of its testimony about the closing speed.

Staffeldt, who was handicapped throughout the trial because he lacked a law clerk to help him with research, recessed the trial to read the cases cited by both sides. When he returned, he promptly issued his ruling on what he called "probably one of the toughest issues in the trial" so far.

"The court does have a great deal of discretion," he said. "It would be an abuse of discretion if the court permitted the prosecutor to separate its case-in-chief and its rebuttal." He precluded Cosentino from presenting any evidence "which could have been produced in the case-in-chief and was available at that time." That included any evidence about the closing speed in the crash.

Because of the lack of discovery," Cosentino protested, "the state had no idea of what the defendant would present. We did not believe the defendant could, in any manner, stop the Pinto." He added that some aspects of the case "were not important to the state in its case-in-chief and only became important after the defendant put on its case."

The most Staffeldt would agree to do, though, was to listen to the testimony of Cosentino's witnesses outside the jury's presence and then rule individually whether each one could testify.

During a break, Cosentino looked devastated as he stood with his head bowed, staring at the hallway floor. "My rebuttal case has been destroyed," he said, half in astonishment and half in anguish. For the first time of the trial, he refused to step in front of the television cameras that day.

When court resumed, Cosentino and Wheeler engaged in a stormy exchange over Graves' proposed testimony, with Wheeler accusing Cosentino of lying to the judge and Cosentino calling Wheeler "Mr. Hot Shot." When it was over, Staffeldt excluded virtually all of the rebuttal testimony that Graves intended to give.

For instance, Staffeldt refused to let Graves discuss whether he believed the gas cap, based on its condition, could have rolled across the highway as Woodard had claimed, or explain any of the physical evidence which indicated the Pinto had not been stopped when it was hit. At one point after some testimony in front of the jury, Neal charged Cosentino with going too far and "absolutely defying the court's rulings" during his questioning of Graves.

"I think you are in violation of the order I had made," Staffeldt said sternly. Cosentino apologized.

Cosentino did succeed in getting into evidence the gas cap and the twisted and partially melted set of Judy's keys to show that one of the keys matched the cap that was recovered from the scene. The knotted and scorched set of keys was a grotesque reminder of the reality of the holocaust inside the Pinto, which was an image far removed from the antiseptic legal maneuvering which had consumed two full months in the courtroom.

Dr. Stein was brought in to testify that "extensive injuries would have been found" in his autopsy of Judy in addition to burns if her Pinto had been rear-ended at 55 miles per hour as Habberstad claimed. He said no such evidence of traumatic injuries was found. He added that Lyn Ulrich did not sustain the sort of impact injuries she would have suffered if the collision had been as severe as Habberstad contended.

Staffeldt ruled, however, that Dr. Stein could not repeat his testimony in front of the jurors.

Cosentino thought he might be successful in getting the testimony of his next witness, Frank C. Camps, into evidence because it did not concern the closing speed. Camps, who was 57 years old, worked for 15 years on Ford's engineering staff before he retired in January, 1978.

During his employment at Ford, he participated in more than 200 crash tests conducted to certify compliance with various federal safety standards. He made news several years earlier when he filed a federal lawsuit seeking a court judgment exempting him from any liability in lawsuits stemming from defects in the windshields of the Pinto.

At the time, Camps charged Ford manufactured more than a million Pintos and Mercury station wagons which did not meet the federal safety standard that at least three-quarters of the windshield must be retained in a 30 mile-per-hour frontal crash. Camps charged that his urgings that Ford improve the windshields went unheeded and that he was demoted because he "made waves" over the issue of safety. "You can only criticize your bosses so long before they come down on you," he told the *Detroit News* at the time.

When Wheeler tried preventing Camps even from testifying outside the jury's presence, Cosentino asked, "You mean we can't even show Ford Motor Company rigs its crash tests?"

"He hasn't been in this activity for six years," Wheeler replied. "Camps was nowhere around when Habberstad's tests were run, so this would be proof of some prior alleged bad practices and the jury would be asked to infer that these bad practices were used in these tests."

Staffeldt agreed to hear Camps' testimony before ruling whether the jury could listen to it. Camps testified he was involved in crash-testing Pintos from 1970-74, and he tested about two dozen of the 1973 models. He was primarily involved with windshield testing, although tests sometimes were conducted simultaneously for fuel system integrity and steering column intrusion.

He described that when there was difficulty in complying with the government's windshield standard, "we deviated from normal crash testing procedures."

In one series of tests, he said, Ford engineers crashed five Pintos, and all of them failed because their windshields popped out. After each test, engineers "took out small portions of weight" so that in the sixth crash, the test car was 225 pounds lighter and was able to pass the test due to its decreased mass.

In another instance, Ford engineers found that a dummy's seat-belt harness, attached to the car's roof, would cause part of the roof to buckle in a crash. Instead of strengthening the roof, engineers "took out the dummy so it wouldn't cause the problem."

Also, engineers devised a method of diverting the force of the impact in a crash test to the car's rear so its windshield would stay intact during a front-end crash and pass the safety requirements, he said.

"So you would do whatever was necessary to pass a test?" Cosentino asked.

"That's correct," Camps replied.

He added that when a car failed a crash test, engineers would "continue ordering cars until we found one that would pass by reducing its weight or finessing the way the windshield was put in or by taking dummies out." Any failures were labeled as "developmental test," and only the cars that passed were reported to the government to achieve certification for having complied with safety standards.

Ford engineers, he said, were instructed to report various test results in a special, euphemistic language. For instance, the federal standard for gas leakage was that the car must spill less than one ounce of gas per minute after an impact at a certain speed. Even if one or two gallons gushed from the tank, the engineers were instructed to simply write that the leakage was "more than one ounce per minute." When a dummy was crushed in a steering wheel test, indicating an actual passenger would have been killed, the report was only supposed to say that the test did not meet the minimum federal requirements.

Engineers were also instructed to give many reports verbally instead of in writing because fears that lawyers in civil lawsuits could obtain copies of written reports.

Camps' sworn account corroborated a *Chicago Tribune* article five months earlier which disclosed some internal Ford memos outlining what one federal safety official called an apparent "coverup" involving crash testing.

Wheeler, however, insisted to reporters that Ford did nothing improper in its crash testing. "The man's statements were simply misleading and false in virtually every repect," Wheeler said. For example, he contended that the weight removal discussed by Camps consisted of taking out dummies which were not required to be in the vehicle under government windshield testing standards. He added that the government only required automakers to report the cars that successfully passed safety tests.

Wheeler, who called Camps' testimony "irrelevant" because Camps knew nothing about the crash tests run by Habberstad, warned the judge that "we'd have a whole new trial" if Camps were allowed to testify. "We'd need 10 more witnesses," he said. "We'd just never get through with this case."

Tankersley called that comment "an attempt to intimidate this court into stopping this proceeding."

"The court don't intimidate," Staffeldt replied.

Cosentino maintained that he could not have used Camps as a witness during the prosecution's main case because Ford had not even presented any crash test films at that point. He said Camps' account also raised doubts about Ford's internal 20 mile-per-hour moving-barrier standard which its 1973 Pinto was supposed to meet. Cosentino implied that standard was meaningless if Ford doctored the test cars to achieve compliance.

Staffeldt said that the crash films introduced into evidence were "done by an independent individual," even though Tankersley stressed that they were performed under Ford's guidance and with Ford's facilities. Staffeldt ruled, however, that Camps would not be allowed to testify, thus precluding Cosentino's strongest counterattack to Ford's powerful crash test evidence.

Cosentino had just one more proposed rebuttal witness, a statistician named Jack Moshman of Bestheda, Maryland. With the jurors absent, Moshman said that the statistics shown to Ford's board of directors in early 1978 were "not a good basis" for concluding that the Pinto was as safe as other cars. He criticized some of the data because their "statistical reliability was very small." Then he elaborated on the statistics cited earlier by Cosentino which showed that the Pinto's involvement in fatal rear-end crashes involving fire from 1975-1977 was twice as great as would be expected based on the number of Pintos on the road.

"The point is," Shewmaker told the judge, "the information (shown to Ford's directors) did not specifically relate to rear-end crashes." He said the board could have been shown "reliable information on what the Pinto was doing in rear-end impacts," but that Ford executives instead gave the board "self-serving" information. "They got the figures to show what they wanted them to show," he said. Ford lawyers denied that.

Staffeldt agreed to let Moshman testify and said that Ford could then rebut his testimony with its own statistical experts. After a lunchbreak, though, Cosentino returned and said he was withdrawing Moshman as a witness. "I didn't want to end on our statistics and have them be able to come back with more statistics," he told some reporters in the hallway. "Since my other rebuttal witnesses were shot down, I'd have to end with Moshman, and it would be confusing to end on such a complicated note."

The trial was rapidly coming to a close, but before it was over Cosentino would suffer another significant defeat.

Staffeldt disclosed that he was planning to limit the attorneys to 90 minutes each in their final arguments. Neal quickly agreed.

"I've had a number of homicide cases that were less complicated and we had more time than that," Cosentino complained. Indeed, with this trial consuming 5,611 pages of transcript, 29 days of testimony, 41 witnesses, and about 200 exhibits, Cosentino believed he would need several hours to tie together his case and put it into perspective for the jurors. But Staffeldt was adamant. Ninety minutes would be the limit.

Staffeldt set closing arguments for Monday, March 10. As the lawyers gathered up their papers, Neal remarked that he was going to provide Cosentino with some information "as a matter of courtesy."

"You can strike the courtesy," Cosentino snapped. "I don't want any of your courtesy!"

The hostility which emerged on the first day of jury selection during the bickering over where to put the lecturn had endured to the last day of testimony. Neal sighed, "It goes right to the end the way it started," he said.

Cosentino and his assistants were bitter and depressed. They never expected to get all of their documents, or even most of them, into evidence, but they had counted on doing much better than getting about 20 out of 200 to the jury. The crash tests and internal Ford memos they considered the most crucial had been excluded, as was their planned rebuttal case. Yet there had been a few victories, and they believed the jury had heard enough evidence to warrant a conviction of Ford.

"We haven't been able to tell our entire story," Cosentino complained to reporters. "However, we have told a story. I think the story will be sufficient when we tie it up in final arguments and it goes to the jury. I don't believe they've stopped that Pinto. I didn't believe they could stop it when we rested our case-in-chief, and I don't believe it now."

Over at Lester Wilson's office, where the acrid cigar smoke hung heavily in the air, Ford lawyers were cautious in their optimism. They believed strongly that there was only a slim chance of conviction because they had been triumphant in winning court rulings which severely limited Cosentino's evidence. Their biggest fear was a hung jury. They wanted this case resolved once and for all and off of the front pages, and they wanted it resolved firmly in their favor.

As for the press corps, only Dave Schreiber of Cosentino's hometown newpaper was placing any bets on the prosecution. And he wouldn't go higher than $5.

22

His voice brimming with emotion, Michael Cosentino waved the death certificates of Judy, Lyn, and Donna Ulrich in front of the jurors and exclaimed, "There has to be more to life than these three pieces of paper! It cannot be that when it's all over, this is all that's left.

". . . In a real sense, this jury by its decision can give meaning to these senseless deaths by planting the seeds of change, the needed seeds of corporate moral responsibility and corporate accountability," he continued as he pointed at the jurors. "You and only you can send a message that can be heard in all boardrooms of corporations across this country."

Cosentino wasted little of his limited time for closing arguments before he grabbed the jury's attention with his suddenly passionate oratory, his voice modulating between bursts of outrage and whispered indignation. His audience was the biggest of the trial; extra chairs for spectators were crammed in at odd angles to accomodate the crowd. Sitting in the second row were Earl and Mattie Ulrich.

"Anytime that car was impacted at 26 or 28 miles per

hour, in Ford's own words, you've got the makings of a holocaust," he said. "This is the car Ford built for you to drive, for your families to drive, for your children and grandchildren. . . . Do you think it's right? If you think it's right, you go into that room and find Ford not guilty. But if you think it's wrong, you stand up and say so!"

Cosentino pointed out that every eyewitness testified that the Pinto had been moving at the time of the crash and that the closing speed was about 35 miles per hour or less. "You have to ask yourself, 'Do I believe the eyewitnesses, or do I believe the Elkhart General Hospital employes who said they talked to Judy?'" The eyewitnesses, he remarked, "gave their names and stepped forward." As for the hospital workers, he stressed that "Woodard said Judy saw the van coming and it *didn't* look like it was going to stop; Mrs. Fogo said she said, 'I thought it *would* stop.'"

The physical evidence, he maintained, also helped establish that the Pinto had been moving. The car was found with its transmission in second gear, and its glass and underbody debris was strewn far from the point of impact, as would be expected if the car had been in motion when hit.

Cosentino attacked Habberstad's testimony by saying that "he would have continued to crash test cars until he obtained the results he wanted." Then he posed the question of why Ford never showed what happened to the dummies inside the test Pinto when it was rear-ended at 50 miles per hour. "I can imagine what happened to those dummies, can't you?" he asked. Pointing out that Judy lacked any traumatic injuries and her sister suffered only a few, he said, "Do you think you can go out in a car in front of the courtroom and get hit from behind at 55 miles per hour and have no injuries?"

Had it not been for the Pinto's fire-prone design, the Ulrich girls would still be alive, he said. "If the crash doesn't kill you, the car shouldn't. The crash didn't kill Judy, Donna, and Lyn, and they should be with us."

Ford knew "how to build a safer subcompact car," Cosentino asserted. "Did you hear one word from Ford Motor

Company about the Capri not being safe? Why not use the safer, proven Capri design on the Pinto? In my opinion, the answer is Lee Iacocca and his ambition for a 2,000 pound, $2,000 car."

Cosentino used a chart to compute Ford's profits as an average of $4,301,369 for each day of the year. He wrote the figure with bold, oversized numbers. "If Ford was not so concerned about profit and was more concerned with people, according to Mr. Copp, the fuel system could have been significantly improved for $6.65 per car."

Then he pulled out a brown cardboard box containing a Pinto recall kit and displayed the parts to the jurors. "Does this look like any great scientific breakthrough occurred? Could they have put this 'scientific breakthrough' on that car in 1973? You bet your boots, you know they could. But you know what? This costs money, and if you put this on, then that," he said, pointing at Ford's daily profits, "goes down. It's a matter of dollars and cents."

Later he asked, "Did Ford ever really defend that car? They brought in $300,000 and $400,000-a-year executives who said they bought the car for their wives and children. Remember what I said earlier about using your common sense?" He suggested the jurors should judge whether the lucrative salaries and bonuses of Ford officials and the expensive fees of Ford's expert witnesses "would color their testimony."

"And Ford said the car was comparable to other subcompacts. That's like an accused burglar defending his actions by saying other people burgle, too. The truth is, the 1973 Pinto was the only 1973 car recalled for fuel system problems."

He also mocked Ford's position on the recall, pointing out that Ford executives said they were proud of the Pinto and considered it safe, and yet decided to recall it because of bad publicity and then "rushed around like crazy" to accomplish the recall. "Ford says, 'We voluntarily recalled 1.5 million safe cars.' As their ads say, 'That's incredible,'" Cosentino charged.

Moreover, he said that once Ford chose to recall the car, its officials "decided not to tell the customers until the parts (for the recall modifications) were at the dealers." As a result, Mattie Ulrich was not notified of the recall "until six months after she lost her lovely girls."

Cosentino picked up the certificate showing Ford's 350 convictions for lying to the government and asked why the guilty employes were never fired even though they cost Ford $7 million in fines. "The reason those low-level employes are with them (today)," he charged, "is because they knew too much, or in the alternative, they were instructed to do what they did. . . ."

Cosentino stressed the jurors were not bound by any particular safety standards in deciding the case. "For the first time in the United States, 12 citizens will set their own standards, not regulated by Washington or the large federal bureaucracy. You'll be regulated by your own consciences."

In concluding his summation, which was considerably more stirring than his bland and mechanical opening statement in the case, Cosentino told the jurors that "only you can say to Ford Motor Company, 'You have a moral and legal responsibility to people.'

"It's a great opportunity to speak and be heard. Ford Motor Company – the third largest industrial corporation in America – is listening. Ford Motor Company, the State of Indiana, and all of America awaits your verdict.

"The time is now, the place is here, and the voice is yours."

James F. Neal, holding his black-rimmed glasses in his right hand, told the jurors in response that Ford Motor Company had a laudable goal in mind when it decided to build the Pinto.

"Ford tried building a small car with *American* labor, to keep *Americans* employed and to keep *American* money in *America*," he said, jutting out his chin with pride.

"But that rather admirable effort has a sad ending," he said as he described how Duggar, who admitted he had not been watching the road, plowed into the Ulrich car. "Yet it's not the young man but Ford Motor Company who stands charged with reckless homicide. We're not *killers*. . . . We are not indifferent to human life."

Cosentino, he remarked, virtually wept during his emotional appeal to the jury. "Well, I cry, too," Neal said angrily, as he turned and pointed toward Cosentino. "I cry because Mr. Duggar is driving and you didn't do anything with a record like (his) except to say, 'Come in here and help me convict Ford Motor Company and I won't oppose probation.'" Commenting that Duggar had only one-sixth of a second to judge the Pinto's speed before the crash, Neal observed: "He had time to calculate the speed of the Pinto but no time to apply the brakes."

Neal slipped on his glasses and grasped the lecturn with both hands like a country preacher in his pulpit. He declared that Cosentino's eyewitnesses "offered a kind of smorgasbord – you can take your choice of 15 as the closing speed or 35." He pointed out that it was a defense witness named Levi Woodard, not a prosecution witness, who solved the mystery of why the Pinto had turned around. "If Levi's not right, then what's the explanation?" he said, again glancing at Cosentino.

Neal recalled testimony that the gas cap was found next to where the Pinto's front bumper would have been at the time of the impact, and Habberstad's opinion that the passenger door had been slightly ajar as if someone tried getting out to retrieve the cap. This evidence, coupled with the accounts by Woodard and Mrs. Fogo, helped prove the car was stopped, he said. In addition, Ford's experimental crash tests showed a 50 mile-per-hour crash produced less crush on a Pinto than the Ulrich car sustained.

"It made no difference what kind of car was out there (on the highway)," he concluded. "With the speed of this accident, other cars would have leaked, too."

Concerning the Pinto itself, Neal jabbed his finger toward the jurors as he cited testimony that the 1973 car met Ford's internal standard "and no other company had any standard" at that time.

"Why didn't Ford adopt a higher standard?" he asked. "Mr. MacDonald said he did not feel a higher standard could be met for the 1973 cars without greater handling problems. . . . How unfair it is for Mr. Copp to say we should have put the tank over the axle when Mr. Copp himself didn't reach the conclusion it should be there until four years after the (1973) car was on the road."

Neal claimed that "there's no safe place to put the (gas) tank because there are reckless drivers on the road."

He said that 1980 cars were required to meet a federal rear-end standard equal to a 32 mile-per-hour car-to-car crash, and thanks to Ford's voluntary standard, the 1973 Pinto was "within five or six miles per hour" of that current requirement.

At the time the Pinto was built, he added, "fire on impact was considered a rare occurrence. Mr. MacDonald understood that when they occurred, it was at high speeds. Douglas Toms said he was aware that deaths in rear impacts were rare and at high speeds. . . . I suspect that more people drown in their cars than die by fire."

Neal also cited Toms, the former NHTSA chief, as having testified the Pinto was comparable and even had some superior features than competitive cars. "Has has no ax to grind," he remarked.

Neal stressed in his summation that the essential element of the case was whether Ford acted recklessly in failing to warn about or repair the 1973 Pinto during the 41-day period before the Ulrich crash, which occurred on August 10,1978.

He said Ford decided to recall the car in early June of that year because "the publicity was hurting the company. They thought the government was wrong, but you can't fight city hall." Two months before the Ulrich crash, Ford issued a "widely disseminated press release" about the recall and "thereafter the government regulated what Ford Motor Company did. . . . And the government did not suggest any more warnings."

He scoffed at the prosecution's observation that Ford failed to place advertisements in June, 1978, to warn about the car. "We would have been telling Pinto owners to get out of their cars and into other cars which were no more safe, and maybe less safe, than the Pinto," he said.

He added that Ford did not recall the car earlier because its officials had been shown statistics indicating the car performed as well or better than other comparable cars. Even Toms said he was surprised Ford recalled the car, Neal said.

Concerning Ford's 350 convictions for violating the Clean Air Act, Neal said it was "unfair for Cosentino to imply that Ford could not be trusted just because "four or five low-level employes tried to cut corners out of frustration" with the government.

"Blaming Ford's 500,000 employes because four or five people cut corners would be like blaming every person in Pulaski County because a few people tried cutting corners," he said. As for Cosentino's allegations about why the employes were not fired, Neal huffed, "Where's his proof of that?"

Neal paused as he neared the end of his presentation. "I'm not here to tell you the 1973 Pinto was the strongest car ever built," he said as he stepped from behind the lecturn. "I'm not here to tell you a stronger car could not have been built. . . . But safety is a matter of degree.

". . . If this country is to survive, it's time to stop blaming industry and business, large or small, for our own sins. No car can ever by fully safe from reckless drivers on the road.

"Ford Motor Company is not perfect. But it is *not guilty* of reckless homicide."

In the brief amount of time remaining for the prosecution, Cosentino sent local attorney Dan Tankersley to address the jurors. Tankersley began by conceding that Duggar's actions in driving the van "cannot be condoned," but said it was the car's faulty design, not the impact itself, which caused the fatal fire.

"How can you compare Duggar's brief inattention with six years of (Ford) intentionally failing to warn consumers?" he asked.

Tankersley said that since Ford knew for years about

the Pinto's fuel system hazards, "why was it necessary for the NHTSA investigation to tell them about the problems they had with the car? Why did they have NHTSA tell them it's a dangerous car? If Ford knew, didn't it have a moral and legal responsibility to fix it?"

The force of this critical prosecution argument, however, was substantially weakened because the strongest proof of Ford's long-standing knowledge of the Pinto's problems was buried in the dozens of internal Ford documents which were excluded from evidence in the case.

"Did not Ford Motor Company fail Judy, Donna, and Lyn?" Tankersley asked as his time expired. "I know you won't fail them and all of the other living Judys and Donnas and Lyns in this country."

Neil Graves leaned back in his chair and rubbed his eyes, which were ringed by dark circles. After 18 months of wrestling with the case and nine weeks of listening to lawyers talk, the case was just about over except for the final score.

Before the jurors could begin their deliberations, however, Judge Staffeldt had to read them their instructions on the law to apply in the case. It took 45 minutes for him to read the 43 separate instructions, which included one submitted by Cosentino which undercut Ford's repeated complaint that Duggar alone should have been held responsible. "The defendant is responsible for the deaths. . . if the injury inflicted upon (the girls) by the defendant's recklessness *contributed* to the deaths, and the fact that other causes may also have contributed to their deaths does not relieve the defendant of criminal responsibility," the jurors were told.

Another instruction reminded them that it was their duty "to determine the acceptible standard of conduct in this case and to further determine whether or not the defendant's conduct was a substantial deviation from that standard." They were told that in determining the standard they could "consider whether Ford conformed with relevant internal corporate standards, with industry customs, practice, state of the art, and with the applicable federal, state, and local statutes, if any."

After eating lunch, the jurors walked into the tiny room at the rear of the courtroom, cleared away the giant jigsaw puzzle which had kept them occupied during their breaks from testimony and the cards they used in playing eight-handed euchre, and shut the door. The time was 3:15 on the afternoon of March 10.

Lawyers used their individual techniques for soothing the nervousness that plagues the "jury wait." Wheeler drove to the bowling alley and bowled so many lanes that he injured his thumb. Neal sucked on a cigar in a back room of Wilson's office as he played cards with other Ford lawyers. One Ford attorney, Richard Malloy, caused a commotion by tossing a frisbee around Wilson's reception room. Cosentino and his crew drove to their cottages where they began their own card games. Several of the reporters, afraid to stray too far in case the verdict came soon, brought their portable typewriters into the courtroom, turning it into a makeshift newsroom. Staffeldt remained in his chambers, chatting with other newsmen.

A short while later, the jurors sent out a note asking for a picture of the Ulrich Pinto which had been entered into evidence. Staffeldt replied that they could not see any of the exhibits. "There are too many of them, some are too big to move, and I don't want to give any part of the evidence undue emphasis," the judge said to reporters. The jurors had read each document and viewed each picture at the time the exhibit was submitted into evidence during the trial.

Inside the jury room, the seven men and five women wrote out the first of what would end up to be 25 ballots. The vote was four for conviction and eight for acquittal. That would be the highest tally Cosentino would garner.

Some of the reporters were puzzled by the occasional sound of laughter coming from the jury room, sometimes audible as far as 25 feet away. "Doesn't sound like a hanging jury to me," one remarked.

No verdict was reached Monday, and on Tuesday the

jurors asked Staffeldt to reread the instructions on the law. This time, two jurors scribbled notes on small pads of paper. That afternoon, the vote shifted for the first time. It was now nine to three for acquittal. Again the jurors went home.

The longer the deliberations lasted, the more optimistic Cosentino grew, and the most apprehensive the Ford lawyers became about the possibility of a hung jury. There seemed little doubt where most of the townspeople stood on the case. Although his language may have been harsh, one prankster reflected the community's mood by arranging letters on the motel's outdoor sign to read: "Cosentino Go Directly To Hell; Do Not Pass Go."

A controversy erupted on the third day of deliberations. *The Indianapolis News* carried an Associated Press dispatch from Winamac by reporter Lisa Levitt under the headline, "Trial Sends Message To Industry." The article was based on an interview with Staffeldt in which he was quoted as saying:

"Maybe no precedent-setting will be done here, but I think there is a message. . . . That is, that they (corporations) ought to refrain from doing some of the things they do and have done. To me, it's gotten pretty serious – you hear on the network news about the scandals in international deals. The message here is that people don't like that, and rightly so, I think."

Ford lawyers were aghast at the judge's comments and rushed to his chambers to express their concern. "The implication (of the story) is detrimental to the company," PR man Jerry Sloan told reporters.

Staffeldt decided to force the jurors to deliberate late into the evening instead of sending them home where they might be exposed to the article. By this time, the vote was 10 to 2 for acquittal, but the two hold-outs were steadfast in their opinions. The deliberations dragged on.

As midnight approached, the weary jurors indicated they were deadlocked. After an 11½-hour session which pushed their total deliberations to more than 20 hours, they were exhausted, irritable, and frustrated.

As they filed into the courtroom at 11:30 that night,

several of the jurors looked red-faced and tense. "Do you think you're close to reaching a verdict?" Staffeldt inquired.

The foreman, Arthur Selmer, a 62-year-old farmer from nearby Medaryville and the only juror with prior jury experience, stood and said, "No, you honor."

"Are further deliberations reasonably possible?" the judge asked.

"I don't think so," Selmer replied.

At that point, Staffeldt read the jurors a new instruction intended to prod them in their talks. "This is an important case," he said, "If you should fail to reach a decision, the case is left open and unresolved. Another trial would be a heavy burden for each party. There is no reason to believe that the case can be tried again any better or more exhaustively than it has been." The judge urged them to deliberate "in a spirit of fairness and candor" and "if at all possible, you should resolve any differences and come to a common conclusion so that this case may be completed." He added, though, "this does not mean that those favoring any particular position should surrender their honest convictions... because of the importance of arriving at a decision."

Again the jurors re-entered their room. It wasn't long before one of the two remaining jurors favoring conviction decided to switch her vote to Ford's side. That left one juror still holding out for the prosecution – James A. Yurgilas, a handsome, black-haired mobile home salesman and the father of two children.

At 2 a.m. on Thursday, the jurors emerged again and Selmer reported that "we have gained some; I feel maybe we can come to a decision." For another hour, heated deliberations continued, with Yurgilas remaining adamant in his belief that Ford Motor Company was guilty of producing a "reckless auto."

Once more, the jurors returned to the jury box. Yurgilas, his hands folded in his lap, stared at the floor while Selmer told the judge that the jury was "no closer" to a verdict and that it was "very doubtful" one could be reached. Asked whether it would be helpful to recess for a while and then return, the clearly frustrated Selmer replied, "I don't believe it would."

Despite that answer, Staffeldt decided to send the jurors home with the instruction to return seven hours later to resume deliberations. He knew there was no way he could sequester them at a motel for the night because lawyers and news media had already claimed every spare room in the county.

Cosentino had already concluded that if the jury became hopelessly deadlocked and a mistrial resulted, he would not seek to retry Ford. He did not have the time or the money. What he did not know, however, was that Staffeldt would have used his power to acquit Ford of the charges if the jury could not render a decision. However, the judge would not have overruled the jury if Ford was declared guilty.

The bleary-eyed jurors collected in the jury room at 10:15 on the morning of Thursday, March 13. No laughter floated through the door this time. One reporter tried going through the plastic bags filled with the courthouse garbage in search of clues such as jury ballots or notes, but found nothing except a secretary's furtive love letter.

Yurgilas, who had spent the seven hour recess wide awake and grappling with the issues and evidence in the case, was changing his mind inside the jury room. He still believed strongly that Ford's Pinto was a "reckless auto." However, the central issue in the case was whether Ford had acted recklessly in failing to warn about or repair the car within the time period before the crash. And Ford was in the midst of the recall process during that 41 days. Yurgilas began to conclude that the prosecution fell short of proving that Ford did not do everything within its power to recall the car.

Reluctantly, he changed his vote to innocent. "I had to put aside my personal opinion. I couldn't have lived with a hung jury if my being the only dissenter had caused it," the 32-year-old Yurgilas would recall later. "*They got off only through a loophole.*"

An hour and 10 minutes after the jurors resumed their deliberations, at the end of 25 hours of frequently turbulent discussions which stretched over four days, Arthur Selmer peeked his head out the door. "We have a verdict," he told the bailiff with a smile.

The news shot through the town in minutes. Reporters alerted their editors to stand by. Merchants scurried from their stores, filling the courtroom seats and standing three-deep along the back and sides. At 12 noon, the solemn jurors trooped out and Selmer handed the bailiff three white envelopes, which were given to Staffeldt. Cosentino searched the faces of the jurors for clues; they avoided his gaze.

Staffeldt ripped open the first envelope. "As to count one, we, the jury, find the defendant *not guilty*," he announced, sending an audible sigh of relief through the townspeople. Cosentino and Graves simultaneously slumped back into their chairs. Staffeldt opened the second and third envelopes and read the identical verdicts. "Do you want to poll the jury?" he asked the prosecutor.

Cosentino cleared his throat. "No, your honor," he said softly.

Trooper Graves, the only person in the courtroom who knew what it was like to look inside the gutted Pinto that horrible night, turned his head from the crowd so no one would see the tears.

It was quite a while before Cosentino and his assistants emerged from a side room, walked down the creaky wooden staircase, and waded into the crowd of reporters and microphones. Cosentino's fiery anger was gone, replaced by a grim acceptance of defeat.

"The jury has spoken," he said. "That's our system of government. We're disappointed, of course, but we have to accept the jury's verdict."

"Does this vindicate the Pinto's safety?" one reporter called out. "It vindicates Ford Motor Company on this case," Cosentino replied.

Asked what he believed the verdict meant for manufacturers, Cosentino said, "I suppose it means. . .they can make any kind of car they want to and it's up to the public to buy it or not. I do not personally think corporations are doing what they can to help this country and its people. Those 12 people up there evidently believe that they are."

He still believed, though, that the trial served a positive purpose. "I would hope, at least, if nothing else, that large corporations will understand that they can be brought to trial, they can have 12 citizens sit in judgment on their acts and make a decision as to whether or not what they've done is correct. And therefore all the decisions made in the boardrooms throughout the country may someday be scrutinized by a jury."

James Neal was bursting with pride as he strutted up to the microphones after Cosentino's departure. With Harwell, Wheeler, and Wilson flanking him, he declared he was "grateful, relieved, proud, and I thought it was a verdict that was fully justified.

"The Pinto has been maligned for years by articles that are unfair and one-sided. We had a chance to present our side of the story to a jury of 12 people in the heartland of America and all 12 found us not guilty. . .The message (of the case) may be that if you bring in the people who manufacture the product, and if they've got a fair, reasonable story to tell, then the people of this country will acquit you."

"Would you drive a Pinto?" someone shouted.

"Well, I prefer a Lincoln Continental," Neal replied. "I don't prefer small cars for safety. I said the Pinto was as safe or safer than other subcompacts of its era. I'm not saying you're as safe in a Pinto as a Lincoln Continental."

Ford's board of directors heard about the verdict during the middle of a meeting in Dearborn and reacted with cheering and a standing ovation. "Everybody said, 'That's great, good news!' " a grinning Henry Ford II told reporters when he emerged.

In Osceola, Indiana, Earl Ulrich was told about the jury's vote in a telephone call from one of the prosecutors. "I'm very disappointed," he said later. "The prosecutors were limited in their evidence. They couldn't get their story told; they couldn't get their evidence in."

23

The jury's verdict in the Ford Pinto trial was a clear-cut victory for Ford Motor Company, but it was a far cry from being a vindication of the automaker's controversial subcompact car.

That became clear during an extraordinary "meet the press" session held by the entire jury within hours after returning its verdict. Staring out at more than a dozen television cameras and speaking into a bundle of microphones, the jurors discussed many of the factors which led to their decision. Although a few balked at answering some questions they considered too prying, the mass interview provided exceptional insights into the panel's deliberative process. The highly unusual encounter was set up for the news media by Judge Staffeldt, whose kindness remained abundant despite some battering he suffered in the press during the trial.

The jurors emphasized that they based Ford's acquittal not on any agreement that the Pinto was a reasonably safe car, but on the narrow ground that prosecutors were unable to prove Ford acted recklessly in failing to warn about the car during the 41-day period before the crash. "We felt that (Ford) did notify people," foreman Selmer said in acting as an occasional spokesman for the panel.

Ray Schramm, a brawny steelworker with salt-and-pepper hair who owned a 1976 Pinto, explained that it was testimony by Ronald Hoffman, Ford's recall supervisor, that helped convince him "Ford did all it could" to recall the car during the crucial time period. Ironically, Hoffman was considered by many observers to be the automakers's most lackluster witness. In fact, during his testimony Neal turned to the spectators and mouthed the word, "*Boring.*"

Even though Staffledt blocked from evidence most internal Ford documents and crash tests directly relating to the issue of safety and design, some of the jurors apparently concluded the car was unreasonably dangerous based on the limited testimony that was successfully admitted.

Yurgilas, for example, labeled the car "reckless," but added: "They (the prosecutors) couldn't actually prove that Ford didn't do everything in its power to recall (the car)." Another juror said privately that "at least a few" other jurors reached conclusions similar to Yurgilas' judgment.

Other opinions about the car's safety varied widely among the jurors. Selmer commented that he "wouldn't feel safe" in a 1973 Pinto and that "there's room for improvement on the gas tank." Roger Tanner, a youthful-looking farmer who had lived all of his 31 years in Pulaski County, concluded, "By my standards, it was not safe enough." But then he added, "I do feel that the American public has the right to choose if it wants to purchase that product."

That philosophy was echoed by Janet Olson, a 31-year-old mother of three who earned a living driving semi-trailer trucks with her husband. "We, as Americans, should have the freedom to choose whether we get in a larger, safer car or a smaller, not as safe car," she said.

Schramm, a life-long Pulaski County resident who lived with his wife and five children about a mile from the courthouse, said "there's an inherent danger in just the fact that (the Pinto) is small." As for his 1976 model of the Pinto, he lamented, "I have to have the gas mileage to live and support my family. I can't drive a big car. I'm just stuck with it." The trial, he added, prompted him to adopt a new driving habit: "I look in my rearview mirror a lot now."

Selmer said that several of the jurors, including Schramm, felt "a little shortchanged" because Staffeldt excluded the bulk of the prosecution's documents. "I think we should have been able to see Pinto crashes of models other than the '73," Schramm said, because they would have been beneficial in reaching a verdict.

What about the closing speed? Interestingly, almost the entire jury concluded that the Pinto was *moving* at the time of the crash, although individuals differed on the impact speed. Tanner and several others maintained the closing speed was about 35 miles per hour, which would fall into the upper range of Cosentino's contention. Others, Selmer said, believed the crash was "at a higher rate of speed than the state said it was." He pegged the closing speed at 40 to 45 miles per hour, adding, "No Pinto with a recall package would have withstood that accident anyway."

Jay Chamness, a balding, 35-year-old telephone repairman with brown mutton chops, believed the Pinto was moving "very slowly" and was impacted by the van at about 50 miles per hour. He was among those complaining that Cosentino's eyewitnesses "never came up with a set speed."

The general reaction to Ford's expensive and impressive crash test films was that they were "entertaining," but the jurors expressed a considerable amount of skepticism because they were conducted at a Ford facility. "It should have been done at an independent place," Tanner said. "And why didn't we get to see the (dummies) inside?" Although virtually every juror rejected Ford's argument that the Pinto had been stopped and the closing speed was 55 miles per hour or faster, it was unclear how much the films might have influenced some of them to increase their estimate of the closing speed.

Selmer added that the jurors appreciated Woodard's testimony because "it gave us the first chance to figure out why the girls turned around." He said he believed the prosecutors "were a little negligent on that."

Alan Lenhoff, the Detroit reporter who speculated at the trial's outset about the effect of Neal's exaggerated "aw-shucks, down-home" mannerisms on the jury, finally got his chance to clear up this irrelevant but interesting issue. The verdict was mixed. "I enjoyed Mr. Neal," said Janet Olson, who tended to laugh the most at Neal's quips during the trial. "I thought he was a very, very nice and generous man, and Cosentino was quite the opposite." Schramm, however, thought Neal went a little too far. "I got the impression he was patronizing us a bit," he remarked.

From the trial's beginning, it was clear that the Ulrich crash was not what many people saw it to be – an ideal criminal case to help resolve the wide-ranging Pinto controversy which had raged since 1977.

First, the crash involved a 1973 car, and there was no dispute that this model was a little safer than the two previous ones. Indeed, the earlier models started leaking gasoline when hit from behind at a mere 18 miles per hour or so. An ideal case would have addressed one of these earlier models, which would have opened the door for many of Ford's most damning internal documents to be admitted into evidence because they dealt with those models. As the astronomical verdict by the outraged jurors in the Grimshaw case demonstrated, those documents can be devastating to Ford.

Second, the case presented significant difficulties in establishing the crucial question of closing speed. Cosentino's lowest estimate by an eyewitness was 5 to 15 miles per hour, and Ford's experts concluded it was 55 or 60 miles per hour. Each side was able to marshal physical evidence in support of its contention. The result was that some jurors concluded that the crash occurred at a substantially higher speed than Cosentino claimed.

Third, Indiana law prevented Cosentino from trying Ford on the most critical issue – whether Ford acted recklessly in designing and building its Pinto. This was the original thrust of the case, but judicial interpretations changed its focus to the bizarre question of whether Ford was reckless in failing to warn during that peculiar 41-day time frame.

This twist created a new batch of obstacles for the prosecution, especially since the recall was publicly announced two months before the crash and, at least according to Ford's witnesses, was at full steam during the 41-day period. Staffeldt compounded the difficulties by barring from the jury the very documents which supported the prosecution's central claim that Ford knew of the hazard years earlier and should have acted long before the NHTSA investigation forced the belated recall.

And then there was the problem of money. Surely Ford cannot be faulted for devoting whatever resources it considered necessary to present a vigorous defense against serious charges. But the disparity between Ford's outlay and Cosentino's paltry budget – even though he was aided by some free help from the state and volunteers – created a lopsided battle which hindered a full airing of the case.

The biggest impact on the prosecution, though, was the string of rulings by Judge Staffeldt which excluded the key crash tests and other internal documents. Was Staffeldt correct in his decisions or did he abuse his discretion?

Staffeldt was in the unenviable position of trying to feel his way through a gray twilight zone of unchartered law where products liability and criminal prosecution came together in an uncertain embrace. Legal scholars can debate the propriety of his rulings, but it probably will take future cases or legislation to sharply define the appropriate limits of this hybrid legal development.

The important point, though, is that these documents *were* excluded, and thus the verdict was rendered without consideration of evidence which was crucial to the Pinto story. Contrary to a commonly held belief, the Ford Pinto trial certainly cannot be seen as a case in which the jury fully examined the Pinto controversy and concluded the car should be vindicated once and for all.

Although Cosentino suffered repeated and crippling losses in his attempts to get the documents to the jurors and then lost the verdict itself, the trial still represents a major achievement.

During the pretrial wrangling, Cosentino won the far-reaching victories which made the Pinto case so significant in the criminal law and which took important new steps toward increasing corporate responsibility and accountability. These legal points, established when Judge Jones denied Ford's request to dismiss the indictment, have been described as:

(1) Corporations can be prosecuted for any crime, including homicide; (2) corporations can be prosecuted criminally for failing to warn users of their products of dangers known to corporate executives; and (3) like any citizen, corporations are criminally accountable for their actions to the people of the state sitting as a jury.

After successfully setting up this framework, Cosentino went on to lose the Ford Pinto case based on its particular set of facts. But the legal structure has remained for others to use in future cases of the same nature. Outside of Indiana, his success in getting his case to the verdict stage was hailed by prosecutors as shattering a psychological barrier. The achievement was certain to encourage other prosecutors to pursue similar criminal cases against companies – and individual executives – when lives are forfeited through corporate callousness.

On Thursday, April 10, 1980, the *State of Indiana vs. Ford Motor Company*, Case Number 11-431, was officially put to rest after 19 months. At a meeting with his volunteer law professors, Cosentino decided against pursuing any appeals from the case. Since the constitutional guarantee against double jeopardy would preclude Ford from being tried again in the Ulrich tragedy, the only issue left for appeal would be Staffeldt's evidentiary and procedural decisions.

"Rules of evidence and procedure are not what this case was all about," Cosentino said in announcing his decision. "The case from the beginning has been principally about corporate responsibility and accountability directly to the people. On these central issues. . . . the prosecution has been successful. An appeal based on less important issues would only divert attention away from the issues which made this case truly significant."

Small-town, part-time prosecutor Michael Cosentino and his crew of volunteers lost the battle. But they sparked a potential revolution in the expanding area of consumer protection. They demonstrated how the powerful criminal law could be forged into a tool capable of requiring a major corporation to answer to a jury for marketing a product widely denounced as lethal. It was a concept which could achieve major reform and whose mere existence would serve as a forceful deterrent to corporate misconduct. It also could turn into a devastating weapon if abused. As a recent development, it still raised some complex issues in need of resolution.

Now that Cosentino has broken the barrier of pioneering this novel legal force, the next case – involving whatever type of product – will be far easier to pursue. Indeed, the enduring significance of the Ford Pinto case was not that Ford Motor Company won the trial, but that the case was tried at all.

Ford Motor Company

PRODUCT DEVELOPMENT ENGINEERING OFFICE

FINAL TEST REPORT

MESSRS:

F. Andreu (Van Dyke + 1)
L. E. Arnett (Van Dyke + 1)
R. J. Berton
K. H. Gropp
G. C. Hedges
S. C. Jonas
E. P. Kennedy (2)
J. C. King
M. W. Lunsford
J. V. Markell
R. W. Trotter

TEST ORDER NO. T-0775
DATE OF ORDER 10/[illegible]/70
TEST AUTH NO. 518
WORK TASK/W O NO. [illegible]
FILE CODE 10
TEST DATES 10-[illegible]-70
DATE REPORTED 10-1[illegible]
SHEET 1 OF 8

SUBJECT: Crash Test 1615 (Barrier, Rear End Impact, 31.1 MPH) - 1970 Capri 2-Door Sedan

REQUESTED BY: Custom Vehicle Development Department - Product Development Car Engineering Office - F. Andreu

OBJECT: To develop a test procedure to be used to provide baseline data on vehicle fuel system integrity

SYNOPSIS: The test vehicle was towed rearward and impacted the barrier at 31.1 mph. No leakage was observed from the fuel tank or lines during and immediately after impact. A tank pressure increase of 9 psi was recorded. Approximately 30 minutes after impact the vehicle was rolled over on the ground on its right side, top and left side (in that order) remaining at each position for a minimum of 5 minutes. While positioned on the right side, stoddard dripped from the filler cap area. Leakage was also observed at the filler p[illegible] rubber sleeve connection and at the carburetor air cleaner. Stoddard also leaked from the carburetor air cleaner while the vehicle was positioned on its left side.

B J Andrews
B. J. Andrews, Principal Engineer
Vehicle Crash Test Engineering Section

R. J. Slempek
R. J. Slempek/jld

1673-2

FIGURE 1: Ford's Capri successfully passes equivalent of 45 mph car-to-car rear-end crash a month after Pinto's introduction.

( )

CONFIDENTIAL

Ford Motor Company,

PRODUCT DEVELOPMENT ENGINEERING OFFICE

FINAL TEST REPORT

MESSRS:
F. Andreu (Van Dyke + 1)
L. E. Arnett (Van Dyke + 1)
R. J. Berton
K. H. Gropp
G. C. Hedges
S. G. Jones
E. P. Kennedy (2)
J. C. King
M. V. Lunsford
J. V. Markell
R. W. Trotter

TEST ORDER NO. T-0738
DATE OF ORDER 10-2-70
TEST AUTH NO. 517
WORK TASK/W O NO. A-TANK
FILE CODE 10
TEST DATES 10-10-70
DATE REPORTED 10-14-70
SHEET 1 OF 8

SUBJECT: Crash Test 1616 (Barrier, Rear End Impact, 21.5 MPH) 1971 Pinto 2-Door Sedan

REQUESTED BY: Custom Vehicle Development Department - Product Development Car Engineering Office - F. Andreu

OBJECT: To develop a test procedure to be used to provide baseline data on vehicle fuel system integrity

SYNOPSIS: The test vehicle was towed rearward, impacting the barrier at a velocity of 21.5 mph. The filler pipe pulled out of the fuel tank and the fluid discharged through the outlet. Additional leakage occurred through a puncture in the upper right front surface of the fuel tank which was caused by contact between the fuel tank and a bolt on the differential housing. Also, there was a slight discharge of fluid through the carburetor fuel vent tube but this leakage was contained in the air cleaner.

H. P. Snider
H. P. Snider, Principal Engineer
Vehicle Crash Test Engineering Section

W. D. Horn
WDH:jld

FIGURE 2: Crash test conducted a month after Pinto's introduction demonstrates pattern of hazardous gas leakage when car is backed into a wall at 21½ miles per hour.

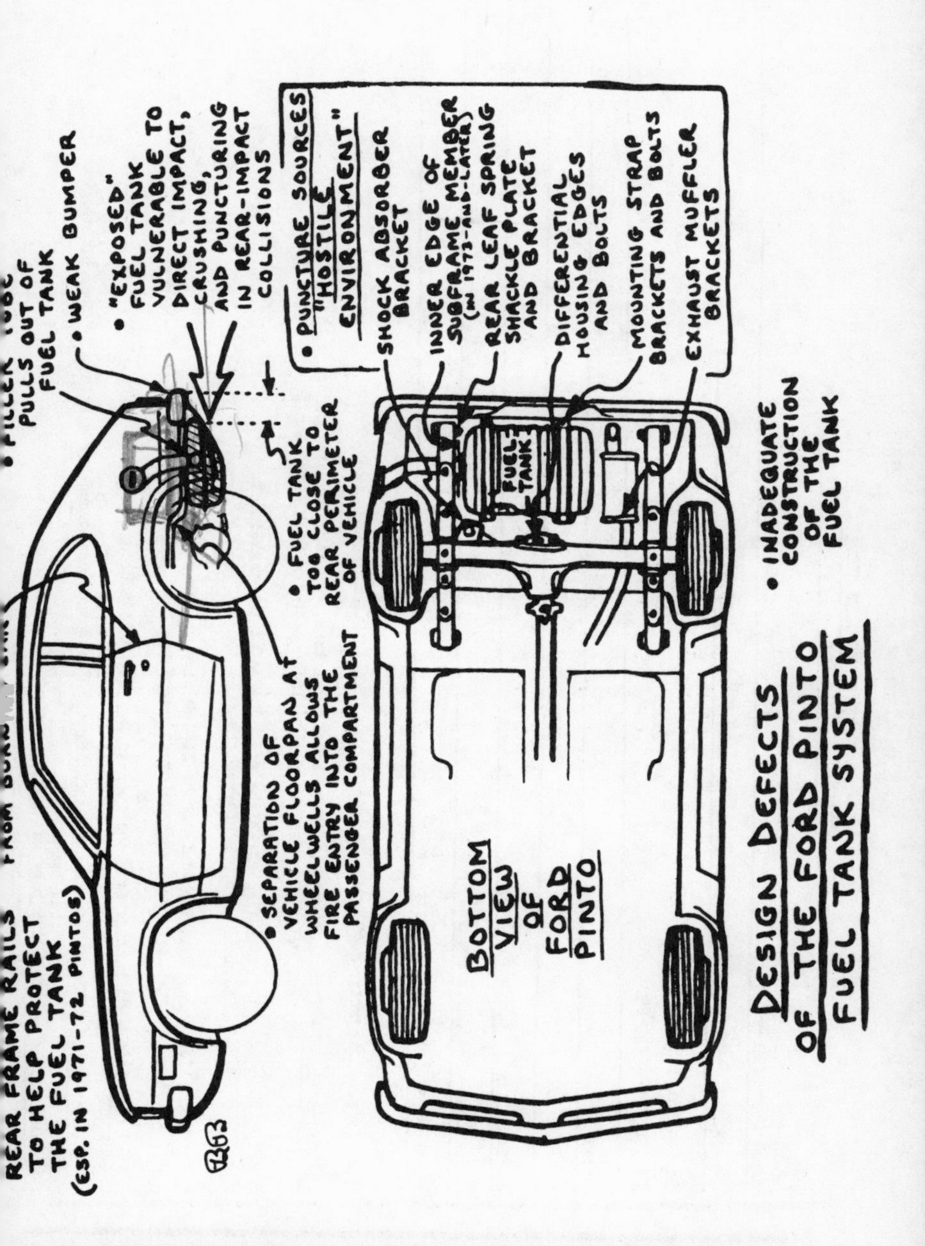

FIGURE 3: Pinto design flaws as illustrated by consultant Byron Bloch

REAR END CRASH TEST RESULTS
1971-1972 Pinto Car, At Fixed Barrier

Crash Test Number	2157	2025	1716	1682	1657	1616
Impact Velocity At Fixed Barrier, Mph	16.8	15.5	26.3	20.8	21.0	21.5
Equivalent Impact Velocity with Moving Barrier, Mph	21.8	20.0	34.7	27.4	27.9	28.3
Model of Vehicle	S.W.	3-Drs.	2-Drs.	2-Drs.	2-Drs.	2-Drs.
Test Weight, Lbs.	2800	2605	2998	2917	3045	2946
Maximum Dynamic Collapse, In.	13.5	10.5	22.0	12.5	16.7	17.9
Static Rear End Collapse, In.	11.0	7.6	19.5	8.7	8.3	12.8
Maximum "B" Pillar Deceleration, g	15	14	22	20	19	19

Fuel System Integrity:

Crash 2157 - Slight leakage in the rear of fuel tank. The axle housing deformed the fuel tank. The filler pipe pulled out of the tank.

Crash 2025 - Slight leakage from the filler pipe at the tank inlet. The axle housing deformed the fuel tank.

Crash 1716 - The tank leaked from the filler pipe. Leakage also occurred at the carburetor. Severe deformation of the fuel tank. Rubber bladder was installed in the steel tank.

Crash 1682 - No leakage from the fuel tank. The axle housing deformed the fuel tank. Two longitudinal side rails of a hat section were added in the rear of car.

Crash 1657 - Slight leakage at the filler cap (less than one ounce per minute). Rubber bladder was installed in the steel tank.

Crash 1616 - The filler pipe was pulled out of the fuel tank. Puncture of the fuel tank with the axle housing bolt.

FIGURE 4: Six Pinto crash tests, dating back to shortly after the car's introduction, are summarized by Ford engineers.

Intra Company

Product Development Group

Car Engineering

January 31, 1969

To: Mr. T. J. Feaheny

cc: Mr. G. E. Adams
Mr. R. B. Alexander
Mr. F. W. Bloom
Mr. H. F. Copp
Mr. K. W. Cunningham
Mr. S. Dabich
Mr. O. D. Dillman
Mr. M. L. Jurosek
Mr. C. L. Knighton
Mr. H. C. MacDonald
Mr. R. E. Maugh (6)
Mr. W. C. McDonald
Mr. F. G. Olsen
Mr. J. A. Pflug
Mr. G. F. Stirrat
Mr. J. D. Velte

Subject: Light Vehicle Weekly Information Report

Attached is the Light Vehicle Weekly Information Report for the week of January 27, 1969.

H. R. Freers

SIGNIFICANT ACCOMPLISHMENTS

A one-day, 1971 Phoenix, evaluation trip was conducted January 21, 1969, to familiarize Advanced Vehicle Personnel and Product Planning with four of the Phoenix image vehicles. The Vauxhall Viva, Volkswagen, Toyota Corolla and Fiat 850 were evaluated.

Phoenix fuel tank and spare tire package proposals were evaluated showing the tank located over the rear axle. Due to the undesirable luggage space attained with these proposals, it was decided to continue with the strap-on tank arrangement as base program. Further studies will be conducted to establish structural requirements for fuel tank crash protection, rail shipping tie-downs, and rear end towing.

FIGURE 5: Ford engineers reject above-the-axle gas tank design for Phoenix (later renamed the Pinto) because of decrease in luggage space.

Attachment II

REVISIONS TO PROVIDE INTEGRITY FOR 30 MPH REAR IMPACT WITH A MOVING BARRIER AND/OR ROLLOVER

Carline	Projected Design Changes	Recommended Effective Point
Pinto	*. Package fuel tank over rear axle kick-up . Solid bulkhead behind rear seat and under package tray . Filler pipe opening in area of left "C" pillar . Safety release fuel cap . New fuel sender . Provision to contain fuel in carburetor or air cleaner	Job 1, 1975
Pinto 3-Door Model and Station Wagon	. Package fuel tank behind rear axle with added structure in body . Possible sheet metal gauge increase . Improved retention or break-away feature for filler pipe . Increase fuel tank metal gauge . Add shields for protrubances adjacent to fuel tank . Safety release fuel cap . New fuel sender . Provision to contain fuel in carburetor or air cleaner	Job 1, 1975
Maverick-Comet-Cougar Mustang (except fold down rear seat model)	*. Package fuel tank over rear axle kick-up . Solid bulkhead behind rear seat and under package tray . Add heat shield to floorpan below tank . Filler pipe opening in area of left "C" pillar . Safety release fuel cap . New fuel sender . Provision to contain fuel in carburetor or air cleaner	Job 1, 1974
Mustang - Fold Down Rear Seat Models	. Eliminate this model or . Package fuel tank behind rear axle with added structure in body . Possible sheet metal gauge increase . Left side fill	Job 1, 1974

* See Attachment III

FIGURE 6A: Two months after Pinto's introduction, engineers develop suggestions for significantly improving its safety in rear-end crashes.

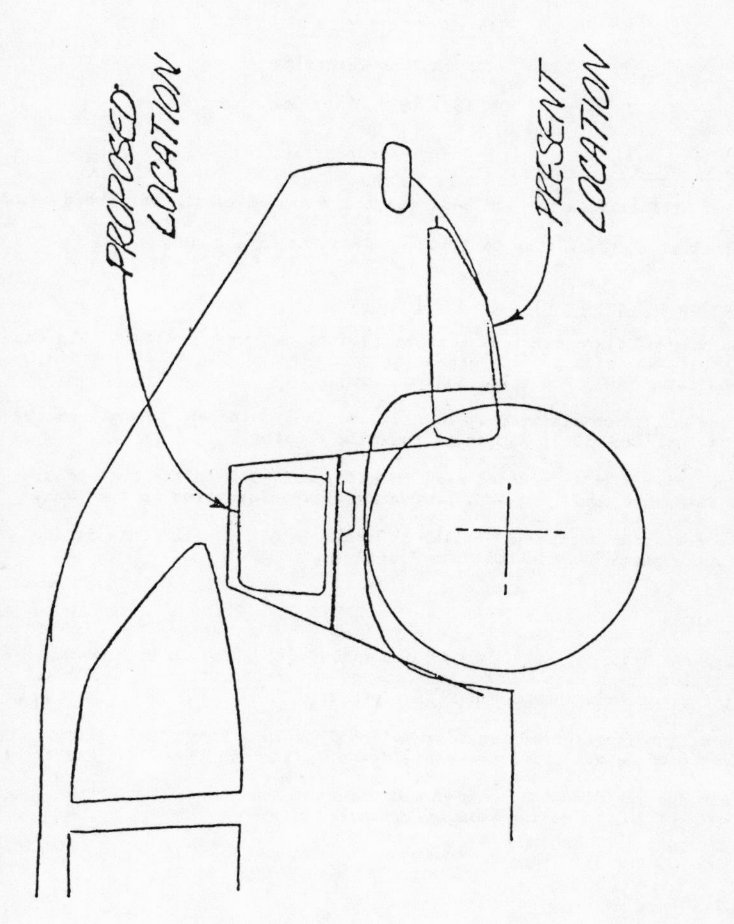

FIGURE 6B: In attachment to 6A, engineers show how the Pinto's gas tank could be relocated above the rear axle in position prosecutors claimed would improve the car's safety.

REAR END CRASH TEST RESULTS

Fuel Tank Integrity

1971-1972 Pinto Car

Status of Present Design

1. Rear of fuel tank is 5 inches from the rear end of the car sheet metal.

2. Front of the fuel tank is 3 inches from the axle housing.

Evaluation of Test Results

1. Summary of six crash test results is attached in Appendix. Only the latest two tests are corresponding to 20 mph moving barrier crash condition (1973 Federal Standard case).

2. Rear end crush distance is large, more than 8 inches. In all cases, the fuel tank is impacting in the axle housing.

3. The spare tire is mounted next to and parallel with the fuel tank: a favorable configuration, producing less deformation in the tank.

4. Deceleration of the "B" pillar is small in all cases. This is due to the large dynamic collapse length.

Conclusions

1. Present rear end structure is not satisfactory for 20 mph movable barrier crash case because of leakage and deformation in the fuel tank, and damaging of the filler pipe.

2. A slight revision of the rear underbody with 2.5 mph bumper system may produce acceptable results in the 1973 Pinto cars.

3. A major revision of the rear end structure is required for the case of 30 mph moving barrier crash.

NOTES:

1. Design change in the 1973 Pinto rear structure: a side rail is added on the left side to protect the filler pipe in the rear end crash.

2. The 1974 Pinto will have side rails on both sides. The section of rail is of the ⅃⌈ type which is poor, undesirable for energy absorption.

J. Valukonis
Advanced Compact Car
4-26-72

FIGURE 7: Ford document concludes that "major revision" is necessary to enable Pinto to withstand a 30 mile-per-hour rear-end crash. Also, rear structure planned for 1974 model is described as "poor, undesirable for energy absorption."

The following is an evaluation of test results obtained through actual crash test observations, reference crash tests, instrumentated data, movie films and photographs.

. Spare Tire

In the crash tests of the Capri, indications are that the tire does act as an absorber of kinetic energy. The fuel tanks did not leak in either crash but without the tire there was more fuel tank deformation.

As indicated earlier, energy absorbtion of from 5-10% is possible with correct treatment of spare tire location.

Direct axle impact along the vehicle centerline should be avoided as driveline failure may occur (Crash #1665), resulting in excessive body structure collapse.

Body Structure

Results indicated a body rail structure is necessary to absorb and control vehicle collapse on a predictable basis. Proper rail structure can serve as protecting arms preventing surrounding sheet metal from total collapse.

The 5 mph Menasco bumper system was simulated by the short absorber cans in Tests #1660 and #1693. The cans collapsed uniformly and served their purpose as energy absorbing devices.

Fuel Tank

Desirable fuel tank location appears to be approximately 3.5 inches behind the differential housing and 13-17 inches forward of the rear bumper extremity. The tank should be under the floor and between the body rails.

Crash Test #1693 was at 23.4 mph fixed barrier which simulates better than a 30 mph moving barrier. Since the fuel tank is vulnerable to impacting the axle housing, a 30 mph fixed barrier crash may result in fuel tank contact with the axle, however, the rear structure is designed to lift the tank over the axle upon rear impact.

A fuel tank bladder may be the answer to small tears in the tank due to impacting. Test #1657, a Pinto 20 mph rear end fixed barrier crash shows three metal tears in the fuel tank but the bladder within the tank was not punctured. Fuel tank bladders were not incorporated in the four crash tests by Advanced Light Car.

Indications are that a side fill and flexible filler connection are most desirable. Present production Capri employs these features today. Body sheet metal displacement and fuel tank displacement on impact is such that a one piece rigid filler pipe invites fuel leakage.

A summary chart of vehicle crash tests is enclosed for a comparison study. Individual crash test reports can be obtained from the Vehicle Crash Test Engineering Section on extension 30147.

Alan J. Pricor

A. J. Pricor
Advanced Light Car Department
February 4, 1971
34808

FIGURE 8: Ford engineer A. J. Pricor discusses methods of increasing safety from gas spillage in rear-end crashes.

.FIDENTIAL

-3-

Design Cost (Average Car Versus Prior Year)

	1973	1974	1975	1976	Total Average Car
. 20 MPH Movable	$(1.44)	x	x	x	$(1.44)
. 30 MPH Movable	-	$(2.01)	$(3.62)	$(11.22)	(16.85)
. Rollover	-	-	-	(4.00)	(4.00)
Total Design Cost	$(1.44)	$(2.01)	$(3.62)	$(15.22)	$(22.29)
Memo: Prior Design (3-4-71 PRM)	$(1.41)	$(3.00)	$(3.00)	$(3.00)	$(10.41)

Note: Estimates do not include possible penalties for tires, suspension, or other chassis changes necessary due to increased vehicle weights.

n summary, revised assumptions and estimates for Corporate Fuel System Integrity pro-rams indicate that a reduction of $55.0 million in tooling versus the prior 1973-1976 cycle lan can be accomplished. Current estimates require $13.5 million in tooling and .8 million in facilities to provide a final system which will meet the in-house 30 mph ovable barrier objective on all car lines by 1976. Design cost is estimated at over 22) per unit after all changes are completed in 1976, which includes $(4) on all cars to et rollover requirements in 1976 and $(8) for flak suits or bladders on affected cars.

.r the 1973-1976 cycle, these design cost estimates represent a total of $(100.0) million variable cost. The estimated total financial effect of the Fuel System Integrity gram is to reduce Company profits over the 1973-1976 cycle by $(109) million, but this vel is only $(2.4) million more than present profit levels (Exhibit III).

OMMENDATION

is recommended that the following product plan be approved:

- Continue with engineering programs to implement 20 mph movable barrier capability on all car lines in 1973.
- Proceed with programs to meet 30 mph movable barrier capability on all car lines by 1976 as indicated in the revised cycle plan.
- Defer adoption of all rollover hardware until 1976 to realize a design cost savings of $10.7 million between 1974 and 1975. Package provisions for rollover should be provided concurrent with car line changes to meet 30 mph movable barrier. Carburetor modifications should be accomplished in-cycle by 1976 with all-new carburetor programs required to meet emissions standards.
- Defer adoption of the "flak" suit or bladder on all affected cars until 1976 to realize a design cost savings of $20.9 million compared to incorporation in 1974. Package provisions for the flak suits and bladder should be accomplished in 1974 and 1975 concurrent with changes to meet 30 mph movable barrier capability.
- Continue with engineering testing and development to assure that final design approaches can be contained with minimum financial impact.

Product Review Meeting
Safety Planning
Car Product Planning
April [illegible]

FIGURE 9: Ford executives in 1971 urge delay in adopting proposed safety feature until 1976 to save $20.9 million dollars compared to adding the change in 1974.

GENERAL
PRODUCT DEVELOPMENT
SAFETY PROGRAM LETTER

NO. 73S-4-32

DATE October 26, 1971

SUBJECT Corporate Fuel System Integrity Objectives
MEETING NAAO Working Safety Com. Mtg.-9/23, 10/21/71
SUPERSEDES LETTER 73S-4-31
SUPPLEMENTS LETTER

INDICATING PROTOTYPES
APPEARANCE AFFECTED
APPEARANCE NOT AFFECTED
PRIORITY
[X] ACTION - RELEASE
OTHER - SEE BELOW

This letter supersedes the direction given in the Product Review Meeting of April 22, 1971 to provide in-cycle package provisions for 30 mph 4000# movable rear barrier impact and 90°/180°/270° rollover fuel system integrity starting with the new 1974 cars (incorporated in all cars by 1976).

The new Corporate Fuel Tank Integrity Program approved on September 23, 1971 is as follows:

> The fuel systems for all 1973 passenger cars must meet a 30 MPH front impact with a fixed barrier.
>
> The fuel systems for all 1973 passenger cars, except Mustang and Cougar, must meet a 20 MPH 4000# movable rear barrier impact. The Mustang and Cougar must meet the requirements by 1974.
>
> Note: This direction does not affect current Company design guidelines on lateral impacts.

Test Weight

- Vehicle curb weight plus 335 pounds (2 - 50th percentile adult male dummies - SAE J-963).

Fuel Leakage Acceptance Standard

- Maximum fuel loss of one ounce during front or rear crash and one ounce/minute maximum loss rate after front or rear crash.

In addition, it is requested that the rollover "rig" be used in a minimum development program to obtain baseline data on representative models.

Additional fuel system integrity requirements will be incorporated or packaged for 1973 and later vehicles when required by law.

for R. C. Graham 10/27

Concur for Car: J. A. Capolongo

CONFIDENT

FIGURE 10: Policy-setting memo directs no additional safety features be adopted for 1973 and later until required by law.

Table 3

BENEFITS AND COSTS RELATING TO FUEL LEAKAGE ASSOCIATED WITH THE STATIC ROLLOVER TEST PORTION OF FMVSS 208

BENEFITS:

Savings - 180 burn deaths, 180 serious burn injuries, 2100 burned vehicles.

Unit Cost - $200,000 per death, $67,000 per injury, $700 per vehicle

Total Benefit - 180x($200,000)+180x($67,000)+2100x($700) = $49.5 million.

COSTS:

Sales - 11 million cars, 1.5 million light trucks.

Unit Cost - $11 per car, $11 per truck.

Total Cost - 11,000,000x($11)+1,500,000x($11) = $137 million.

FIGURE 11: Cost-benefit analysis sent by Ford in opposition to proposed federal standard intended to reduce the number of deaths by fire in rollover crashes. Chart concludes it is not cost-efficient to add an $11 part per car in order to prevent 180 burn deaths and 180 serious burn injuries per year.